ALL
THAT DWELL
THEREIN

ALL THAT DWELL THEREIN

Animal Rights and Environmental Ethics

Tom Regan

University of California Press
Berkeley—Los Angeles—London

University of California Press
Berkeley and Los Angeles, California

University of California Press, Ltd.
London, England

Library of Congress Cataloging in Publication Data

Regan, Tom.
  All That Dwell Therein.

  "Papers and lectures written and delivered over
the past six years or so on the general topic of
human obligations to nonhumans"—Pref.
  Bibliography: p. 241
  Includes index.
  Contents: The moral basis of vegetarianism—
Utilitarianism, vegetarianism, and animal rights—
Animal experimentation—Animal rights, human
wrongs— [etc.]
  1. Animals, Treatment of—Addresses, essays,
lectures. 2. Animals, Treatment of—Law and
legislation—Addresses, essays, lectures. I. Title.
HV4711.R36   179'.3   81-16469
ISBN 0-520-04571-8   AACR2

To
George A. Lear, Jr.
Who Would Have Agreed With Many of the Conclusions
But Few of the Premises

Contents

Preface ix

1. The Moral Basis of Vegetarianism 1

2. Utilitarianism, Vegetarianism, and Animal Rights 40

3. Animal Experimentation: First Thoughts 61

4. Animal Rights, Human Wrongs 75

5. Why Whaling Is Wrong 102

6. An Examination and Defense of One Argument Concerning Animal Rights 113

7. Animals and the Law: The Need for Reform 148

8. What Sorts of Beings Can Have Rights? 165

9. The Nature and Possibility of an Environmental Ethic 184

10. Environmental Ethics and the Ambiguity of the Native American's Relationship with Nature 206

Bibliography 241

Index 247

Preface

This collection of essays brings together papers and lectures written and delivered over the past six years or so on the general topic of human obligations to nonhumans. The nonhumans at issue include not only nonhuman animals, though our obligations to animals, and their rights against us, are major themes in most of the essays; also at issue is the question of the foundations of our moral relations to nature generally, "the land" in Aldo Leopold's sense. This latter question comes into full flower in the last three essays, but it is a question that is growing just beneath the surface throughout.

There are some things—and these not a few!—said in these pages which I would not say now, because they are not well said, are false, or worse. As nice as it would be to disassociate myself from my past errors, I have resisted the temptation to revise, thinking it best to let the essays stand on their own feet, warts and all. Except for a very few additions, which are explicitly noted, and some minor stylistic changes, the papers or lectures appear here in the form in which they were originally published or delivered. The introduction accompanying each selection attempts to highlight the main philosophical themes of the work that follows, sketch some of the history behind it, indicate where its arguments have been challenged and by whom, and direct the interested reader to other relevant sources. A particularly important bibliographical resource, one that is relevant to each and every issue discussed in these essays, is Charles R. Magel, *A Bibliography on Animal Rights and Related Matters* (Washington, D.C.: University Press of America, 1981).

Also relevant is a second bibliography prepared by Magel. "An Updated Bibliography," devoted mainly to recent works relating to animals, appears as an appendix in the recent timely reissue of Henry S. Salt's *Animals' Rights* (Clarks Summit, Pa.: Society for Animal Rights, 1980). A third, less extensive bibliography, jointly prepared by Magel and myself, is reproduced at the end of this volume.

The essays do not contain fully worked out theories of the central ideas they examine. There is no settled theory of rights, for example, or of animal rights in particular, and neither is there a comprehensive account of what an environmental ethic must be like, let alone an example of such a theory. What I think the essays do contain are currents of thought which flow toward the development and testing of such theories. My hope is that collecting the essays in one place, as others have encouraged me to do, will make them more accessible to others interested in pursuing the same theoretical questions that have exercised my attention. But I would be less than candid if I failed to acknowledge, to borrow words from the first essay, that "fundamentally . . . my intentions are practical, not theoretical." How we answer the theoretical questions helps determine how we view the world, and this in turn helps determine how we *act* in relation to all that dwell therein, including all that is not human. The theoretical questions, in short, *can* make a practical difference, and that in my view is why they are important.

It is a pleasure to thank all those who have granted permission to reprint these essays; Sheila Berg, editor, the University of California Press, for her enthusiastic support of the project; Lucy W. Kluckhohn for her valuable help in preparing the manuscript; Ruth Boone and Anne Rives for their expert typing; Agnes Denes for her permission to use "The Snail" on the jacket and my wife Nancy for first suggesting its use; and the National Endowment for the Humanities, which, by supporting my research on a related topic, afforded me the time to prepare the several introductions that accompany the essays collected here. As always, I owe most to my wife and children; I can only hope that my work is of a quality that repays them for their abundant tolerance. But I should also like to acknowledge my great debt to my university, whose officials have never failed to be supportive of my work, and, in particular, my department head, Robert S. Bryan, who has been a friend besides.

North Carolina State University   Tom Regan
Raleigh, N.C.
April 1981

1
The Moral Basis of Vegetarianism[1]

My initial interest in vegetarianism grew out of my study of the life and writings of Mahatma Gandhi. Gandhi, as is well known, was an advocate of nonviolence (*ahimsa*), not only in political affairs but in the conduct of one's life generally. The extreme pacifistic position he advocated, from which he derived the obligatoriness of vegetarianism, struck me as inadequate, and I sought a less radical moral basis for vegetarianism, one that those of us in the Western world would find more hospitable. Since the leading theories were (and remain) one or another version of utilitarianism, on the one hand, and, on the other, theories that proclaim basic moral rights, it seemed to me that the moral basis of vegetarianism would have to be found somewhere among these options. That such a basis may be provided by a rights-based theory is what "The Moral Basis of Vegetarianism" attempts to show. Both the moral right not to be caused gratuitous suffering and the right to life, I argue, are possessed by the animals we eat if they are possessed by the humans we do not. To cause animals to suffer cannot be defended merely on the grounds that we like the taste of their flesh, and even if animals were raised so that they led generally pleasant lives and were "humanely" slaughtered, that would not insure that their rights, including their right to life, were not violated. Despite the Western custom of supposing that vegetarians must defend their "eccentric" way of life, the essay attempts to shift the burden of proof onto the shoulders of those who should bear it—the nonvegetarians.

"The Moral Basis of Vegetarianism" originally appeared in the *Canadian Journal of Philosophy* 5, 2 (October 1975): 181–214 and is reprinted here with the permission of that journal. When I reread it today I am struck by how very G. E. Moorish is its style. This was deliberate. Because I wanted to provide vegetarianism with a moral basis without resting it on extremely controversial moral views (e.g., the radical pacifism of Gandhi), I was determined not to let any extravagance, any emotion, any "rhetorical device" find a place in the argument. This was to be hard core philosophy—clear, rigorous, dispassionate, written in an appropriate style, a style that might be fairly characterized as "ponderously prodding." I hope the essay's highly analytic tone will be read and understood against this background.

But it is the essay's arguments, not its style, which ultimately matter most, and it will be useful to cite their principal critics, both those who accept the essay's conclusion (i.e., that vegetarianism is morally obligatory) and those who deny this. In the former category are Peter Singer, "Animals and the Value of Life," in Tom Regan, ed., *Matters of Life and Death* (New York: Random House, 1980, paperback, and, in a hardbound edition, Philadelphia: Temple University Press, 1980), esp. pp. 244–246, and Singer, "Utilitarianism and Vegetarianism," *Philosophy and Public Affairs* 4 (1980): 325–337; and Cora Diamond, "Eating Meat and Eating People," *Philosophy* 206 (1978): 465–480. Among those who reject the obligatoriness of vegetarianism and who dispute this essay's arguments are R. G. Frey, *Interests and Rights: The Case Against Animals* (Oxford: Clarendon Press, 1980); Michael A. Fox, " 'Animal Liberation': A Critique," *Ethics* 88, 2 (1978): 106–118; Jan Narveson, "Animal Rights," *Canadian Journal of Philosophy* 7, 2 (1977): 161–178; and Michael Martin, "A Critique of Moral Vegetarianism," *Reason Papers*, 3 (Fall 1976): 13–43, and "Vegetarianism, The Right to Life and Fellow Creaturehood," *Animal Regulation Studies* 2 (1979/80): 205–214. I have replied to Fox in "Fox's Critique of Animal Liberation," *Ethics* 88, 2 (1978): 126–133; to Diamond in "Cruelty, Kindness, and Unnecessary Suffering," *Philosophy* 55, 4 (1980): 532–541; to Narveson in "Narveson on Egoism and the Rights of Animals," *Canadian Journal of Philosophy* 7, 2 (1977): 179–186; and to Singer in "Utilitarianism and Vegetarianism Again," *Ethics and Animals* 2, 1 (1981): 2–7. Though I have not yet responded to the arguments of Frey's book, the two of us have exchanged some thoughts on animal rights in the past. See his "Interests and Animal Rights,"

Philosophical Quarterly 27, 108 (1977): 254–257, and my "Frey on Interests and Animal Rights," *Philosophical Quarterly* 27, 109 (1977): 335–337. See also a note jointly authored with Dale Jamieson, "Animal Rights: A Reply to Frey," *Analysis* 38, 1 (1978): 32–36, and Frey's "Animal Rights," *Analysis* 37 (June 1977): 186–189. Jamieson defends Narveson against some of my objections while urging new ones in his "Rational Egoism and Animal Rights," *Environmental Ethics* 3, 2 (Summer 1981): 167–171. Section II of "The Moral Basis of Vegetarianism" appears in Tom Regan and Peter Singer, eds., *Animal Rights and Human Obligations* (Englewood Cliffs, N.J.: Prentice-Hall, 1976) and in Richard Wasserstrom, ed., *Today's Moral Problems*, 2d ed. (New York: Macmillan, 1979), pp. 572–581. My reasons for rejecting Gandhi's pacifism are set forth in my somewhat misleadingly entitled paper, "A Defense of Pacifism," *Canadian Journal of Philosophy* 2, 1 (1972): 73–86; reprinted in Richard Wasserstrom, ed., *Today's Moral Problems* (New York: Macmillan, 1975), pp. 452–465.

The bay was sunlit and filled with boats, many of them just returned from early-dawn trips to the open sea. Fish that a few hours before had been swimming in the water now lay on the boat decks with glassy eyes, wounded mouths, bloodstained scales. The fishermen, well-to-do sportsmen, were weighing the fish and boasting about their catches. As often as Herman had witnessed the slaughter of animals and fish, he always had the same thought: in their behavior toward creatures, all men were Nazis. The smugness with which man could do with other species as he pleased exemplified the most extreme racist theories, the principle that might is right. Herman had repeatedly pledged to become a vegetarian, but Yadwiga wouldn't hear of it. They had starved enough in the village and later in the camp. They hadn't come to rich America to starve again. The neighbors had taught her that ritual slaughter and Kashruth were the roots of Judaism. It was meritorious for the hen to be taken to the ritual slaughterer, who had recited a benediction before cutting its throat (from *Enemies, A Love Story*. By Isaac Bashevis Singer [New York: Farrar, Straus and Giroux, 1971], pp. 256–257).

I trust it is not a moral stigmatism that leads me to see Everyman, or at least every sensitive person, in Singer's Herman. Not that each of us necessarily made Herman's pledge to become a vegetarian, only to postpone repeatedly giving the pledge life by our deeds. Rather, I cannot help but think that each of us has been struck, at one moment or another, and in varying degrees of intensity, by the ruthlessness, the insensitivity, the (to use Singer's word) smugness with which man inflicts untold pain and deprivation on his fellow animals. It is, I think, a spectacle that resembles, even if it does not duplicate, the vision that Herman calls to mind—that of the Nazi in his treatment of the Jew. "In their behavior toward creatures," he says, "all men [are] Nazis." A harsh saying, this. But on reflection it might well turn out to contain an element of ineradicable truth.

Of course it is possible to suppose that the Hermans of the world suffer from a perverse sentimentality—that they really should not be troubled by the common lot of many animals—that, in short, there are no rational grounds on which to rest their admirable, if lamentably misplaced, emotions. Vegetarianism, in particular, might seem to represent a way of life where an excessive sentimentality has spilled over the edges of rational action. For my own part, I cannot accept such a view. My belief is that a vegetarian way of life can be seen, from the moral point of view, to have a rational foundation. This is what I shall try to show in what follows. At the outset, however, I want to avoid possible misunderstanding. I do not intend to argue, nor do I believe, that it is absolutely or irredeemably wrong to eat meat. What I do intend to show is that we are entitled to presume and required to act as if it is wrong, given that certain conditions are fulfilled. What these conditions are, I shall try to make clear as I proceed. If a title was demanded for the position I shall try to defend, then, it might be called "conditional vegetarianism." But lest this appear to be a preamble to a tedious logical exercise devoid of practical significance, let me say that I think that most of those who should happen to read this essay will be leading lives that, if my argument is sound, ought to be changed in a quite fundamental way. Fundamentally, then, my intentions are practical, not theoretical.

I

A natural place to begin the philosophical defense of any form of vegetarianism is with Descartes. Descartes, as is well known, held the view that animals are like automata or machines: they have no mind (or incorporeal soul); they are unable to think; they are altogether lacking in consciousness. Like the motions of machines, animal behavior can be explained in purely mechanical terms. That animals do some things better than we do, says Descartes, "does not prove that they are endowed with mind. . . . It is nature which acts in them according to the disposition of their organs, just as a clock, which is only composed of wheels and weights, is able to tell the hours and measure the time more correctly than we can do with our wisdom."[2]

All this is common knowledge. What perhaps is not so widely known is that Descartes was well aware of the practical implications of his view. On the matter of killing and eating animals, for example, Descartes, in a letter to More, observes that "my opinion is not so much cruel to animals as indulgent to men—at least to those who are not given over to the superstitions of Pythagoras (a vegetarian)—since it absolves them from any suspicion of crime when they eat or kill animals."[3] Second, and relatedly, the view that animals do not feel pain might be expected to erase any moral qualms, any "suspicion of crime" we might have in using animals as subjects in scientific research. Descartes, himself, was an active participant in such research, as may be inferred from his discussion of the circulation of the blood in the *Discourse on Method*, and it is significant that the first champions of his views on the nature of animals, as Leonora Rosenfield has noted,[4] were physiologists. That Descartes was taken literally by these pioneers of science may be seen from a passage describing their work at the Jansenist seminary of Port Royal during the seventeenth century.[5]

> There was hardly a *solitaire* who didn't talk of automata. . . . They administered beatings to dogs with perfect indifference, and made fun of those who pitied the creatures as if they felt pain. They said the animals were clocks; that the cries they emitted when struck, were only the noise of a little spring that had been touched, but that the whole body was without feeling. They nailed poor animals up on boards by their four paws to vivisect them and see the circulation of the blood which was a great subject of controversy.

It is not without good reason, then, that we may suppose that Descartes was familiar with the practical implications of his views on the nature of animals, and though, in this essay, I confine my attention to defending the "superstitions" of Pythagoras and other vegetarians, I believe that the argument that follows could be applied with equal force to the practice of using animals as subjects in "scientific" research.[6]

Now, there can be no doubt that animals[7] sometimes appear to be in pain. On this point, even Descartes would agree. In order for us to be rationally entitled to abandon the belief that they actually do experience pain, therefore, especially in view of the close physiological resemblances that often exist between them and us, we are in need of some rationally compelling argument that would demonstrate that this belief is erroneous. Descartes's principal argument in this regard fails to present a compelling case for his view. Essentially, it consists in the claim that, since animals cannot speak or use a language, they do not think, and since they do not think, they have no minds; lacking in these respects, therefore, they have no consciousness either. Thus, since a necessary condition of a creature's being able to experience pain is that it be a conscious being, it follows, given Descartes's reasoning, that animals do not experience pain.[8]

There are two ways in which this argument can be challenged. First, one might dispute Descartes's claim that no animals can speak or use a language; second, one might dispute the view that being able to use a language is a necessary condition of being a conscious being. I think the second challenge is the stronger of the two. The first must sooner or later stand on the shifting sands of our concept of language, a topic that, for reasons too evident to enumerate here, I cannot discuss adequately.[9] I do not think this constitutes a serious defect, however, since whether man is or is not unique in possessing the capacity to use a language is logically irrelevant to the morally significant questions that arise concerning his treatment of his fellow animals. This is a point I shall seek to make clearer in what follows. First, though, there is the matter of the connection between using language and experiencing pain to be looked into.

Let us ask, then, whether Descartes is correct in holding that only a being who can use a language can experience pain. It seems he is not. Infants, for example, are not able to describe the location and character of their pains, and yet we do not, for all that, suppose that, when they fill the air with their piercing cries, they are not (or, stronger still, cannot possibly be) in pain. True, we can say of infants, what we may not be in a position to say of animals, that they have the *potential* to learn to use a language. But this cannot help the Cartesian. For when the infant screams for all he is worth, and when we find the diaper pin piercing his side, we do not say "My oh my, the lad certainly has a fine potential for feeling pain." We say he really is feeling it. Or imagine a person whose vocal chords have been damaged to such an extent that he no longer has the ability to utter words or even make inarticulate sounds, and whose arms have been paralyzed so that he cannot write, but who, when his tooth abcesses, twists and turns on his bed, grimaces and sobs. We do not say, "Ah, if only he could still speak, we could give him something for his pain. As it is, since he cannot speak, there's nothing we need give him. For he feels no pain." We say he is in pain, despite his loss of the ability to say so.

Whether or not a person is experiencing pain, in short, does not depend on his being able to perform one or another linguistic feat. Why, then, should it be any different in the case of animals? It would seem to be the height of human arrogance, rather than of Pythagorean "superstition," to erect a double standard here, requiring that animals meet a standard not set for humans. If humans can experience pain without being logically required to be able to say so, or in any other ways to use a language, then the same standard should apply to animals as well.

Of course, none of this, by itself, settles the question "*Do* animals experience pain?" But the foregoing does find a place within this larger debate. Animals, I said earlier, certainly appear at times to be in pain. For us to be rationally justified in denying that they ever are in pain, therefore, we are in need of some rationally compelling argument that demonstrates that, though they may appear to suffer, they never really do so. Descartes's argument does not show this. Granted, animals do not verbally express their state of mind when they are in pain. But to be able to do so, it has been argued, is not a necessary condition of a being's being in pain. Moreover, how animals who are physiologically similar to man behave in certain circumstances—for example, how muskrats behave when they try to free themselves from a trap—provides us with all the evidence we *could* have that they are in pain, given that they are not able to speak; in the case of the muskrats struggling to free themselves, that is, one wants to ask what *more* evidence could be rationally required to show that they are in pain in addition to their cries, their whimpers, the straining of their bodies, the desperate look of their eyes, and so on. For my own part, I do not know what else could be required, and if a person were of the opinion that this did not constitute enough evidence to show that the muskrats were in pain, I cannot see how any additional evidence would (or could) dissuade him of his skepticism. My position, therefore, is the "naive" one—namely, that animals can and do feel pain, and that, unless or until we are presented with an argument that shows that, all the appearances to the contrary, animals do not experience pain, we are rationally justified in continuing to believe that they do. And a similar line of argument can be given, I think, in support of the view that animals have experiences that are pleasant or enjoyable, experiences that, though they may be of a low level in comparison to, say, the joys of philosophy or the raptures of the beatific vision, are pleasurable nonetheless.

If, then, we are rationally entitled to believe that animals can and do experience both pleasure and pain, we are rationally compelled to regard animals as beings who count for something, when we attempt to determine what we morally ought or ought not to do. Bentham saw this clearly when he observed that the morally relevant question about animals is not "Can they *reason?* or Can they *talk?* but, Can they *suffer?*"[10] (although even Bentham fails to mention the pleasure animals may enjoy, a view which assumes some importance in my argument below). For if it is true that animals can and do experience pain; and if, furthermore, it is true, as I think it is, that pain is an intrinsic evil; then it must be true that the painful experience of an animal is, considered intrinsically, just as much of an evil as a comparable experience of a human being. As Joel Feinberg has noted,[11]

> if it is the essential character of pain and suffering themselves that make them evil, and evil not for their consequences but in their own intrinsic natures, then it follows that given magnitudes of pain and suffering are equally evil in themselves whenever and wherever they occur. An intense toothache is an evil in a young man and an old man, a man or a woman, a Caucasian or a Negro, a human being or a lion. A skeptic might deny that a toothache hurts a lion as much as it does a human being, but once one does concede that lion pain and human pain are equally pain—pain in the same sense and the same degree—then there can be no reason for denying that they are equally evil in themselves. All this follows necessarily from the view that pain as such is an intrinsic evil.

Now, an essential part of any enlightened morality is the principle of noninjury. What this principle declares is that we are not to inflict pain on, or otherwise bring about or contribute to the pain in, any being capable of experiencing it. This principle, moreover, is derivable from the more general principle of nonmaleficence, which declares that we are not to do or cause evil, together with the value judgment that pain, considered in itself, is intrinsically evil. It is, I think, possible to hold that it is *always* wrong to cause pain, but the objections raised against this view, from Plato onward, seem to me to be decisive. The parent who causes pain to the child in the course of forcing him to take some essential medicine does cause pain, but does not do wrong; for the pain caused in this case is necessary if greater pain is to be avoided. More reasonable, then, is the view that causing pain is always prima facie wrong—that is, wrong in the absence of any other overriding moral consideration. Such a view leaves open the possibility that, in some actual or possible cases, a person can be morally justified in causing pain. At the same time, however, by insisting that to do so is always prima facie wrong, it has the important consequence of placing the onus of justification on anyone who is involved in causing pain. In other words, if, as a consequence of my actions, other creatures are made to suffer pain, then I am rationally obliged to show how it is that my failure to observe the principle of noninjury does not constitute any actual wrongdoing on my part.

Now, given the intrinsic evil of pain, and assuming further that pleasure is intrinsically good, it is clear that cases can arise in which the evil (pain) caused to animals is not compensated for by the good (pleasure) caused humans. The classical utilitarians—Bentham, Mill, and Sidgwick—all were aware of this; nor did Mill, for one, flinch from insisting upon the conclusion that he thought utilitarianism required, given such a state of affairs. He writes:[12]

> We (the utilitarians) are perfectly willing to stake the whole question on this one issue. Granted that any practice causes more pain to animals than it gives pleasure to "man": is that practice moral or immoral? And if, exactly in proportion as human beings raise their heads out of the slough of selfishness, they do not with one voice answer "immoral," let the morality of the principle of utility be forever condemned.

I find this argument of Mill's persuasive, as far as it goes. For if, as seems reasonable to assume, animals can experience pain; and if, as seems reasonable to assume, we have a prima facie obligation not to cause pain; and if a practice exists like the one Mill describes; and if, finally (a point that Mill assumes, I think, without explicitly stating), there is no reason to believe that the animals in question have done anything to deserve the pain inflicted on them; then I think it does follow that the practice is immoral and ought to be discontinued in its present form. Thus, one way of trying to show that animals count for something, from the moral point of view, is along the lines of the utilitarian argument outlined by Mill. Whether the force of his argument would be altered by supposing that the pleasures caused by the practice were of a very high "quality" (a point about which Mill, himself, surprisingly is silent), is a matter I take up later on.

This argument of Mill's, then, has much to recommend it, and although I argue that he should have gone further than he does, what Mill does say shows that he is opposed to the view, endorsed by such diverse writers as Saint Thomas and Kant, that we have no direct duties to animals.[13] Recall that Kant, for example, formulates the categorical imperative in such a way that it excludes any reference to nonhuman animals; we are to act in such a way that we treat humanity, both in our own person and in the person of every other, always as an end, never as a means merely. Significantly, there is no mention of the treatment of animals here. Of course, Kant, who rejected the Cartesian idea that animals lack the capacity even to feel pain, did not regard the matter of man's treatment of animals as one of moral indifference. It is wrong, he thinks, as does Aquinas, to be cruel to animals. But what makes it wrong, according to these thinkers, is not that the animals suffer pain. What makes it wrong is that such treatment of animals tends to lead its perpetrators to treat human beings in a similar fashion. Cruelty to animals, in other words, leads to cruelty to humans, and it is because the former leads to the latter that the former is wrong.

Mill, quite rightly, will have none of this. His argument makes clear that he is sensitive to the implications of the view that pain is an intrinsic evil. For if, as Mill imagines, there is a practice that causes more pain to animals than it gives pleasure to man, then the practice is wrong, not *just* because or *only if* there is a rise in the nastiness of some men toward their fellows; it is wrong because of the unjustified pain felt by the animals. To suppose otherwise would do violence to the conception of pain as an intrinsic evil—an evil, that is, no matter when or where it exists, and no matter who experiences it. Thus, even if it is true that cruelty to animals does lead to cruelty to humans—and whether the former does lead to the latter is an empirical question that stands in need of solid factual backing, not armchair speculation—even if this is true, this cannot be the only thing that makes cruelty to animals wrong. For there is also the matter of the pain experienced by the animals that needs to be taken into account.

In this respect, then, Mill appears to me to be correct. And yet he does not go as far as he should. Recall that the case he considers is the one where a practice causes more undeserved pain to animals than it gives pleasure to man. This is just one among a number of possible cases of the comparative distribution of pleasure and pain. I begin by considering three others. These are (1) the case where the amount of undeserved pain caused to animals is equivalent to the amount of pleasure given to man; (2) the case where the amount of undeserved pain caused to animals is slightly exceeded by the amount of pleasure given to man; and (3) the case where the amount of pleasure greatly exceeds the amount of pain. There are other cases that will need to be considered later on.

Let us begin here by first considering a conceivable practice that involves inflicting undeserved pain on human beings. Imagine, then, the following Swiftian possibility. Suppose that a practice develops whereby the severely mentally retarded among us are routinely sent to Human Farms, where they are made to live in incredibly crowded, unsanitary, and confining conditions. Except for contact with one another, they have very little human contact. They are kept in stalls or in cages where they are fed by automated devices. Many of them are kept permanently indoors, and among those who are permitted outside, most of them are deprived of the ordinary means they might employ to secure enjoyment. And imagine, further, that the purpose of all this is to raise these human beings as a source of food for other human beings. At the end of a certain period of time, let us say, or after each has attained a certain weight, they are sold at public auction to the highest bidder and summarily carted off in loathsome vehicles to be "humanely" slaughtered.

Now, given such a practice, let us suppose that the following is true of it: The amount of undeserved pain caused to these human beings is exactly equivalent to the amount of pleasure other human beings secure as a result of the practice. The question is: would we say that this equality of pain and pleasure shows that there are no moral grounds for objecting to the practice in question? I do not think we would. I think we would want to say that this way of treating humans is not morally justified.

Consider, next, the following possibility. Imagine the same practice, only now imagine that the amount of pleasure other humans get from the practice slightly exceeds the amount of undeserved pain experienced by those who suffer. Would we say that, in this case, the practice is morally justified? Once again, I do not think we would. On the contrary, I think we would want to say here, as in the previous case, that the practice is immoral.

Now, if this is true of the two cases just imagined, why would not the same thing be true of cases where the practice imagined involves the treatment of animals? Let us suppose, that is, that there is a practice that involves treating animals in such a way that either (1) the amount of undeserved pain they experience is equal to the amount of pleasure human beings get from the practice or (2) the amount of pleasure humans receive slightly exceeds the amount of undeserved pain the animals suffer. And let us suppose that the pain suffered in either case is comparable to the pain suffered by the humans in the cases previously described. Under either one or both of the hypotheses, why would the practice in question not be just as wrong as in the case of the practice involving human beings? Well, certainly it cannot consistently be said that the intrinsic evil of an animal's pain counts for less than the intrinsic evil of a comparable human pain, and that that is why the practice involving the treatment of animals can be morally accepted while the practice involving humans is not. For it has already been pointd out that the pain an animal feels is just as much pain, and just as much an intrinsic evil, as a comparable pain felt by a human being. So, if there is any rational basis for rendering conflicting judgments about the two practices, it must be looked for in some other direction.

The most likely and, on the face of it, the most plausible direction in which to look is in the direction of rights. "Humans," this line of reasoning goes, "have certain natural rights that animals lack, and that is what makes the two practices differ in a morally significant way. For in the case of the practice involving humans, their equal natural right to be spared undeserved pain is being violated, while in the case of the practice involving animals, since animals can have no rights, *their* rights are not being ignored. That is what makes the two cases differ. And that is what makes the practice involving humans an immoral one, while the practice involving animals is not."

Natural though this line of argument is, I do not think it justifies the differential treatment of the animals and humans in question. For on what grounds might it be claimed that the humans, but not the animals, have an equal natural right to be spared undeserved pain?[14] Well, it cannot be, as it is sometimes alleged, that all and only human beings have this right because all and only humans reason, make free choices, or have a concept of their identity. These grounds will not justify the ascription of rights to all humans because some humans—infants and the severely mentally defective, for example—do not meet these conditions. Moreover, even if these conditions did form the grounds for the possession of rights; and even if it were true that all human beings met them; it still would not follow that *only* human beings have them. For on what grounds, precisely, might it be claimed that no animals can reason, make free choices, or form a concept of themselves? What one would want here are detailed analyses of these operative concepts together with rationally compelling empirical data and other arguments that support the view that all nonhuman animals are deficient in these respects. It would be the height of prejudice merely to assume that man is unique in being able to reason. To the extent that these beliefs are not examined in the light of what we know about animals and animal intelligence, the supposition that *only* human beings have these capacities is just that—a supposition, and one that could hardly bear the moral weight placed upon it by the differential treatment of animals and humans.[15]

Nor will it do to argue that all and only human beings can use a language, and that this is why they can have the right in question while animals cannot. For even if it were true that all and only human beings can use a language, there would be no reason to believe that the possession of this capacity could have anything whatever to do with the possession of this right. For there is neither a logical nor an empirical connection between being able to use a language, on the one hand, and, on the other, being able to experience undeserved pain.

How, then, might we justify the ascription of an equal natural right to be spared undeserved pain to all human beings? This is not easy to say, and all I can do here is indicate what seems to me to be the most plausible line or argument in this regard. A detailed examination of the issues that arise here is beyond the scope of this essay.

Two things, at least, are reasonably clear. First, if the right in question is a *natural* right, then it cannot be one that is conferred upon one human being by other human beings; in particular, it cannot be a right that the governments or their laws can grant to or, for that matter, withhold from their subjects. Second, if the natural right in question is supposed to be one that belongs *equally* to all human beings, it cannot be a right that some human beings can acquire by doing something that other humans are unable to do; it must be a right, in other words, that all human beings have, to an equal extent, just because they are human beings. It is because of this second requirement that most proposed grounds for the right in question fail. For, given that there are some human beings who cannot, say, reason, or speak, or make free choices, it could not be the case that all humans have an equal right to be spared undeserved pain because all humans can reason, speak, or make free choices. Any plausible argument for ascribing this right equally to all human beings, therefore, must invoke a basis that applies equally to all beings who are human.

Now, there is one argument for ascribing this natural right equally to all humans which has a degree of plausibility the others lack. This is the argument that begins with the claim that humans *can* have natural rights because humans *do* have interests.[16] The word "interests" here is used to cover such items as (to use a list of examples given by Perry[17]) liking-disliking, loving-hating, hoping-fearing, desiring-avoiding. As it is used in the present context, "interests" is used to refer to what Perry calls "a certain class of acts or states which have the common characteristic of *being for or against*."[18] Thus, as Feinberg has pointed out,[19] although we may speak of a car as "needing some gas," we do not think that the car can have a right to the gas; and we do not think this because cars are not the kind of being that can have interests—that can *feel* the need to have gas or *desire* to have it. In the case of human beings, however, we do experience desires and needs; we do have a connative life that includes the "acts or states" mentioned above; and it would seem to be because we do have such interests that we are the kind of being that can have rights.

A critic might object to this by saying that not all human beings have interests, from which it would follow that not all human beings can have rights, if a necessary condition of having rights is that one have interests. I do not find this criticism very persuasive. For it does seem to be the case that, when we are confronted with individuals who never have and never will manifest any interests whatsoever—where, that is, there is no reason to believe that they experience needs or wants, affection or aversion, hopes or fears, as in the case of those individuals who "vegetate"—then I think we have good reason to withhold the rubric "human being," though they are the offspring of human parents. To be a subject of interests, in short, does appear to be a necessary condition of being human.

Of course, even if this much is true, it does not follow that we have any rights; all that follows is that we *can* have them. So the question is, "Assuming that we can have rights, do we have any? In particular, do we all have the equal natural right to be spared undeserved pain?" The most plausible basis for supposing that we do would, I think, have to show the following.

First, it would have to show that, in the absence of any wrongdoing on the part of any individual human being, A, in terms of which it might be judged that A deserves to be punished—that is, that A deserves to be made to suffer pain—no one human being is any more deserving of being made to experience pain than is any other. Thus, to cause an innocent human being undeserved pain, on this account, will be to treat him *unjustly*; it is to cause a human being to suffer an evil, in the form of pain, which he does not deserve.

Second, the most plausible argument here would have to show that there is a necessary connection between injustice and rights, such that, if it is true that a person has been treated unjustly, it follows that one of his rights has been violated. At least for a subset of our duties, in other words, a correlation between duties and rights would have to be established, so that, though it will not always follow from my duty to do something (say, act benevolently) that someone has a corresponding right to demand that I act in this way toward him, this entailment will hold true in some cases; that is, because I have a duty to act justly, it will follow that specific individuals are entitled to demand that I act justly toward them.

Thus, assuming that all human beings are the kind of being that can have rights; and assuming that to cause any human being undeserved pain is to treat him unjustly; and assuming, finally, that any time we treat a person unjustly we violate one of his rights; then it could be inferred that to cause a human being undeserved pain is to violate his natural right to be spared undeserved pain. and it could also be argued that this is a right that all human beings have, to an equal extent, just because they are human beings.

I am not sure what to say about this argument. In some respects, at least, it represents an improvement over the others. In particular, it does not presuppose that all human beings have to be able to excercise certain high-grade capacities, such as making free choices, in order to be human beings. Humans may have vastly different interests, and still it could remain true that the having of some interests is a necessary condition of being human. And, too, this argument does not commit us to the dubious position that the concept of a right is just the other side of a duty—that, in other words, one person may be said to have a right to demand x if another person can be said to have a duty to do x.

On this basis, then, it might be argued that all human beings have an equal right to be spared undeserved pain. Whether such an argument would succeed, I cannot say. All that I can say is, first, that it has a degree of plausibility that the other arguments lack, and, second, that precisely the same line of reasoning can be used in support of the contention that animals have an equal natural right to be spared undeserved pain. For animals, too, are the kind of being who have interests; we have no reason to believe, that is, that the contents of their conscious life are matters of uniform indifference to them; on the contrary, we have every reason to believe that there are many things toward which they are, in Perry's terms, "for or against"; unlike cars, they have needs, for example, which we have every reason to believe that they experience the desire to fulfill. Moreover, if it is unjust to cause a human being undeserved pain (and if what makes this unjust is that pain is evil and that the human is innocent and thus does not deserve the evil he receives), then it must also be unjust to cause an innocent animal undeserved pain. If it be objected that it is not possible to act unjustly toward animals, though it is possible to do so toward humans, then, once again, what we should demand is some justification of this contention; what we should want to know is just what there is that is characteristic of all human beings, and is absent from all other animals, that makes it possible to treat the former, but not the latter, unjustly. In the absence of such an explanation, I think we have every reason to suppose that restricting the concepts of just and unjust treatment to human beings is a prejudice.

If, then, the most plausible basis for attributing an equal natural right to be spared undeserved pain to all human beings turns on the idea that it is unjust to cause pain to an undeserving human being, then, given that it is unjust to do this to an innocent animal, it likewise would follow that animals have an equal natural right to be spared undeserved pain.

A critic will respond that all that this argument could show is that, among themselves, each animal has an equal natural right to be spared undeserved pain. What this argument could not show, this critic will contend, is that any animal could have a right that is equal to the right that any human being has to be spared undeserved pain. I do not think this criticism is justified. For assuming that the grounds for ascribing the right in question are the same for humans and animals, I do not understand how it can be logically inferred that humans possess this right to a greater extent than do animals. Unless or until we are given some morally relevant difference that characterizes all humans but no animals—a difference, that is, on the basis of which we could justifiably allege that our right to be spared undeserved pain is greater than the right that belongs to animals—unless or until we are given such a difference, I think reason compels us to aver that if humans have this right to an equal extent, for the reasons given, then animals have this right also, and have it to an extent that is equal to that in which humans possess it.

Now, none of this, even if it is correct, establishes that animals (or humans) have an equal natural right to be spared undeserved pain. For my arguments in the preceding are arguments *about* arguments for and against the ascription or withholding of this right to humans and animals; they are not intended to show that humans or animals do or do not have this right. What I have argued, however, provides a sufficient basis to respond to the thesis that it is because human beings have an equal natural right to spared undeserved pain, while animals do not, that we can be justified in treating them differently. What I have argued is that, at least in view of the arguments considered here, there is no good reason to believe this. For the grounds that might be invoked for denying that animals have this right—for example, that they cannot reason or make free choices—would also show that some humans do not have this right either, whereas what appear to be the most plausible grounds on which to rest the claim that all humans have this right are grounds that would equally well support the claim that animals do too. If I am correct, therefore, none of these arguments provides us with a good reason for believing that it would be wrong to treat, say, mentally defective human beings in the way I described earlier, but morally permissible to treat animals in a similar way, because such a practice would violate a right that all humans have but which all animals lack.

Two objections should be addressed before proceeding. Both involve difficulties that are supposed to attend the attribution of rights to animals. The first declares that animals cannot have rights because they lack the capacity to *claim* them.[20] Now, this objection seems to be a variant of the view that animals cannot have rights because they cannot speak, and, like this more general view, this one too will not withstand a moment's serious reflection. For there are many human beings who cannot speak or claim their rights—tiny infants, for example—and yet who would not be denied the right in question, assuming, as we are, that it is supposed to be a right possessed by *all* human beings. Thus, if a human being can possess this (or any other right) without being able to demand it, it cannot be reasonable to require that animals be able to do so, if they are to possess this (or any other) right. The second objection is different. It declares that the attribution of rights to animals leads to absurdity.[21] For if, say, a lamb has the natural right to be spared undeserved pain, then the wolf, who devours it unmercifully, without the benefit of anesthetic, should be said to violate the lamb's right. This, it is alleged, is absurd, and so, then, is the attribution of rights to animals. Well, absurd it may be to say that the wolf violates the lamb's right. But even supposing that it is, nothing said here implies that such deeds on the part of the wolf violate the lamb's rights. For the lamb can have rights only against those beings who are capable of taking the interests of the lamb into account and trying to determine, on the basis of its interests, as well as other relevant considerations, what, morally speaking, ought to be done. In other words, the only kind of being against which another being can have rights is a being that can be held to be morally responsible for its actions. Thus, the lamb can have rights against, say, most adult human beings. But a wolf, I think it would be agreed, is not capable of making decisions from the moral point of view; nor is a wolf the kind of being that can be held morally responsible; neither, then, can it make sense to say that the lamb has any rights against the wolf. This situation has its counterpart in human affairs. The severely mentally feeble, for example, lack the requisite powers to act morally; thus, *they* cannot be expected to recognize our rights, nor can *they* be said to violate our rights, even if, for example, they should happen to cause us undeserved pain. For as they are not the kind of being that can be held responsible for what they do, neither can they be said to violate anyone's rights by what they do.

Of course, even if it is true that animals and humans have an equal natural right to be spared undeserved pain, it would not follow that it is always wrong to cause them undeserved pain. For a right may always be overridden by more stringent moral demands. Thus, even if we assume that both human beings and animals have an equal natural right to be spared undeserved pain, questions can arise concerning when we would be justified in engaging in or supporting practices that cause undeserved pain to either humans or animals. Now, I have already suggested that we would not approve of engaging in or supporting practices that cause undeserved pain to some human beings merely on the grounds that these practices bring about an amount of pleasure equal to or slightly in excess of the amount of pain these humans are made to suffer. And I think that, if someone believes that human beings have an equal natural right to be spared undeserved pain, one of the reasons he would give for disapproving of these practices is that they would violate their right. For to cause a human being pain simply on the basis that it will give others an equivalent amount of pleasure, or an amount of pleasure slightly in excess of the amount of pain involved, is not to show that he deserves to suffer any more than anyone else, and it is not to go any way toward justifying, therefore, overriding his equal right not to suffer undeserved pain, assuming that all humans have this right. I have also observed, however, that what appears to be the most plausible argument in support of the view that all human beings have an equal natural right to be spared undeserved pain would provide an equally compelling basis for ascribing this right to animals also. Accordingly, if we would object to the practice in question, when it involves the treatment of human beings, on the grounds that their right is being violated, and assuming that we are unable to cite any grounds that would justify the claim that all humans but no animals have this right, then we must, if we are to be consistent, condemn any similar practice, for the same reasons, when it involves the treatment of animals.

But there is, of course, a third type of case to be considered. This is the case where the amount of undeserved pain caused by a practice is *greatly* exceeded by the amount of pleasure the practice brings about. And the question we must ask is whether, under these circumstances, the practice could be morally justified. And here, I think, a case might be made for the position that such a practice could be justified, if the undeserved pain involved is of a very trivial variety. Imagine, that is, that the world was such that, by inflicting a very slight, momentary, unde-served pain on animals, the human population, or a large segment of it, would experience an incredible amount of long-lasting pleasure. Then, I think, we might submit that, though it might be better if the world allowed us to get this incredible pleasure without causing the animals the pain in question, still, the pain they experience is so slight and lasts for such a very short time that, though it is undeserved, the vast amount of good that is brought about more than compensates for their very modest suffering. We might argue, in other words, that, even if animals do have a right to be spared undeserved pain, their right would be justifiably overridden in a situation such as this.

Now, I am not sure whether even this use of animals would be justified. But assuming that it is, there are two points I want to make. The first is that, if such a practice is justified in the case where those who suffer are animals and those who secure the pleasure are humans, then, given the soundness of my argument up to now, and assuming that no one is able to show that there is a morally relevant difference between all humans and all animals, the same would be true of a practice where *both* those who suffer *and* those who secure the pleasure are humans. And, of course, the same thing would be true, given the conditions I have just stated, of a practice where those who receive the pain are humans and those who secure the pleasure are *animals*.[22]

But the second thing I would say here is that, although this is true, it is not particularly relevant to defending conditional vegetarianism. And this is because the undeserved pain that animals experience, in the course of being raised and slaughtered as a source of food, frequently is not of the "trivial" variety. I shall have more to say on this score shortly. What is highly relevant to the conditional vegetarian's defense, then, is the case where the undeserved pain we are talking about is not trivial— where beings are made to suffer intense or long-lasting pain, both physical and psychological. Imagine, then, that we have a practice that causes a given amount of nontrivial and undeserved pain for some human beings; and imagine, further, that this practice brings about an amount of pleasure greatly in excess of the pain these humans are made to suffer. Would we suppose that this practice was justified, simply on the ground that the pleasure greatly exceeded the pain? I do not think we would. For even if we happen to be of the opinion that inflicting undeserved, trivial pain might be justified in this way, I do not think we would be inclined to suppose that causing undeserved, nontrivial pain can be. I think we would be inclined to submit here, as in the earlier cases, that the equal right of humans not to suffer undeserved pain, assuming we have this right, is being unjustifiably overridden. But I also think that, if this is our considered opinion in this case, then, in the absence of any morally relevant difference that exists between the humans and animals in question, we could not consistently render a different judgment if the practice in question caused nontrivial, undeserved pain to the animals. Certainly none of the arguments considered earlier succeeds in providing us with a credible basis on which to rest the belief that humans have a greater claim to an equal right to be spared undeserved pain than do animals.

I can anticipate several objections that might be raised here. The first does not pass muster. The others raise more serious problems that I will try to answer.

First, then, it might be alleged that I have overlooked altogether two points: pleasures can differ qualitatively, and not just quantitatively, and it is human beings who are so endowed by nature that they can experience the higher quality pleasures. Then, it might be alleged, we could justify practices that cause undeserved, nontrivial pain to animals on the grounds that they bring about an amount of high quality pleasure that is equal to, or slightly or greatly exceeds, the amount of pain the animals experience.

Well, I do not think this criticism will stand up under even the briefest reflection. For even if we assume, what is debatable, that pleasures can differ qualitatively one from another, this objection must, I think, offend a moral principle to which we would all subscribe. This is the principle that no practice that causes undeserved, nontrivial pain can be justified *solely* on the grounds of the amount of pleasure it brings about for others, no matter how "high" the quality of the pleasure might be supposed to be. To test this contention we need merely to ask whether we would approve of a practice that causes some humans to suffer nontrivial, undeserved pain but which brings about, say, high intellectual pleasures for other human beings; more particularly, we need to ask whether we would approve of such a practice *simply* on the grounds that it produces this kind of pleasure in whatever amount might be hypothesized. My belief is that we would not approve of it. My belief is that the pain is not justified by these higher pleasures—that the pain is, therefore, gratuitous and that the natural right to be spared undeserved pain, assuming that humans have this right, is being violated.

But, now, if this is true in the case of human (sentient) beings, then, in the absence of any morally relevant difference, it must also be true in the case where the sentient beings involved are nonhuman animals. For the pain that an animal might feel would be just as much pain and just as much an evil as any comparable pain felt by a human being; and since animals appear to have as much claim to the natural right to be spared undeserved pain as do humans, it would be inconsistent to deny that their rights are being violated, if the rights of humans are being violated by a similar practice.

The second criticism is more difficult to answer. This is the objection that we need to take intrinsic values other than pleasures into account, and that, if we do, then it could easily be the case that a practice that causes some undeserved, nontrivial pain to animals could be justified, not because of the amount of pleasure it brings about for humans, but, rather, because of the amount of pleasure and other intrinsic goods we humans reap as a result of it.

But can such practices be justified in this way? I do not think they can. At least I do not think they can so long as the prevention, reduction, or elimination of evil are not considered to be intrinsic goods. And I do not think they are. To begin with, I think those philosophers are right who maintain that it is only certain states of consciousness, certain experiences that can be intrinsically good or evil. So far as the *prevention* of evil is concerned, therefore, though an act or practice that does prevent evil would be a good thing, it would not, I think, be something that is intrinsically good. For preventing evil is a property of certain actions or practices; it is not itself a state of consciousness; neither, then, can it be an intrinsically valuable state of consciousness.

The status of reducing or eliminating evil is more controversial. Since pain, for example, cannot be reduced or eliminated unless it exists, and since it cannot exist unless someone is conscious of it, it certainly seems to be possible to speak of people *experiencing* its reduction or elimination, as when, for example, we say that our headache is "going away" or "is gone." Our question is, then, whether these experiences, these states of consciousness, are intrinsically good. I do not think they are. For, first, though it is true that the value such experiences have is not contingent upon what their *future* consequences happen to be, the value that they have does not seem to reside just in themselves either. Rather, they seem to have the value they have because they provide us with this or that degree of *relief* from the states of consciousness we have had to endure in the past. Take away all considerations about the pain that has gone before, as we must, if we are to ask whether these states of consciousness are *intrinsically* good, and I think we see that they are not desired for their own sake, but for the sake of the relief they bring from the painful experiences that preceded them.

Second, if we were to suppose that such experiences—the experiences of the dimunition or elimination of pain—were intrinsically good; and if, further, we were to agree, as seems reasonable, that we have a prima facie obligation to bring intrinsically good states of affairs into the world; and if, finally, it is the case, as surely it is, that we could not experience the reduction or elimination of pain unless some pain exists; then it would seem to follow that we have a prima facie obligation to make sure that some pain exists so that we can bring about the allegedly intrinsically good experiences that are supposed to attend its reduction or elimination. And this, I think, is a consequence that runs counter to our most basic moral convictions. And since a similar consequence would follow if we took evils other than pain into account, I think we are justified in denying that the reduction or elimination of any evil is, in itself, intrinsically good.

If, then, the foregoing is correct, the question we have before us is *not* "Might we conceivably justify a practice that causes animals undeserved, nontrivial pain if, by doing so, we could thereby prevent, reduce or eliminate evil—for example, evil in the form of pain?" to which the answer is "yes." I have more to say on this matter shortly. Our question is, rather, "Might we be able to justify such a practice *solely* on the grounds of the amount or variety of intrinsically good experiences it brought into being?" And here, I think, the answer is "no." At least this must be our answer if (1) we agree, as I think we would, that no practice that brought these intrinsic goods into being would be justified, on that account alone, if the recipients of the undeserved, nontrivial pain were *human* beings, and if (2) we are unable to show that there is a morally relevant difference that exists between all those animals who are human and all those others who are not.

How, then, might we justify a practice of the kind in question? I have already indicated what seems to be the general direction in which such a justification would have to proceed. In general, what one would have to show is that such a practice would prevent, reduce, or eliminate evil—for example, pain. But more than this surely would be required. For imagine a practice where the recipients of the nontrivial, undeserved pain are humans. And suppose that the evil the practice prevents, reduces, or eliminates is equal to or only slightly exceeds the amount of pain these humans are made to suffer. Then I think we would say that the practice was not morally justified—that the natural right to be spared undeserved pain, which belongs to these human beings if it belongs to all human beings, is being violated. For it is only if the amount of evil prevented, reduced, or eliminated would be *considerably* (perhaps *vastly*) more than the amount of pain caused the human recipients—it is only then, if at all, I think, that we would seriously consider approving the practice. But even more than this would have to be the case, if we were to be tempted to approve it. For I think we would want to be convinced, by rational means, that, realistically speaking, it was *only* by having such a practice that we could bring about these consequences, *and* that we have *very good* reason to believe that these consequences will obtain. Only then, I think, would we seriously consider approving and supporting the practice. And so it is that, in the absence of any morally relevant difference between all humans and other animals, and in view of the argument of the preceding pages, we must, if we are to be consistent, insist that these same conditions must be met, if a practice that causes undeserved, nontrivial pain to animals ought seriously to be considered worthy of our approval.

Now the preceding does, I think, contribute to our understanding of the obligation to be vegetarian. To make this clearer, let us first note that animals who are raised to be eaten by human beings very often are made to suffer. Nor is it simply that they suffer only when they are being shipped to the slaughterhouse or actually being slaughtered. For what is happening is this: The human appetite for meat has become so great that new methods of raising animals have come into being. Called intensive rearing methods, these methods seek to insure that the largest amount of meat can be produced in the shortest amount of time with the least possible expense.[23] In ever increasing numbers, animals are being subjected to the rigors of these methods. Many are being forced to live in incredibly crowded conditions. Moreover, as a result of these methods, the natural desires of many animals often are being frustrated. In short, both in terms of the physical pain these animals must endure, and in terms of the psychological pain that attends the frustration of their natural inclinations, there can be no reasonable doubt that animals who are raised according to intensive rearing methods experience much nontrivial, undeserved pain. Add to this the gruesome realities of "humane" slaughter and we have, I think, an amount and intensity of suffering that can, with propriety, be called "great."

To the extent, therefore, that we eat the flesh of animals that have been raised under such circumstances, we help create the demand for meat that farmers who use intensive rearing methods endeavor to satisfy. Thus, to the extent that it is known that such methods will bring about much undeserved, nontrivial pain on the part of the animals raised according to these methods, anyone who purchases meat that is a product of these methods—and almost everyone who buys meat at a typical supermarket or restaurant does this—is *causally implicated* in a practice that causes pain that is both nontrivial and undeserved for the animals in question. On this point too, I think there can be no doubt.

It is on these grounds that the conditional vegetarian can base at least part of his moral opposition to eating meat. First, he can point out that the onus of justification is always on anyone who supports a practice that is known to inflict nontrivial, undeserved pain on a sentient creature to show that, in doing so, he is not doing anything wrong. And he can point out, furthermore, that the onus of justification is always on those who support a practice that causes a sentient creature nontrivial, undeserved pain to show that, in doing so, the sentient creature's right to be spared this pain is not being violated (assuming that sentient creatures have this right). The conditional vegetarian, in short, is in a position where he can rationally demand that those who lead a life contrary to his show how it is that *their* way of life can be morally justified, just as we are all rationally entitled to demand that those who are causally implicated in a practice that causes nontrivial, undeserved pain to human beings must show how it is that the practice, and their role in it, is not immoral. Contrary to the habit of thought which supposes that it is the vegetarian who is on the defensive and who must labor to show how his "eccentric" way of life can even remotely be defended by rational means, it is the nonvegetarian whose way of life stands in need of rational justification. Indeed, the vegetarian can, if I am right, make an even stronger claim than this. For if the previous argument is sound, he can maintain that unless or until someone does succeed in showing how the undeserved, nontrivial pain animals experience as a result of intensive rearing methods is not gratuitous and does not violate the rights of the animals in question, then he (the vegetarian) is justified in believing that, and acting as if, it is wrong to eat meat, if by doing so we contribute to the intensive rearing of animals and, with this, to the great pain they must inevitably suffer. And the basis on which he can take this stand is the same one that vegetarians and nonvegetarians alike can and should take in the case of a practice that caused great undeserved pain to human beings—namely, that we are justified in believing that, and acting as if, such a practice is immoral unless or until it can be shown that it is not.

And there is another thing the vegetarian can aver, if I am right. He can point out that though those who contribute to the suffering of animals by purchasing meat in the usual way might conceivably be able to justify their buying and eating habits, they cannot do this by arguing that the nontrivial, undeserved pain these animals experience is a small price to pay for the variety and amount of human pleasure or other intrinsic goods brought into being by treating animals as we do. Such a "justification" will not work, if my preceding argument is sound, any more than will the "justification" that it is all right to cause nontrivial, undeserved pain to human beings so long as other human beings are able thereby to secure an abundant crop of pleasures or other intrinsic goods from the garden of earthly delights.

Now, there are, as I mentioned earlier, two further objections that might be raised, both of which, I think, uncover important limitations in the argument of this section. The first is that a meat eater might be able to escape the thrust of my argument by the simple expedient of buying meat from farms where the animals are not raised according to intensive rearing methods, a difficult but not impossible task at the present time. For despite the widespread use of these methods, it remains true that there are farms where animals are raised in clean, comfortable quarters, and where the pain they experience is the natural result of the exigencies of animal existence rather than, to use an expression of Hume's, of "human art and contrivance." Or one might secure one's meat by hunting. And it is true, I think, that, judging from what some vegetarians have said,[24] such expedients would escape the net of their moral condemnation, provided the animals were killed "humanely"—that is, as painlessly as possible. For my own part, however, I think that a vegetarian, if he were to concede this much, would be conceding more than he should. For it is not merely considerations about the pain that an animal may feel that should form the moral basis of vegetarianism. It is also the routine killing of animals, whether "humanely" or not. Of course, nothing that I have said in this section goes any way toward justifying this contention of mine, which is why I think my argument up to this point is deficient in an important respect. This is a deficiency I hope to remedy in the following section.

My response to the second objection also must be deferred to the section that follows. This is the objection that reads thus: "Granted, the amount of pain animals experience in intensive rearing units is deplorable and ought to be eliminated as far as is possible; still, it does not follow that we ought to give up meat altogether or to go to the trouble of hunting or buying it from other farmers. After all, all we need do is get rid of the pain and our moral worries will be over. So, what we should do is this; we should try to figure out how to *desensitize* animals so that they do not feel any pain, even in the most barbarous surroundings. Then, if this could be worked out, there would not be any grounds for worrying about the 'morality' of eating meat. Remove the animals' capacity for feeling pain and you thereby remove the possibility of their experiencing any pain that is gratuitous."

Now, I think it is obvious that nothing that I have said thus far can form a basis for responding to this objection, and though I think there are alternative ways in which one might try to respond to it, the case I try to make against it evolves out of my response to the first objection; I try to show, in other words, that an adequate response to this objection can be based upon the thesis that *it is the killing of animals, and not just their pain, that matters morally.*

Before turning to this matter, however, there is one final point I want to make about the argument of this section. This is that, despite the deficiencies to which I have just alluded, it would, if sound, make a strong case for altering the purchasing habits of many of us. If sound, it would show that we cannot suppose that it is a matter of moral indifference where we buy our meat or from whom. If sound, it would show that we are justified in believing that, in the absence of any compelling argument to the contrary, it is wrong to buy meat from sources who rely on farms that use intensive rearing methods. And this, though it may not be the final, would at least be a first step in the direction of "animal liberation."[25]

II

My argument in this section turns on considerations about the natural "right to life" that we humans are sometimes said uniquely to possess, and to possess to an equal degree. My strategy here is similar to my strategy in the previous section. What I try to show is that arguments that might be used in defense of the claim that all human beings have this natural right to an equal extent would also show that animals are possessors of it, whereas arguments that might be used to show that animals do not have this right would also show that not all human beings do either. Just as in the preceding section, however, so here too, a disclaimer to completeness is in order. I have not been able to consider all the arguments that might be advanced in this context; all that I have been able to do is consider what I think are the most important ones.

Let us begin, then, with the idea that all humans possess an equal natural right to life. And let us notice, once again, that it is an *equal natural* right that we are speaking of, one that we cannot acquire or have granted to us, and one that we all are supposed to have just because we are human beings. On what basis, then, might it be alleged that all and only human beings possess this right to an equal extent? Well, several familiar possibilities come immediately to mind. It might be argued that all and only human beings have an equal right to life because either (*a*) all and only human beings have the capacity to reason, or (*b*) all and only human beings have the capacity to make free choices, or (c) all and only human beings have a concept of "self," or (d) all and only human beings have all or some combination of the previously mentioned capacities. And it is easy to imagine how someone might argue that, since animals do not have any of these capacities, *they* do not possess a right to life, least of all one that is equal to the one possessed by humans.

I have already touched upon some of the difficulties such views must inevitably encounter. Briefly, it is not clear, first, that no non-human animals satisfy any one (or all) of these conditions, and, second, it is reasonably clear that not all human beings satisfy them. The severely mentally feeble, for example, fail to satisfy them. Accordingly, *if* we want to insist that they have a right to life, then we cannot also maintain that they have it because they satisfy one or another of these conditions. Thus, *if* we want to insist that they have an equal right to life, despite their failure to satisfy these conditions, we cannot consistently maintain that animals, because they fail to satisfy these conditions, therefore lack this right.

Another possible ground is that of sentience, by which I under-stand the capacity to experience pleasure and pain. But this view, too, must encounter a familiar difficulty—namely, that it could not justify restricting the right *only* to human beings.

What clearly is needed, then, if we are to present any plausible argument for the view that all and only human beings have an equal natural right to life, is a basis for this right that is invariant and equal in the case of all human beings and only in their case. It is against this backdrop, I think, that the following view naturally arises.[26] This is the view that the life of every human being has "intrinsic worth"—that, in Kant's terms, each of us exists as "an end in himself"—*and* that this intrinsic worth that belongs *only* to human beings, is shared *equally* by all. "Thus," it might be alleged, "it is because of the equal intrinsic worth of all human beings that we all have an equal right to life."

This view, I think, has a degree of plausibility which those pre-viously discussed lack. For by saying that the worth that is supposed to attach to a being just because he or she is human is intrinsic, and that it is because of this that we all have an equal natural right to life, this view rules out the possibility that one human being might give this right to or withhold it from another. It would appear, therefore, that this view could make sense of the alleged *naturalness* of the right in question. Moreover, by resting the equal right to life on the idea of the equal intrinsic worth of all human beings, this view may succeed, where the others have failed, in accounting for the alleged *equality* of this right.

Despite these apparent advantages, however, the view under consideration must face certain difficulties. One difficulty lies in specifying just what it is supposed to mean to say that the life of every human being is "intrinsically worthwhile."[27] Now, it cannot mean that "each and every human being has a natural right to life." For the idea that the life of each and every human being has intrinsic worth was introduced in the first place to provide a basis for saying that each and every human being has an equal right to life. Accordingly, if, say, "Jones's life is intrinsically worthwhile" ends up meaning "Jones has an equal right to life," then the claim that the life of each and every individual is equally worthwhile, judged intrinsically, cannot be construed as a *basis* for saying that each and every human being has an equal right to life. For the two claims would mean the same thing, and one claim can never be construed as being the basis for another, if they both mean the same.

But a second and, for our purposes, more important difficulty is this: On what grounds is it being alleged that each and every human being, and only human beings, are intrinsically worthwhile? Just what is there, in other words, about being human, and only about being human, that underlies this ascription of unique worth? Well, one possible answer here is that there is not "anything" that underlies this worth. The worth in question, in short, just belongs to anyone who is human, and only to those who are. It is a worth that we simply recognize or intuit, whenever we carefully examine that complex of ideas we have before our minds when we think of the idea, "human being." I find this view unsatisfactory, both because it would seem to commit us to an ontology of value that is very difficult to defend, and because I, for one, even after the most scrupulous examination I can manage, fail to intuit the unique worth in question. I do not know how to prove that the view in question is mistaken in a few swift strokes, however. All I can do is point out the historic precedents of certain groups of human beings who have claimed to "intuit" a special worth belonging to their group and not to others within the human family, and say that it is good to remember that alluding to a special, intuitive way of "knowing" such things could only serve the purpose of giving an air of intellectual respectability to unreasoned prejudices. And, further, I can only register here my own suspicion that the same is true in this case, though to a much wider extent. For I think that falling into talk about the "intuition of the unique intrinsic worth of being human" would be the last recourse of men who, having found no good reason to believe that human beings have an unique intrinsic worth, would go on believing that they do anyhow.

Short of having recourse to intuition, then, we can expect those who believe that human beings uniquely possess intrinsic worth to tell us what there is about being human, in virtue of which this worth is possessed. The difficulty here, however, as can be anticipated, is that some familiar problems are going to raise their tiresome heads. For shall we say that it is because humans can speak, or reason, or make free choices, or form a concept of their own identity that underlies this worth? These suggestions will not work here, any more than they have before. For there are some beings who are human who cannot do these things, and there very well may be some beings who are not human who can. None of these capacities, therefore, could do the job of providing the basis for a kind of worth that all humans and only humans are supposed to possess.

But suppose we try to unpack this notion of intrinsic worth in a slightly different way.[28] Suppose we say that the reasons we have for saying that all and only human beings exist as ends in themselves are, first, that every human being has various positive interests, such as desires, goals, hopes, preferences and the like, the satisfaction or realization of which brings intrinsic value to their lives, in the form of intrinsically valuable experiences; and, second, that the intrinsic value brought to the life of any one man, by the satisfaction of his desires or the realization of his goals, is just as good, judged in itself, as the intrinsic value brought to the life of any other man by the satisfaction or realization of those comparable desires and goals he happens to have. In this sense, then, all men are equal, and it is because of this equality among all men, it might be alleged, that each man has as much right as any other to seek to satisfy his desires and realize his goals, so long, at least, that, in doing so, he does not violate the rights of any other human being. "Now, since," this line of argument continues, "no one can seek to satisfy his desires or realize his goals if he is dead, and because every man has as much right as any other to seek to satisfy his desires and realize his goals, then to take the life of any human being will always be prima facie to violate a right that he shares equally with all other human beings— namely, his right to life."

What shall we make of this argument? I am uncertain whether it can withstand careful scrutiny. Whether it can or not, however, is not a matter I feel compelled to try to decide here. What I do want to point out is that, of the arguments considered here, this one has a degree of plausibility the others lack, not only because, as I have already re-marked, it addresses itself both to the alleged naturalness and the alleged equality of the right in question, but also because it rests on what I take to be a necessary condition of being human—namely, that a being must have interests. For these reasons, then, I do not think I can be accused of "straw-man" tactics by choosing this as the most plausible among a cluster of possible arguments that might be urged in support of the contention that all human beings have an equal natural right to life. At the same time, however, as can be anticipated, I believe that, whatever plausibility this argument might have in this connection, it would also have in connection with the claim that animals, too, have an equal natural right to life.

For even if it is true that this argument provides us with adequate grounds for ascribing a natural right to life equally to all human beings, there is nothing in it that could tend to show that this is a right that belongs *only* to those beings who are human. On the contrary, the argument in question would equally well support the claim that any being who has positive interests that, when satisfied, bring about experi-ences that are just as intrinsically valuable as the satisfaction of the comparable interests of any other individual, would have an equal right to life. In particular, then, it would support the view that animals have an equal right to life, if they meet the conditions in question. And a case can be made for the view that they do. For, once again, it seems clear that animals have positive interests, the satisfaction or realization of which would appear to be just as intrinsically worthwhile, judged in them-selves, as the satisfaction or realization of any comparable interest a human being might have. True, the interests animals have may be of a comparatively low grade, when we compare them to, say, the contem-plative interests of Aristotle's virtuous man. But the same is true of many human beings: their interests may be largely restricted to food and drink, with occasional bursts of sympathy for a few. Yet we would not say that such a man has less of a right to life than another, assuming that all men have an equal right to life. Neither, then, can we say that animals, because of their "base" interests, have any less of a right to life.

One way to avoid this conclusion and, at the same time, to chal-lenge part of the argument in Section I, is to deny that animals have interests.[29] But on what basis might this denial rest? A by now familiar basis is that animals cannot speak; they cannot use words to formulate or express anything; thus, they cannot have an interest in anything. But this objection obviously assumes that only those beings who are able to use words to formulate or express something can have interests, and this, even ignoring the possibility that at least some animals might be able to do this, seems implausible. For we do not suppose that infants, for example, have to learn to use a language before they can have any interests. Moreover, the behavior of animals certainly seems to attest not only to the possibility that they can, but that they actually do have interests. Their behavior presents us with many cases of preferential choice and goal-directed action, in the face of which, and in the absence of any rationally compelling argument to the contrary, it seems both arbitrary and prejudicial to deny the presence of interests in them.

The most plausible argument for the view that humans have an equal natural right to life, therefore, seems to provide an equally plausible justification for the view that animals have this right also. But just as in saying that men and animals have an equal right to be spared undeserved pain, so here, too, we would not imply that the right in question can never be overridden. For there may arise circumstances in which an individual's right to life could be outweighed by other, more pressing moral demands, and where, therefore, we would be justified in taking the life of the individual in question. But even a moment's reflection will reveal that we would not condone a practice that involved the routine slaughter of human beings simply on the grounds that it brought about this or that amount of pleasure, or this or that amount of intrinsically good experiences for others, no matter how great the amount of good hypothesized. For to take the lives of individuals, for this reason, is manifestly not to recognize that their life is just as worthwhile as anybody else's, or that they have just as much right to life as others do. Nor need any of this involve considerations about the amount of pain that is caused the persons whose lives are taken. Let us suppose that these persons are killed painlessly; that still would not alter the judgment that they have been treated wrongly and that the practice in question is immoral.

If, then, the argument in this section is sound; and assuming that no other basis is forthcoming which would support the view that humans do, but animals do not, have an equal right to life; then the same is true of any practice involving the slaughter of animals, and we have, therefore, grounds for responding to the two objections raised, but not answered, at the end of the first section. These objections were, first, that since the only thing wrong with the way animals are treated in the course of being raised and slaughtered is that they are caused a lot of undeserved pain, the thing to do is to desensitize them so that they do not feel anything. What we can see now, however, is that the undeserved pain animals feel is not the only morally relevant consideration; that they are killed must also be taken into account.

Similarly, to attempt to avoid the force of my argument for conditional vegetarianism by buying meat from farms that do not practice intensive rearing methods or by hunting and killing animals oneself—expedients that formed the basis of the second objection at the end of Section I—these expedients will not meet the total challenge vegetarians can place before their meat-eating friends. For the animals slaughtered on even the most otherwise idyllic farms, as well as those shot in the wild, are just as much killed, and just as much dead, as the animals slaughtered under the most ruthless of conditions.

Unless or until, then, we are given a rationally compelling argument that shows that all and only human beings have an equal right to life; and so long as any plausible argument that might be advanced to support the view that all human beings have this right can be shown to support, to the same extent, the view that animals have this right also; and so long as we believe we are rationally justified in ascribing this right to humans and to make reference to it in the course of justifying our judgment that it is wrong to kill a given number of human beings simply for the sake of bringing about this or that amount of good for this or that number of people; given all these conditions, then I believe we are equally committed to the view that we cannot be justified in killing any one or any number of animals for the intrinsic good their deaths may bring to us. I do not say that there are no possible circumstances in which we would be justified in killing them. What I do say is that we cannot justify doing so in their case, any more than we can in the case of the slaughter of human beings, by arguing that such a practice brings about intrinsically valuable experiences for others.

Once again, therefore, the onus of justification lies not on the shoulders of those who are vegetarians but on the shoulders of those who are not. If the argument of the present section is sound, it is the nonvegetarian who must show us how he can be justified in eating meat, when he knows that, to do so, an animal has had to be killed. It is the nonvegetarian who must show us how his manner of life does not contribute to practices that systematically ignore the right to life which animals possess, if humans are supposed to possess it on the basis of the most plausible argument considered here. And it is the nonvegetarian who must do all this while being fully cognizant that he cannot defend his way of life merely by summing up the intrinsic goods—the delicious taste of meat, for example—that come into being as a result of the slaughter of animals.

This is not to say that practices that involve taking the lives of animals cannot possibly be justified. In some cases, perhaps, they can be, and the grounds on which we might rest such a justification would, I think, parallel those outlined in the preceding section in connection with the discussion of when we might be morally justified in approving a practice that caused animals nontrivial, undeserved pain. What we would have to show here, I think, in order seriously to consider approving of such a practice, is (1) that such a practice would prevent, reduce, or eliminate a much greater amount of evil, including the evil that attaches to the taking of the life of a being who has as much claim as any other to an equal natural right to life; (2) that, realistically speaking, there is no other way to bring about these consequences; and (3) that we have very good reason to believe that these consequences will, in fact, obtain. Now, perhaps there are some cases in which these conditions are satisfied. For example, perhaps they are satisfied in the case of the Eskimo's killing of animals and in the case of having a restricted hunting season for such animals as deer. But to say that this is (or may be) true of *some* cases is not to say that it is true of all, and it will remain the task of the nonvegetarian to show that what is true in these cases, assuming that it is true, is also true of any practice that involves killing animals which, by his actions, he supports.

Two final objections deserve to be considered before ending. The first is that, even assuming that what I have said is true of *some* nonhuman animals, it does not follow that it is true of *all* of them. For the arguments given have turned on the thesis that it is only beings who have interests who can have rights, and it is quite possible that, though some animals have interests, not all of them do. I think this objection is both relevant and very difficult to answer adequately. The problem it raises is how we can know when a given being has interests. The assumption I have made throughout is that this is an empirical question, to be answered on the basis of reasoning by analogy—that, roughly speaking, beings who are very similar to us, both in terms of physiology and in terms of nonverbal behavior, are, like us, beings who have interests. The difficulty lies in knowing how far this analogy can be pushed. Certain animals, I think, present us with paradigms for the application of this reasoning—the primates, for example. In the case of others, however, the situation is less clear, and in the case of some, such as the protozoa, it is very gray indeed. There are, I think, at least two possible ways of responding to this difficulty. The first is to concede that there are some beings who are ordinarily classified as animals who do not have interests and who cannot, therefore, possess rights. The second is to insist that all those beings who are ordinarily classified as animals do have interests and can have rights. I am inclined to think that the former of these two alternatives is the correct one, though I cannot defend this judgment here. And thus I think that the arguments I have presented do not, by themselves, justify the thesis that *all* animals have interests and can, therefore, possess rights. But this exaggeration has been perpetrated in the interests of style, and does not, I think, detract from the force of my argument, when it is taken in context. For the cases where we would, with good reason, doubt whether an animal has interests—for example, whether protozoa do—are cases that are, I think, irrelevant to the moral status of vegetarianism. The question of the obligatoriness of vegetarianism, in other words, can arise only if and when the animals we eat are the kind of beings who have interests. Whatever reasonable doubts we may have about which animals do and which do not have interests do not apply, I think, to those animals that are raised according to intensive rearing methods or are routinely killed, painlessly or not, preparatory to our eating them. Thus, to have it pointed out that there are or may be some animals who do not have interests does not in any way modify the obligation not to support practices that cause death or nontrivial, undeserved pain to those animals that do.

Finally, a critic will object that there are no natural rights, not even natural rights possessed by humans. "Thus," he will conclude, "no animals have natural rights either and the backbone of your argument is broken." This objection raises problems too large for me to consider here, and I must content myself, in closing, with the following two remarks. First, I have not argued that either human beings or animals do have natural rights; what I have argued, rather, is that what seem to me to be the most plausible arguments for the view that all humans possess the natural rights I have discussed can be used to show that animals possess these rights also. Thus, if it should turn out that there is no good reason to believe that we humans have any natural rights, it certainly would follow that my argument would lose some of its force. Even so, however, this would not alter the principal logical points I have endeavored to make.

But, second, even if it should turn out that there are no natural rights, that would not put an end to many of the problems discussed here. For even if we do not possess natural rights, we would still object to practices that caused nontrivial, undeserved pain for some human beings if their "justification" was that they brought about this or that amount of pleasure or other forms of intrinsic good for this or that number of people; and we would still object to any practice that involved the killing of human beings, even if killed painlessly, if the practice was supposed to be justified in the same way. But this being so, what clearly would be needed, if we cease to invoke the idea of rights, is some explanation of why practices that are not right, when they involve the treatment of people, can be right (or at least permissible) when they involve the treatment of animals. What clearly would be needed, in short, is what we have found to be needed and wanting all along—namely, the specification of some morally relevant feature of being human which is possessed by *all* human beings and *only* by those beings who are human. Unless or until some such feature can be pointed out, I do not see how the differential treatment of humans and animals can be rationally defended, natural rights or no. And to dismiss, out of hand, the need to justify this matter or the seriousness of doing so, would be to be a party to the "Nazism" that Singer's Herman attributes to us all.[30]

NOTES

1. The title of this essay comes from Gandhi. (See his *The Moral Basis of Vegetarianism* [Ahmedabad: Navajivan Publishing House, 1959.]) Though the substance of my essay differs considerably from Gandhi's, it was through a study of his work, made possible by a Summer Stipend from the National Endowment for the Humanities for the summer of 1972, that I first saw the need to think seriously about the moral status of animals. I am indebted to the National Endowment for the opportunity to carry out my research, and to Gandhi for the inspiration of his work and life. I do not think the grounds on which I endeavor to rest the obligation to be vegetarian are the only possible ones. Perhaps a more accurate title of my essay would be "A Moral Basis for Vegetarianism."

2. René Descartes, *The Discourse on Method* in Elizabeth S. Haldane and G. R. T. Ross, trans., *The Philosophical Works of Descartes* (New York: Dover, 1955), p. 115. Relevant portions of the works cited in this footnote and in footnotes 3, 6, 7, 9, 10, 12, 13, and 21 are included in Tom Regan and Peter Singer, eds., *Animal Rights and Human Obligations* (Englewood Cliffs, N.J.: Prentice-Hall, 1976).

3. Anthony Kenny, trans. and ed., *Descartes: Philosophical Letters* (Oxford: Clarendon Press, 1970), p. 245.

4. Leonora Rosenfield, *From Animal Machine to Beast Machine* (New York: Octagon Books, 1968), pp. 27 ff.

5. Quoted in ibid., p. 54.

6. On the use of animals as subjects in research, see Richard Ryder's "Experiments on Animals," in Stanley and Roslind Godlovitch, and John Harris, eds., *Animals, Men, and Morals* (London: Taplinger, 1972).

7. Unless otherwise indicated, I use the word "animal" to refer to animals other than human beings. That this is an ordinary use of the word, although humans *are* animals, suggests that this is a fact that we are likely (and perhaps eager) to forget. It may also help to account for our willingness to treat (mere) animals in certain ways that we would not countenance in treating humans. On this and other points pertaining to how we talk about animals and humans, see, for example, Mary Midgley, "The Concept of Beastliness," *Philosophy* 48 (1973): 111–135 and Arthur Schopenhauer's *The Basis of Morality*, trans., with introduction and notes, Arthur Broderick Bullock (London: George Allen and Unwin, 1915), pp. 219–221. See also my further comments on my use of the word "animal" toward the end of this essay.

8. See Descartes, *Discourse*, pp. 116–117. But see also his letter to More, alluded to above, where Descartes seems to soften the earlier position of the *Discourse*, stating that "though I regard it as established that we cannot prove that there is any thought in animals, I do not think it is thereby proved that there is not, since the human mind does not reach into their hearts." Descartes then goes on to talk about what is "probable in this matter."

9. On the topic of "talking chimpanzees," see, for example, Peter Jenkins's essay "Ask No Questions," *The Guardian* (London), Tuesday, July 10, 1973.

10. Jeremy Bentham, *The Principles of Morals and Legislation*, chap. 17, sec. 1, n. to par. 4.

11. Joel Feinberg, from "Human Duties and Animal Rights," in Richard K. Morris and Michael W. Fox, eds., *The Fifth Day: Animal Rights and Human Duties* (Washington, D.C.: Acropolis Press, 1978), pp. 45–69.

12. "Whewell on Moral Philosophy," from Mill's *Collected Works*, eds. F. E. L. Priestley et al. (Toronto: University of Toronto Press), 19 volumes, 10:187.

13. See Kant's "Duties Toward Animals and Spirits" in his *Lectures on Ethics*, trans. Louis Infield (New York: Harper and Row, 1963), pp. 239–241. For Aquinas's views, see, for example, *Summa Theologica*, literally translated by

the Dominican Fathers (Benziger Brothers, 1918), Part II, Question 25, Third Article and Question 64, First and Second Articles.

14. I am especially indebted to my colleague, Donald VanDeVeer, for many helpful conversations on the general topic of rights. I also am indebted to H. J. McCloskey's paper, "Rights," *Philosophical Quarterly* 15, 1 (1965): 115–127, and to Joel Feinberg's essays, "Human Duties and Animals' Rights," alluded to above, and "What Kinds of Beings Can Have Rights?," an expanded version of his paper, "The Rights of Animals and Unborn Generations," in William Blackstone, ed., *Philosophy and Environmental Crisis* (Athens: University of Georgia Press, 1974), pp. 43–68. So far as I am aware, the position that only beings who have interests can have rights, and that animals have them, was first set forth by Leonard Nelson in *A System of Ethics*, trans. N. Gutermann (New Haven: Yale University Press, 1956). The relevant portion of Nelson's book has been reprinted in Godlovitch, Godlovitch, and Harris, eds., *Animals, Men, and Morals*.

15. For arguments in support of the thesis that at least some nonhuman animals satisfy these conditions, see, for example, Jane Goodall's *In the Shadow of Man* (New York: Dell, 1971), esp. chap. 19.

16. See, for example, the essays by McCloskey, "Rights," and Feinberg, "Human Duties and Animal Rights."

17. Ralph Barton Perry, *Realms of Value* (Cambridge, Mass.: Harvard University Press, 1954), p. 7.

18. Ibid.

19. Feinberg, "What Kinds of Beings Can Have Rights?"

20. Ibid.

21. See, for example, D. G. Ritchie's *Natural Rights* (London: George Allen and Unwin, 1889).

22. Nelson, *A System of Ethics*, makes a similar point.

23. See, for example, Ruth Harrison's *Animal Machines* (London: Stuart, 1964).

24. One gets this impression, sometimes, when reading Salt's work. See his *The Humanities of Diet* (Manchester: Vegetarian Society, 1914). I have received the same impression from some things said and written by Peter Singer. See his "Animal Liberation," *The New York Review of Books* 20, 3 (April 5, 1973): 17–21. I am uncertain whether Salt or Singer actually hold this view, however.

25. An expression first given currency by Peter Singer.

26. For an example of this kind of argument, see Gregory Vlastos, "Justice and Equality," in Richard B. Brandt, ed., *Social Justice* (Englewood Cliffs, N. J.: Prentice-Hall, 1962), pp. 31–72.

27. This is a point that first became clear to me in discussion with Donald VanDeVeer.

28. Vlastos, "Justice and Equality."

29. See, for example, the essay by McCloskey, "Rights." McCloskey denies that

animals have interests, but does not, so far as I can see, give any reason for believing that this is so.

30. I want to thank my colleagues, W. R. Carter, Robert Hoffman, and Donald VanDeVeer for their helpful criticisms of an earlier draft of this paper. I am also much indebted to Peter Singer for bringing to my attention much of the literature and many of the problems discussed here.

Lastly, John Rodman of the Political Science Department at Pitzer College put me onto some dimensions of the debate over Descartes's view that I was unaware of. See John Rodman, "The Dolphin Papers," *North American Review* 259, 1 (Spring 1974): 13–26.

2
Utilitarianism, Vegetarianism, and Animal Rights

In the summer of 1973 Peter Singer and I met for the first time while I was in Oxford, England, where Singer was then teaching. In April of that year Singer published his powerful review of *Animals, Men, and Morals* (Roslind and Stanley Godlovitch, and John Harris, eds., London: Gollancz, and New York: Taplinger, 1972). (Singer's review appeared in the *New York Review of Books* 20, 3 [April 3, 1973]: 17–21.) Singer's review, the book he reviewed, and, most especially, the pioneering work of Ruth Harrison in *Animal Machines* (London: Stuart, 1964) provided me with increased incentive to finish "The Moral Basis of Vegetarianism," the first draft of which was by then nearing completion, and gave that essay's first section a firm empirical basis. Singer was aware of some material on the moral status of animals which had eluded me in my research—I have expressed my debt to Singer in this regard on several occasions in the past and am pleased to do so yet another time—and I had come across other sources that were new to him. Though we met and discussed our views and aspirations only twice during that summer, we both lamented that the comparatively small body of literature (at that time) on the moral status of animals was so little known and not readily accessible, and we resolved to remedy the situation by putting together a collection of the most important readings then extant. Thus arose our coedited *Animal Rights and Human Obligations* (Englewood Cliffs, N.J.: Prentice-Hall, 1976), which, even while

Singer moved from Oxford back to his native Australia, we managed to put together through the mail.

Despite our mutual concerns and shared projects, Singer and I have significant philosophical differences, differences that go to the very foundation of accounting for our duties to animals. These differences, present even in our earliest work, have not always been recognized by critics of vegetarianism in particular and of "animal liberation" in general. The "Singer-Regan position" has not infrequently been attacked, as if there *were* such a position. (See, for example, Cora Diamond, "Eating Meat and Eating People," *Philosophy* 53, 206 [1978]: 465–480; Michael Fox, " 'Animal Liberation': A Critique," *Ethics* 88, 2 [1978]: 106–118; and Jan Narveson, "Animal Rights," *Canadian Journal of Philosophy* 7, 2 [1977]: 161–178.) In fact, however, our philosophical differences are as deep as our similar concerns, and it was to set these matters straight that I wrote "Utilitarianism, Vegetarianism, and Animal Rights." In this essay I show why it is erroneous to credit Singer with the view that animals have rights, and why, once his position is seen in the light in which he intends it—as, that is, a form of utilitarianism—his case for the moral obligatoriness of vegetarianism is, in my view, very weak indeed. The basis for that obligation, I believe, is not to be found where Singer attempts to locate it, but rests on the recognition that animals have moral rights.

Singer has published a reply to my criticisms in his "Utilitarianism and Vegetarianism," *Philosophy and Public Affairs* 9, 4 (1980): 325–337, and I have answered some of his objections in my "Utilitarianism and Vegetarianism Again," *Ethics and Animals* 2, 1 (1981): 2–7. The debate is not likely to abate, at least so long as each of us continues to be skeptical of the other's position. Of course, neither of us wants or intends to divide the political movement for securing better treatment of animals, and there is no reason why our philosophical differences must spill over into the political arena. For though we may disagree over why it is wrong to treat animals as they are treated in, for example, factory farming or cosmetic tests, we do not disagree about whether it is wrong or whether it ought to stop. And it is the cessation of this treatment which the political movement seeks.

Donald VanDeVeer challenges my rights-based approach because of its appeals to consequences at key places in his "Animal Suffering," *Canadian Journal of Philosophy* 10, 3 (1980): 463–472. I defend the propriety of combining rights and appeals to consequences in my "On the Right to be Spared Gratuitous Suffering," ibid., pp. 473−478.

Persons unfamiliar with Singer's work on animals are encouraged to read his now classic *Animal Liberation* (New York: A New York Review Book, distributed by Random House, 1975; New York: Avon Books, 1977), and *Animal Factories*, co-authored with Jim Mason (New York: Crown Publishers, 1980).

"Utilitarianism, Vegetarianism, and Animal Rights" originally appeared in *Philosophy and Public Affairs* 9, 4 (summer 1980). Copyright © 1980. Reprinted by permission of Princeton University Press.

Philosophy is notorious for its disagreements. Give two philosophers the same premises and we are not surprised that they disagree over the conclusion they think follows from them. Give them the same conclusion and we expect them to disagree about the correct premises. My remarks in this essay fall mainly in this latter category. Peter Singer and I both agree that we have a moral obligation to be vegetarians. This is our common conclusion. We do not agree concerning why we have this obligation. Important differences exist between us regarding the premises from which this conclusion should be derived.[1] My position implies *both* that (*a*) the idea of animal rights is intelligible[2] *and* that (*b*) the view that certain animals have certain rights must play a role in adequately grounding the obligation to be vegetarian. I have more to say about my position in the second section of this essay. To begin I note that Singer, for his part, might accept (*a*); that is, he might accept the view that the idea of animal rights is at least logically coherent. Clearly, however, he does not accept (*b*).

Readers familiar with some of Singer's earlier writings might be forgiven for thinking otherwise. For example, in his well-known essay "All Animals Are Equal," he quotes Bentham's famous passage: "the question is not, Can they (that is nonhuman animals) reason? nor Can they *talk?* but, *Can they suffer?*" Singer then comments:

> In this passage Bentham points to the capacity for suffering as the vital characteristic that gives a being the right to equal consideration.[3]

Here, it perhaps bears emphasizing, Singer points to a particular capacity—namely, the capacity for suffering or, as he says a few lines later, the capacity for "suffering and/or enjoyment"—as the basis for the right to equal consideration. No mention is made of utilitarian considerations. On the contrary, it would not be an unnatural, even if it should turn out to be an incorrect, interpretation to say that Singer thinks that certain beings have the right to equal consideration of interests *because of their nature*—because, as a matter of their nature, they have the capacity to suffer or to enjoy or both. Arguably, Singer could be interpreted as thinking that some animals, at least, have one natural right: the right to equal consideration of their interests.

Nor is this right the only right Singer mentions. To avoid the prejudice that Singer, following Richard Ryder,[4] calls "speciesism," we must "allow that beings which are similar (to humans) in all relevant respects have a similar right to life."[5] At least some animals *are* sufficiently similar to humans in "all relevant respects"; thus, at least some animals have a right to life, Singer implies. But if we ask what those respects are in virtue of which the humans and animals in question have an equal claim to the right to life, these are the natural capacities of the beings in question, which further supports interpreting Singer as believing that at least some animals have, as all or at least most humans do, certain natural rights—in this case, the natural right to life.

Natural though this interpretation appears, Singer has since stated clearly that it fails to capture his considered position. In response to a recent critic's complaint that he has little to say about the nature of rights, Singer writes as follows:

> Why is it surprising that I have little to say about the nature of rights? It would only be surprising to one who assumes that my case for animal liberation is based upon rights and, in particular, upon the idea of extending rights to animals. But this is not my position at all. I have little to say about rights because rights are not important to my argument. My argument is based on the principle of equality, which I do have quite a lot to say about. My basic moral position (as my emphasis on pleasure and pain and my quoting Bentham might have led [readers] to suspect) is utilitarian. I make very little use of the word "rights" in *Animal Liberation*, and I could easily have dispensed with it altogether. I think that the only right I ever attribute to animals is the "right" to equal consideration of interests, and anything that is expressed by talking of such a right could equally well be expressed by the assertion that animals' interests ought to be given equal consideration with the like interests of humans. (With the benefit of hindsight, I regret that I did allow the concept of a right to

intrude into my work so unnecessarily at this point; it would have avoided misunderstanding if I had not made this concession to popular moral rhetoric.)

To the charge of having embroiled the animal liberation debate in the issue of animals' rights, then, I plead not guilty. As to who the real culprit might be . . . .[6]

This passage leaves little room for doubt as to what Singer thinks. His previous references to "animal rights," he thinks, not only were unnecessary for his utilitarian position; they were lamentable, something he now "regrets," a "concession to popular moral rhetoric" rather than a reasoned appeal.

Perhaps this is so. Perhaps appeals to "the rights of animals" must bear the diagnosis Singer gives of his own earlier efforts. I do not know. But I do not think so. Granted it is not uncommon for those mounting the box for some cause or other to invoke gladly the idea of rights; granted also that this appeal is part of the stock-in-trade of the moral rhetorician, "a rhetorical device," in D. G. Ritchie's words, "for gaining a point without the trouble of proving it"—a "device" that, Ritchie goes on to observe, "may be left to the stump-orator or party-journalist but which should be discredited in all serious writing".[7] Nevertheless, despite the testimony of Ritchie and Singer to the contrary, there remains the possibility that we are driven to invoke the idea of rights for serious-minded, theoretical, nonrhetorical reasons. I believe this is true some of the time. In particular, I believe this is true in the case of arguing well for the obligation to be vegetarian. I return to this topic in the second section. My immediate interest, however, lies in paving the way for rational acceptance of this possibility. This I propose to do by arguing that, shorn of appeals to the rights of animals, Singer fails to justify the obligation to be vegetarian or to treat animals in a more humane manner.

I

Anyone writing on the topic of the treatment of animals must acknowledge an enormous debt to Singer. Because of his work, as well as the pioneering work of Ruth Harrison, the gruesome details of factory farming are finding a place within the public consciousness.[8] All of us by now know, or at least have had the opportunity to find out, that chickens are raised in incredibly crowded, unnatural environments; that veal calves are intentionally raised on an anemic diet, are unable to move enough even to clean themselves, are kept in the dark most of their lives; that other animals, including pigs and cattle, are being raised intensively in increasing numbers. Personally, I do not know how anyone pretending to the slightest sensitivity or powers of empathy can look on these practices with benign indifference or approval. In any event, Singer's position, growing out of his professed utilitarianism, is that we have a moral obligation to stop eating meat, to become vegetarians. Here is the way he brings his case to its moral destination:

> Since, as I have said, none of these practices (of raising animals intensively) cater for anything more than our pleasures of taste, our practice of rearing and killing other animals in order to eat them is a clear instance of the sacrifice of the most important interests of other beings in order to satisfy trivial interests of our own . . . we must stop this practice, and each of us has a moral obligation to cease supporting the practice.[9]

I wonder about this. First, I wonder on what grounds Singer judges that "our pleasures of taste" are "trivial interests." Most of the people I know, including many quite thoughtful persons, do not regard the situation in this way. Most of them go to a great deal of trouble to prepare tasty food or to find "the best restaurants" where such food is prepared. Singer might say that people who place so much importance on the taste of food have a warped sense of values. And maybe they do. But that they do, if they do, is something that stands in need of rather elaborate argument, which will not be found in any of Singer's published writings. This is not to say that the interest we have in eating tasty food is as important an interest as we (or animals) have in avoiding pain or death. It is just to say that it is unclear, and that Singer has given no argument to show, that our interest in eating tasty food is, in his words, "trivial."

Second—and now granting to Singer his assumption that our interest in eating pleasant-tasting food is trivial—it is unclear how, as a utilitarian, he can argue that we have a moral obligation to stop supporting the practice of raising animals intensively (this practice is henceforth symbolized as *p*) because of some statement about the *purpose* of *p*. The question the utilitarian must answer is not, (*a*) What is the purpose of *p*?. It is, (*b*) All things considered, what are the consequences of *p*, and how do they compare to the value of the consequences that would result if alternatives to *p* were adopted and supported? Thus, when Singer objects to *p* on the ground that it does not "cater for anything more than our pleasures of taste," he gives us an answer to (*a*), not, as we should expect from a utilitarian, an answer to (*b*). The difference between the two questions and their respective answers is not unimportant. For though the purpose of *p* might be correctly described as that of catering to our (trivial) pleasures of taste, it does not follow *either* that this is a utilitarian objection one might raise against *p*—it is not, so far as I understand utilitarianism—*or* that, when a distinctively utilitarian objection is forthcoming, it will dwell on Singer's characterization of *p*'s purpose. His characterization also leaves out much that, from a utilitarian point of view, must be judged to be highly relevant to determining the morality of *p*.

What I have in mind here is this. The animal industry is big business. I do not know exactly how many people are involved in it, directly or indirectly, but certainly the number must easily run into the many tens of thousands. There are, first and most obviously, those who actually raise and sell the animals; but there are many others besides, including feed producers and retailers; cage manufacturers and designers; the producers of growth stimulants and other chemicals (for example, those designed to ward off or to control disease); those who butcher, package, and ship the meat or eggs or other animal products to which Singer might (and does, as in the case of eggs from battery hens) take moral exception; and the extension personnel and veterinarians whose lives revolve around the success or failure of the animal industry. Also consider all the members of the families who are the dependents of these employees or employers. Now, the interests that these persons have in "business-as-usual," in raising animals intensively, go well beyond pleasures of taste and are far from trivial. These people have a stake in the animal industry as rudimentary and important as having a job, feeding a family, or laying aside money for their children's education or their own retirement. What do these people do about a job, a means of supporting themselves or their dependents, if we or they see the error of their or our ways and become vegetarians? Certainly it is no defense of an immoral practice to plead that some people profit from it. In the case of slavery, for example, we would not cease to condemn it merely because we were apprised that plantation owners found it beneficial. But Singer, as a utilitarian, cannot *just* appeal to our moral intuitions or *assume* that our intuitions can be given a utilitarian basis. In the particular case of the morality of raising animals intensively, Singer, as a utilitarian, cannot say that the interests of those humans involved in this practice, those whose quality of life presently is bound up in it, are irrelevant. As a utilitarian, Singer, I believe, must insist on the relevance of their interests as well as the relevance of the interests of other persons who are not directly involved in the practice but who might be adversely affected by its sudden or gradual cessation. For example, the short and long term economic implications of a sudden or gradual transition to vegetarianism, by large numbers of persons, must seriously be investigated by any utilitarian. It is not enough to point out, as vegetarians sometimes do, that grains not used to feed intensively raised animals *could* be used to feed the starving masses of humanity; a utilitarian must have the hard data to show that this *possibility* is at least probable *and*, judged on utilitarian grounds, desirable. The debate between Singer and Garrett Hardin over the desirability of famine relief, judged on utilitarian principles, is relevant here and points to the enormity of the task that confronts anyone who would rest vegetarianism on utilitarianism.[10] Though the issues involved are enormously complicated and cannot receive anything approaching even a modest airing on this occasion, one thing is certain: It is not *obviously* true that the consequences for everyone affected would be better, all considered, if intensive rearing methods were abandoned and we all (or most of us) became (all at once or gradually) vegetarians. Some nice calculations are necessary to show this. Without them, a utilitarian-based vegetarianism cannot command our rational assent. Even the most sympathetic reader, even a "fellow traveler" like myself will fail to find the necessary calculations in Singer's work. They simply are not there.

Singer, or a defender of his position, can be expected to protest at this point by noting that utilitarianism, as he understands it, involves acceptance of a principle of equality. There is some unclarity concerning how we should interpret Singer's understanding of this principle. Sometimes he writes as though this principle applies to interests; sometimes he writes as though it applies to treatment. I shall consider the latter alternative below. For the present I shall consider how this principle is thought by him to apply to interests.

At one point Singer explains the principle of equality as follows: "The interests of every being affected by an action are to be taken into account and given the same weight as the like interests of any other being" ("All Animals Are Equal," p. 152). I propose to call this "the equality of interests principle." Abstractly, this principle states that equal interests are (and ought to be considered) equal in value, no matter whose interests they are, and that the interests of all affected parties are to be taken into account. Thus, if a human's interest in avoiding pain is a nontrivial, important interest, then, given this principle, the like interest of a nonhuman animal also is (and ought to be considered) nontrivial and important.

Suppose this principle is accepted and is conjoined with the principle of utility. Have we then been given a utilitarian basis for the obligation to be vegetarian? I do not believe so. The problem with the equality of interests principle is that it does not tell us what we ought to do, once we have taken the interests of all affected parties into account and counted equal interests equally. *All* that *it* tells us is that this is something we must do. If, in addition to this principle, we are also supplied with the principle of utility, we are still some distance from the obligation to be vegetarian. For what we would have to be shown, and what Singer fails to show, as I have argued in the above, is that the consequences of all or most persons adopting a vegetarian way of life would be better, all considered, than if we did not. *That* is *not* shown *merely* by insisting that equal interests are equal.

A defender of Singer might object that I have overlooked an important argument. On several occasions (for example, "All Animals Are Equal," p. 156) Singer argues that we would not allow to be done to human imbeciles what we allow to be done to more intelligent, more self-conscious animals; for example, we would not allow trivial, painful experiments to be conducted upon these humans, whereas we do allow them to be conducted on primates. Thus, we are guilty of a gross form of prejudice ("speciesism"): we are grossly inconsistent from the moral point of view.

This view of Singer's is not without considerable moral weight. But how does it strengthen his avowedly *utilitarian* basis for vegetarianism or, more generally, for more humane treatment of animals? Not at all, so far as I understand the issues. In order for this argument for moral consistency to provide a utilitarian basis for more humane treatment of animals, Singer would have to show that it would be just as wrong, *on utilitarian grounds*, to treat animals in certain ways as it is to treat humans in comparable ways. Singer, however, does not show, first, that, on utilitarian grounds, it would be wrong to treat humans in the ways described (here he merely appeals to our settled conviction that it would be wrong to do this) and, second, that it would be wrong at all, on utilitarian grounds, to treat animals in certain ways, let alone, again on utilitarian grounds, that it would be just as wrong to treat them in these ways as it would be to treat humans. In short, Singer fails to give anything resembling a utilitarian basis for the argument for moral consistency.

Nor will it do, as a defense of Singer, merely to assume that the equality of interests principle must be violated by the differential treatment of the humans and animals in question. *That* would have to be shown, not assumed, on utilitarian grounds, since, a priori, the following seems possible. The interests of animals raised intensively are counted as equal to the interests of human imbeciles who might be raised as a food source under similar circumstances, but the consequences of treating the animals in this way are optimific (i.e., are the best for all affected by the outcome, all considered), whereas those resulting from raising imbeciles intensively would not be. More generally, dissimilar treatment of beings with equal interests might well have greatly varying consequences. So, even granting that we would not approve of treating imbecilic humans in the ways animals are routinely treated, and even assuming that the humans and animals themselves have an equal interest in avoiding pain or death, it does not follow that we have been given a utilitarian basis for vegetarianism or the cause of more humane treatment of animals generally. If by the principle of equality Singer means what I have called the equality of interests principle, we must conclude that he has failed to ground the obligation to be vegetarian on utilitarianism.

As mentioned earlier, Singer, in addition to arguing that equality applies to interests, also sometimes writes as if equality applies to treatment. Thus, for example, we find him at one point saying that the principle of equality, as it applies to humans, "is a prescription of how we should *treat* humans" ("All Animals Are Equal," p. 152, my emphasis). It is possible, therefore, that, in addition to the equality of interests principle, Singer also recognizes another principle of equality, what I call the equality of treatment principle. Abstractly this principle might be formulated thus: beings with equal interests ought to be treated equally. This principle has an advantage over the equality of interests principle, in that it does profess to tell us how we ought to act: we ought to treat beings with equal interests equally. This principle, however, suffers from a certain degree of vagueness, in that, by itself, it does not tell us how to determine what constitutes equal treatment. Certainly it cannot be interpreted to mean (and I do not mean to suggest that Singer thinks that it means) that beings with equal interests ought to be treated identically; that, for example, we ought to give dancing lessons to pigs if we give them to little girls on the grounds that pigs and little girls both enjoy dancing. Still, what counts as equal treatment is far from clear. Nevertheless, whatever the appropriate criteria are, I think it is fair to say that Singer would agree to the following—namely, that if we think it wrong to inflict unnecessary pain on humans who have an interest in avoiding it, then we must also think it just as wrong to inflict unnecessary pain on nonhuman animals who have an equal interest in avoiding it. Not to think it just as wrong in the case of animals as in the case of humans, if I understand Singer, would be a breach of the equality of treatment principle.

My question now is this. Suppose that the equality of treatment principle strengthens the case for the obligation to be vegetarian. How, if at all, does Singer provide *this* principle with a utilitarian basis? If I understand him correctly, I believe we must conclude that he fails to provide this principle with such a basis.

Abstractly, there appear to be three possibilities. (1) The equality of treatment principle is identical with the principle of utility. (2) The equality of treatment principle follows from the principle of utility. (3) The equality of treatment principle is presupposed by the principle of utility. I examine each alternative in its turn.

(1) It is implausible to maintain that the equality of treatment principle is identical with the principle of utility. Utility directs us to bring about the greatest possible balance of nonmoral good over nonmoral evil; a priori, whether treating beings with equal interests equally would be conducive to realizing the utilitarian goal is an open question. In other words, a priori, it is at least conceivable that systematic violations of the principle of equality of treatment could be optimific. If this is so, then it cannot plausibly be maintained that the two principles are identical.

(2) Possibly it will be thought that the equality of treatment principle follows from utility in two ways: (*a*) the equality principle follows logically from (is logically entailed by) the principle of utility; (*b*) the equality principle, when supplied with certain factual premises, can be justified by an appeal to utility. As for the first alternative, it must again be said that it is implausible to maintain that the equality of treatment principle is entailed by the principle of utility. Certainly it *appears* possible that someone might affirm the principle of utility and, at the same time, deny the equality of treatment principle without thereby contradicting himself. To put the point differently, someone might maintain that we ought to act so as to bring about the greatest possible

balance of nonmoral good over nonmoral evil *and* maintain that to realize this objective it may be necessary to treat some beings unequally. If this is so, then the equality of treatment principle is not logically entailed by the principle of utility.

The second argument for the equality of treatment principle following from utility is that the utilitarian objective is assisted if this principle is accepted. On this view, we ought to treat beings with equal interests equally because, as a matter of fact, this is optimific. Now, it is certainly open to a utilitarian to argue in this way. Indeed, what I want to emphasize is that, *if* this is how the equality of treatment principle is supposed to follow from the principle of utility, then *it must be argued for*.

No such argument is forthcoming from Singer, I believe, despite certain appearances to the contrary. There are occasions, alluded to earlier, where Singer argues that we are morally inconsistent when we allow things to be done to animals which we would not allow to be done to less developed humans. In doing this, Singer thinks, if I understand him correctly, we violate the equality of treatment principle. But, for this finding to strengthen his allegedly utilitarian basis for vegetarianism and animal liberation generally, Singer would first have to show (at least) that practices that violate this principle also violate the principle of utility. It is not adequate merely to *assume* that this is so, since one thereby begs the question at issue—namely, whether the equality of treatment principle does follow from the principle of utility, in the sense of "follows from" under discussion. By merely noting that the way we allow animals to be treated violates the equality of treatment principle, assuming that it does, Singer fails to give us any argument for opposing this treatment of animals on distinctively *utilitarian* grounds.

How, then, might he argue, on utilitarian lines, against treating animals as they are treated? The question is enormously complicated. I have already alluded to its difficulty earlier, when I mentioned the animal industry. What Singer would have to show, I believe, is that the consequences of treating animals as they are at present being treated are worse, all considered, than those that would result if we treated them differently—for example, if they were not raised intensively. *Possibly* this could be shown. I do not know. Singer, however, has not even begun to show this. And yet, if I am right, this is precisely what he must show, if he is to give the case for animal liberation a utilitarian basis. And this is as much as to say that, judged on his published writings, he fails to give this liberation movement a basis of this kind.

(3) In defense of Singer one might say that, though the equality of

treatment principle is not identical to, is not entailed by, and is not shown by Singer to be justified by the principle of utility, it remains true that utility presupposes equality. Thus, it is by means of this presupposition that the principle of equality of treatment makes its entrance into utilitarian theory. And since equality enters in this, a logically respectable way, Singer's use of the equality of treatment principle has a utilitarian basis after all.

I do not believe this argument holds. What grounds there are for thinking that utility presupposes the equality of treatment principle turn on ignoring the difference between this principle and the equality of interests principle. It is arguable that utilitarianism presupposes the equality of interests principle, that principle being, again, that equal interests are equal—that is, have like importance or value—and that the interests of all affected parties are to be taken into account. Thus, the equality of interests principle directs us, as utilitarians, not to attempt to justify treating different beings differently on the grounds that, for example, though *A* and *B* have a like interest in *C*, *A*'s interests are more important than *B*'s. Like interests have like importance. That is something utilitarianism must presuppose even to get off the ground.

Suppose this is true. What, then, of the equality of treatment principle? Nothing follows concerning its status within utilitarian theory. Certainly it does not *follow* that we ought to treat beings with equal interests equally just because they have equal interests. More conspicuously, this does not follow logically given a utilitarian-based ethic. Nor is the equality of treatment principle presupposed by utilitarianism. If it were, there would be another, more fundamental principle than utility—namely, the principle of equality of treatment. And that, so far as I understand utilitariansim, would be inconsistent with that theory. One cannot hold *both* that the principle of utility is the one and only fundamental moral principle *and* that this principle presupposes another, different, and more fundamental principle, that of equality of treatment. So, this attempt to defend Singer's utilitarian basis for vegetarianism, and for animal liberation generally, just will not do.

The upshot of this is as follows. If Singer actually is to give a utilitarian basis for vegetarianism, he must argue in a quite different way. In particular, the equality of treatment principle must be given a solid utilitarian justification *before* he can be justified in using it, as a utilitarian, in support of vegetarianism. Now, to justify this principle on utilitarian grounds, Singer must show that accepting it and extending its scope to the treatment of animals would bring about better results than are now obtained by treating animals as though they are not covered by this principle. It is *possible* that this can be shown. But to show it would require enormous amounts of complicated empirical data, concerning, for example, the long-term economic implication of Western society's giving up meat eating. Singer gives us no such data. Thus, if the preceding is sound, he fails to give a utilitarian justification of the equality of treatment principle, most especially of extending this principle to animals; and thus he fails to give a utilitarian basis for his objections against meat eating.

Of course, if Singer were to insist that, whatever the consequences of treating animals differently, the fact remains that treating them as they are treated now is a clear violation of their rights and so ought to be stopped—were he to insist on this, apart from considerations about long-term consequences, *then* he would have a decidedly different argument, one that did not turn out, after all, to be utilitarian. For one can hardly argue as a utilitarian and say, in effect, the devil take the consequences, it is the animals' rights that are being violated. So, Singer could dispense with the need to investigate systematically the probable consequences of changing our eating habits, but he could do this only by paying a certain price: giving up his belief in an exclusively utilitarian basis for vegetarianism. In a word, then, the dilemma I think Singer must face is this: if he is a utilitarian, then he must give a radically different argument from the one he has actually given; whereas, if he rests his case for vegetarianism on the argument he has actually given, then he cannot continue to believe that he has given a utilitarian basis for the moral obligation to be vegetarian. Possibly the appeal to the rights of animals is not a "concession to popular rhetoric" after all. That it may not be is what I hope to explain in the next section.

II

My argument begins by considering the situation of those unfortunate humans to whom Singer draws our attention—namely, severely mentally enfeebled humans. (For convenience's sake I shall normally refer to these humans as group *G*.) Like Singer, I shall assume that thoughtful people would agree that it is wrong to treat the humans in question in certain ways—for example, to use them in painful, trivial research or to raise them intensively as a "gourmet" food source (again, as a matter of convenience, I shall normally refer to these practices as treatment *T*). So, the question that divides Singer and me is not whether this is wrong but how, theoretically, its wrongness can most adequately be grounded.

Now, suppose we were to concede, what is far from certain, that, given the condition of the world at present, subjecting group *G* to treatment *T* is not optimific. The point that needs emphasis is that, even if this should happen to be true now, there is no guarantee that it will continue to be so in the future. Thus, if the treatment *T* of group *G* should, in the future, become optimific, as it might, then, if we accepted the principle of utility as our sole fundamental principle, we would have no rational choice but to change our mind about the wrongness of the treatment in question. We would have to say that using the *G*'s in painful, trivial research or raising them intensively as a gourmet food source, although this once was wrong, has ceased to be so. And if we asked how this change in the morality of the practices had come to pass, what we would have to say, as utilitarians, is that it resulted from a change in the value of the consequences of the practices. It was because practices that previously had not been optimific had become so.

I resist such a change in moral judgment. I do not think that persons not already committed to utilitarianism would, on reflection, be willing to change their judgment about the wrongness of the practices in question *merely* on the grounds that these practices had become optimific whereas previously they were not. I think those who are not already committed to utilitarianism would want to know much more than just how much the value of the consequences had changed with the passage of time and circumstances. But if thoughtful people would not change their judgment on utilitarian grounds alone; and if utilitarianism requires that they should change their judgment in the face of these imagined changes in consequences; then the grounds for thinking it wrong *now* to treat the humans in question in the ways in question are not adequately illuminated by the principle of utility. Even granting, that is, that the practices are not now or ever will be optimific, there is, it would appear, something else involved over and above and distinct from how good or bad are the consequences. [11]

The argument just sketched, I believe, spells trouble for theories other than utilitarianism. Ethical egoism, or what Jan Narveson calls "rational egoism," runs into similar problems. The grounds underpinning our objection to treatment *T* of group *G*, Narveson argues, are that, though *G*'s are not rational and thus have no rights themselves, they nevertheless are the object of the sentimental interests of other human beings who, because they are rational, do have rights, including the right to have others respect their sentimental interests.[12] Narveson's claims about the sentimental interests of people at the present time are, I think, highly speculative. However much we might wish to deny or conceal it, a lot of human beings would rather have done with group *G*'s, including those conventionally "closest" to them—for example, relatives. But even conceding that *G*'s are the object of the sentimental interests of other (rational) human beings, there is no guarantee that they will continue to be so in the future. Perhaps rational humans might all cease to have such an interest; and severely mentally enfeebled, orphaned humans might come to be regarded as kin to vermin or worse. Thus, if our judgment that we ought not to subject group *G* to treatment *T* were founded on rational egoism, we should be prepared to say that it would become morally permissible or even morally obligatory to treat them in these ways if the future sentimental interests of rational egoists happened to change as described. I do not believe that thoughtful people not already committed to the position of rational egoism would be prepared to say this, however, which leads me again to the position that something other than and distinct from the interests of rational human beings underlies our judgment that it would be wrong to subject group *G* to treatment *T*.

Similar remarks apply to Kant's position, I believe, though this is conjectural; I am not certain what his position would be. His theory, we know, places constraints on how one rational being may treat himself or herself as well as other rational beings: we are always to treat rational free beings as ends, never merely as means. The problem is, severely mentally enfeebled humans are not rational and so, given Kant's views on free will (or my understanding of his views), they also lack free will. What constraints, then, could Kant consistently place on how we may treat them? I conjecture that his position could be analogous to his position on the treatment of animals.[13] We ought not to maltreat severely mentally enfeebled humans, Kant could hold, because doing so will eventually lead us to maltreat rational free beings. We owe nothing to these humans themselves. Rather, we owe it to ourselves, and to other rational free beings that we do not do those things that in the future will lead us to treat rational free beings as mere means.

My objection to my (conjectural) interpretation of Kant is this. Even granting that treating the humans in question in certain ways *now* leads to the sort of future Kant supposes—one where the perpetrators treat themselves or other rational free beings as mere means—there is no reason why this must continue to be so in the future. In the future, rational free beings might draw a very sharp line indeed between (say) moronic and nonmoronic human beings, and, as a consequence of this distinction, they might have radically different attitudes and feelings about members of the two classes. From a psychological point of view it does not seem implausible to suggest that, if people drew a sharp enough distinction between what they believed about and felt toward moronic and nonmoronic human beings, there would cease to be a strong or widespread tendency (assuming it exists at present) that leads those who treat morons as mere means to treat themselves or other rational free beings as mere means also. If, however, this actually were to come to pass; and if the grounds for judging it wrong to treat morons in the ways in question were Kantian, then we should be prepared to alter our judgment accordingly: though it is wrong *now* to treat them thus, it would *cease* to be so in the future, if the future held the consequences we have imagined. Once more, though, I do not think anyone not already committed to a Kantian-type theory would alter the judgment for these reasons. This leads me once again to conjecture that there is something else that underlies our present judgment that it is wrong to subject group *G* to treatment *T*.

It is not only utilitarianism, therefore, that must face the kind of difficulty I have been tracing. But now, if I ask myself how to avoid this difficulty, I find that I am ineluctably drawn to the idea that morons (even) have certain rights, that we *owe it to them* not to treat them in certain ways, not out of niceness, or sentimental interest, or because they provide a sort of "warm-up" for the really serious moral game played between rational free beings,[14] or because treating them thus is optimific—rather, we owe it to them not to treat them in certain ways because they themselves have a moral right not to be treated in these ways. It is only, I think, if rights are postulated *even* in the case of morons that we can give a sufficiently firm theoretical basis for our conviction that it is wrong to treat them in the ways in question.

For a certainty there is much in the preceding that is left up in the air. For example, I have not shown that human morons do have any rights. To do this I would have to show that what I believe is true, actually is true—namely, that (1) it is *only* if they have rights that we can give a sufficiently firm theoretical basis for the conviction in question; (2)

that this conviction is true; and (3) that the adequacy of theories depends on their ability to illuminate and account for such convictions. To show this, however, I would have to show that *every* alternative theory fails to give this conviction a sufficiently firm basis. I have not shown this. I am not even sure how I might try. That effort, if it comes, will have to come at some later date.[15] Moreover, I have not ventured any analysis of what rights are (Are they valid claims? Entitlements? Powers?), nor have I advanced anything approaching a complete account of the range of rights morons can or do have, assuming they they can or do have some. For example, I have not endeavored to argue for or against the view that they have a right to life, or to pursue happiness.[16] There are many complicated questions that would have to be considered in each of these (and other) cases. I cannot explore them here. But, while conceding (or, rather, insisting) that there is much in the preceding that is left unsaid, the relevance of what has been said to the question of animal rights can now be brought into sharper focus. For if, as I think, in our search for the most adequate theory to account for our settled moral convictions we are driven to postulate that morons (even) have certain rights, it remains to be asked what there is about them that could serve as the grounds or basis of the rights they have, if they have them. Singer, I believe, has argued persuasively that it cannot be that they are human beings, that they belong to the species homo sapiens, which accounts for this; that is to mark moral boundaries in a way that invites comparisons to racism and sexism. Nor can it be argued that morons have the rights they do, if they do, because they are autonomous or very intelligent; they are not. Nor again will it do to argue that they belong to a species whose members normally are rational and the like.[17] Rather, if there is some basis for their having rights, *it must be something about the capacities of the morons themselves* that forms the grounds of their having them. What this is, is controversial, to be sure, but if we search around for the most promising candidates, what we find is that many, many animals will satisfy the grounds in questions.[18] Take, for example, Singer's mention of "the capacity to experience pain and/or enjoyment." That seems to me to be a very strong candidate for grounding rights in the case of human morons. But if that is so, then we seem to be inconsistent at best if we withhold ascribing any rights whatever in the case of those animals who have the capacity in question. I do not mean to suggest that it is a *simple* matter to say what the grounds are for attributing rights to human morons, or to humans generally. Far from it. What I do mean to suggest is that the strongest arguments describing how it is that human morons have rights will rationally compel us to ascribe similar rights to many animals, if I am correct in thinking that (1) it is wrong to treat human morons in the ways in question; (2) we would not (and should not) change this judgment in the ways utilitarianism, egoism, or Kantianism would require, if the future happened to change in the ways described earlier; (3) if, in our search for the most adequate moral theory on which to ground this belief, we are driven to postulating that human morons (even) have certain rights; and (4) if the grounds underlying their possessing the rights they possess are common grounds, as it were, between them and many other animals. If all this is correct, then I think the case for animal rights is very strong indeed. But even if none of it is right, this must be because my arguments are unsound, not because there are no arguments at all. Though I might be confused in my reasoning, I *think* I can tell the difference between reasoning and rhetoric.

NOTES

1. These differences are brought out most clearly in our respective replies to an essay critical of our views by Michael Fox. See his "Animal Liberation: A Critique," *Ethics* 88:2 (January 1978):106–118. See Singer's "The Fable of the Fox and the Unliberated Animals," and my "Fox's Critique of Animal Liberation," in the same issue. In this regard compare the first chapter of Singer's *Animal Liberation* (New York: A New York Review Book, distributed by Random House, 1975; New York: Avon Books, 1977) and my "The Moral Basis of Vegetarianism," *Canadian Journal of Philosophy*, October 1975 (essay 1, above). I discuss some of the differences between us at greater length in my "Animal Rights, Human Wrongs," *Environmental Ethics*, 2 (1980): 99–120 (essay 4, below).

2. On the intelligibility of this idea see, for example, Joel Feinberg, "The Rights of Animals and Unborn Generations" in William Blackstone, ed., *Philosophy and Environmental Crisis* (Athens: University of Georgia Press, 1974); Tom Regan, "Feinberg on What Sorts of Beings Can Have Rights," *Southern Journal of Philosophy* 14:4 (Winter 1976):485–498 (essay 8, below) and "McCloskey on Why Animals Cannot Have Rights," *Philosophical Quarterly* 26:104 (July 1976):251–257.

3. Peter Singer, "All Animals Are Equal" originally appeared in *Philosophic Exchange* 1:5 (Summer 1974):103–115. It was reprinted in Tom Regan and Peter Singer, eds., *Animal Rights and Human Obligations* (Englewood Cliffs, N. J.: Prentice-Hall, 1976), pp. 148–162. Page citations in the text refer to this version.

4. Richard Ryder, "Experiments on Animals," in Stanley and Roslind God-lovitch, and John Harris, eds., *Animals, Men, and Morals* (London: Gollancz, and New York: Taplinger, 1972). See also Richard Ryder, *Victims of Science* (London: Davis-Poytner, 1975).

5. Singer, *Animal Liberation*, p. 21.

6. Singer, "The Fable of the Fox and the Unliberated Animals," p. 122.

7. D. G. Ritchie, *Natural Rights* (London: George Allen and Unwin, 1894). Relevant passages are included in Regan and Singer, eds., *Animal Rights and Human Obligations*, p. 182.

8. See Ruth Harrison, *Animal Machines* (London: Stuart, 1964). See also her essay, "On Factory Farming," in Godlovitch, Godlovitch, and Harris, eds., *Animals, Men and Morals.*

9. Singer, "All Animals Are Equal," in Regan and Singer, eds., *Animal Rights and Human Obligations*, p. 155.

10. See Garrett Hardin, "Lifeboat Ethics: The Case Against Helping the Poor," *Psychology Today* (September 1974): 38–43, 123–126; Peter Singer, "Famine, Affluence, and Morality," *Philosophy and Public Affairs* 1, 3 (Spring 1972): 229–243. Both are reprinted in W. Aiken and H. LaFollette, eds., *World Hunger and Moral Obligation* (Englewood Cliffs, N. J.: Prentice-Hall, 1977), pp. 12–21 and pp. 22–36 respectively. For a discussion of both views see Onora O'Neill, "The Moral Perplexities of Famine Relief," in Tom Regan, ed., *Matters of Life and Death* (New York: Random House, 1980), pp. 260–298.

11. The general point argued for here and in what follows has become clearer to me through conversations with Dale Jamieson. For some first inklings of this line of argument, see my "Narveson on Egoism and the Rights of Animals," *Canadian Journal of Philosophy* 7, 2 (March 1977): 179–186.

12. Jan Narveson, "Animal Rights," *Canadian Journal of Philosophy* 7, 2 (March 1977): 161–178.

13. Immanuel Kant, "Our Duties to Animals and Spirits," in *Lectures on Ethics*, trans. Louis Infield (New York: Harper and Row, 1963). Relevant portions are reprinted in Regan and Singer, eds., *Animal Rights and Human Obligations*. For a critique of Kant's views on the wrongness of cruelty to animals, see my "Exploring the Idea of Animal Rights" in D. A. Paterson and Richard Ryder, eds., *Animals' Rights: A Symposium* (London: Centaur Press, 1979), pp. 73–86. See also Alexander Broadie and Elizabeth Pybus, "Kant's Treatment of Animals," *Philosophy* 49 (October 1974): 375–383. For a defense of Kant against their line of criticism, see my "Broadie and Pybus on Kant," *Philosophy* 51 (October 1976): 471–472.

14. See Ross's analogous observation: "If we think we ought to behave in a certain way to animals, it is out of consideration primarily for *their* feelings that we think we ought to behave so; we do not think of them merely as a practicing-ground for virtue." W. D. Ross, *The Right and the Good* (Oxford: Clarendon Press, 1930), p. 49. Ross's grounds for denying rights to animals

are subjected to a critical review in my "Exploring the Idea of Animal Rights."

15. I have explored some of the relevant problems in my "An Examination and Defense of One Argument Concerning Animal Rights," *Inquiry* 22, 1–2 (Summer 1979); (essay 6, below).

16. I take up this question in my "The Moral Basis of Vegetarianism," Section II (essay 1 above). Singer subjects my views to a careful critical examination in his "Animals and the Value of Life," in Tom Regan, ed., *Matters of Life and Death* (New York: Random House, 1980). See also my "Exploring the Idea of Animal Rights."

17. On this point see my reply to Fox, "Fox's Critique of Animal Liberation," pp. 129 ff.

18. I examine this controversy at length in my "An Examination and Defense of One Argument Concerning Animal Rights" (essay 6, below).

3
Animal Experimentation: First Thoughts

One cannot begin to think about the moral basis of vegetarianism and avoid thinking about the moral propriety of other uses we make of animals. Their routine use in scientific settings (in basic research, toxicology testing, and high school and university laboratory sections) is one use that demands our critical attention. We cannot assume that how we use and treat them in these settings is all right just because it is customary. Slavery, to cite an example that Singer uses to great effect, was once "customary" in the United States; but that did not make that practice morally well founded. For similar reasons, we cannot assume that the use of animals in science is above moral criticism just because, as a society, we support and allow it.

One danger of challenging an established custom is that those who are actively involved in it (in this case, practicing scientists) and those who are critical of it will find it difficult to communicate with one another. Partly this is a result of human psychology. Those who are under attack understandably are inclined not to listen carefully, and those who are attacking, because their views fall (or at least sometimes seem to fall) on deaf ears will, also understandably, think that the remedy is to talk louder and more stridently. A proverbial "shouting match" is almost inevitable. Almost. It need not turn out this way, and the growing willingness of those in the scientific community to listen to the ideas of their critics, in proper settings, with social grace and patience, cannot but be applauded as a healthy development.

It was in one such setting that the third essay was presented. The occasion was the Eleventh Annual Laboratory Animal Medicine Conference held at the University of Cincinnati in April 1979. The theme of the conference, ably organized and chaired by Dr. Steele F. Mattingly, professor and director of Laboratory Animal Medicine in the University's College of Medicine, was "Ethical Issues Related to the Use of Research Animals." My limited objective in my contribution was "to raise the consciousness" of the scientists in attendance. As it turned out, I had my consciousness raised too, as I will explain in a moment.

Two of the most frequently used ideas in discussions and campaigns about our treatment of animals are (1) cruelty and (2) kindness. What I sought to do in the opening sections of my lecture was to explain how terribly inadequate and potentially counterproductive these two ideas are—inadequate because "being against cruelty" cannot explain or account for our negative duties to animals (how they should not be treated), while "being for kindness" cannot explain or account for our positive duties to them (how they should be treated); and potentially counterproductive because both ideas take attention away from *what* people do and start us speculating about *why* they do it. The charge of "cruelty," frequently leveled against practicing scientists, is especially to be discouraged, since it conjures up images of crazed sadists and thus can only serve to intensify the division that already exists between those who use animals in science and those who want this stopped. In this respect, my remarks were intended to disabuse the critics of science and to defend the character of scientists. That was part of the "consciousness raising" project I had in mind.

My consciousness was raised, however, when it came to my use of the word "vivisection"—since deleted from my lecture, I can assure you! As one of the more forceful veterinarians in attendance volunteered, the use of that word "just makes the hairs on the back of my neck stand up!" (I cannot now recall if the observation was greeted with applause, but my memory is not the least bit cloudy concerning the favorable response it generated.) The observation is apt. Not all those who use animals in science are "vivisectors." Not all (the literal meaning of the word) "cut living organisms." For example, many of those who test the toxicological (harmful) effects of various chemicals do not cut animals and thus are not vivisectors. This does not mean that we cannot raise serious moral questions about what they do, or that none of these questions can be the same as those raised about vivisection. What it does mean is that we simply speak inaccurately and in ways that are unnecessarily divisive if we continue to pose all questions about the use of animals in science in terms of "vivisection." To put the questions more clearly is a small price to pay for greasing the wheels for informed, respectful communication, and a necessary preliminary if the questions are to be answered.

This lecture merely scratches the surface of the use of animals in science. A more fully developed essay, co-authored with Dale Jamieson, "On The Ethics of the Use of Animals in Science," is forthcoming in Tom Regan and Donald VanDeVeer, eds., *And Justice for All* (Towota, N. J.: Rowman and Littlefield, 1982). The idea of animal rights, explored briefly in the essay's final section, is explored at greater length in subsequent essays (see, especially, essays 4 and 6). It is interesting and, in some respects, mysterious that, despite the wealth of literature critical of arguments for vegetarianism, no recent philosopher has yet stepped forward to defend the routine use of animals in science. For important contributions to the debate over the use of animals in science, see Richard Ryder, *Victims of Science* (London: Davis-Poynter, 1975) and Peter Singer, *Animal Liberation* (New York: A New York Review Book, distributed by Random House, 1975; New York: Avon Books, 1977). A nicely conceived discussion of the principal arguments may be found in Charles R. Magel, "Humane Experimentation on Humans and Animals: or . . . Muddling Through," The National Anti-Vivisection Society, 1980. The sections on "Cruelty" and "Kindness" in the essay that follows form part of my "Cruelty, Kindness, and Unnecessary Suffering," *Philosophy* 55, 4 (1980): 533−537. Reprinted from *Philosophy* by permission of Cambridge University Press.

There is no mistaking it. Opposition to the prevailing ways animals are treated, including opposition to their routine use in scientific research, is growing. This growing opposition is being spearheaded by diverse forces, some predictable, some less expected. Predictably, there are those organizations that traditionally have had as at least one of their goals the total abolition of, or the significant reduction in, the use of animals in scientific experiments. Through their publications and other activities, these organizations are succeeding in conveying their perception of animal experimentation to the general public. Researchers actively involved in such experimentation may accuse these organizations of bias, deception, dishonesty, or worse, but that is not the point just now. Just now the point to realize is that these organizations are an increasingly powerful voice against the prevailing practice of relying on animals as research "subjects" or "models." If, during their existence, the organizations working for animal welfare have sometimes been a chorus of dissonant voices, have sometimes given the impression of being what one writer has called "one-person organizations, each bitterly jealous of the others,"[1] this is increasingly not the case. Increasingly one can hear a harmonious message. Their voice has found, while at the same time it has helped create, an increasingly restless, aroused general public.

A second force for change is far less expected and, for the most part, speaks to a different audience. Without either the benefits or handicaps of belonging to any formal organization, individual philosophers have, in the last half dozen years or so, examined the morality of our treatment of animals at greater length, and in greater depth, than had previously been done in the entire history of philosophy. That is a bold claim, I know. But I believe it is a true one. During this period more than a handful of books devoted to this topic have appeared or are now in press,[2] and at least a score of individual essays have found a place in the highly competitive pages of professional philosophy journals.[3] (One fact that is not well known outside philosophy, and one that sometimes shocks outsiders, is that the average rate of rejection in our professional journals is about 90 percent; for every ten articles submitted, that is, about nine are rejected. This rejection rate alone goes some way toward suggesting just how very competitive publishing is in philosophy; and it also does much to convey how seriously questions about the moral status of animals are being taken in our discipline. If they were not being taken quite seriously, they would fall conveniently into the 90 percent rejection pile.) But not only do individual essays dot the landscape. Three prestigious journals, from three different countries, have published entire numbers devoted exclusively to questions revolving round the moral status of animals: the journals *Philosophy* (England), *Inquiry* (Norway), and *Etyka* (Poland). True, both the books and the essays tend to speak to a narrower audience—academicians mainly, humanists generally, philosophers in particular. But, like the efforts of the formal organizations mentioned earlier, the message of these individual philosophers has found, and has also helped create, an increasingly aroused audience.

What are these philosophers saying? Well, as is the wont of philosophers, they are saying many different, sometimes incompatible things. As is our wont, these philosophers are slugging it out in print, subjecting arguments and assumptions to the severest test of reflective criticism, in the hope—and this is always the hope in philosophy, as it is the hope in science—that we might find some hypothesis, some argument, some assumption that will stand up under the hardest test. The point I would make, then, is that the issues are very much unsettled at the present moment; philosophy is now in a period of intense dialectic over many of the questions at hand. And yet, despite the unsettledness, despite the incompatibility of certain views, despite the dark corners of issues barely perceived, there are common points of agreement and emphasis. Two in particular stand out. The first is that animals themselves have moral standing—that animals, themselves, have interests, in other words, which must be taken into account, not only if (or just so long as) it is in *our* interest to do so, but because of the interests of the animals themselves. And, second, there is widespread—indeed, so far as I am aware, unanimous—agreement that there are many cases, including many cases in scientific research, where the interests of animals are not counted at all, or counted less than the comparable interests of human beings—cases where, therefore, there is at least prima facie evidence for thinking that the animals are being treated immorally and where the treatment in question must be stopped.

Now, stopping the use of animals in research, either in whole or in part, as mentioned earlier, has been one of the long-standing objectives of what, for the sake of convenience, I shall refer to as "animal welfare organizations." Thus, it might appear that philosophers are rather Johnny-come-latelys, offering an echo, not a choice, serving up the same menu as these organizations, only calling it by a different name. I do not believe this is true. Though the conclusions reached by the philosophers

I have in mind do happen to coincide with the objectives of these organizations, the *grounds* on which these conclusions can be reached can be, and I think are, importantly different. In what follows I try to illustrate this difference by examining two of the central ideas favored by these organizations—namely, cruelty to animals (which they are against), and kindness to animals (which they are for).[4] I hope to be able to explain why those out to improve the lot of animals, especially those out to abolish or reduce their use in science, ought themselves to abolish or reduce their reliance on these ideas. Later on, after I have raised some dust over these matters, I hope to be able to explain how and why the idea of animal rights might legitimately be used to fill the gap left, if and when the habit of relying so heavily on the ideas of cruelty and kindness can be broken.

Cruelty

It would be difficult to find anyone who is in favor of cruelty. Thus, when individuals and organizations champion the cause of animal welfare by denouncing cruelty to animals, they strike a responsive moral chord. Theoretically, however, I do not believe that our negative duties to animals are adequately grounded, if we endeavor to rest them on the prohibition against cruelty. This becomes clear once we become clearer about the idea of cruelty itself.

Cruelty is manifested in different ways. People can rightly be judged cruel either for what they do or for what they fail to do, and either for what they feel or for what they fail to feel. The central case of cruelty appears to be the case where, in Locke's apt phrase,[5] one takes "a seeming kind of Pleasure" in causing another to suffer. Sadistic torturers provide perhaps the clearest example of cruelty in this sense: they are cruel not just because they cause suffering (so do dentists and doctors, for example) but because they enjoy doing so. For convenience I shall term this "sadistic cruelty."

Not all cruel people are cruel in this sense. Some cruel people do not feel pleasure in making others suffer. Indeed, they seem not to feel anything. Their cruelty is manifested by a lack of what is judged appropriate feeling, as pity or mercy, for the plight of the individual whose suffering they cause, rather than pleasure in causing it; they are, as we say, insensitive to the suffering they inflict, unmoved by it, as if they were unaware of it or failed to appreciate it *as suffering*, in the way that, for example, lions appear to be unaware of, and thus are insensitive to, the pain they cause their prey. Indeed, precisely because one expects indifference from animals but pity or mercy from humans; and precisely because the absence of pity or mercy manifests a want of what makes humans human; people who are cruel by being insensitive to the suffering they cause often are called "animals" or "brutes," and their character or behavior, "brutal" or "inhuman." Thus, for example, particularly ghastly murders are said to be "the work of animals," the implication being that these are acts that no one moved by the human feelings of pity or mercy could bring themselves to perform. The sense of "cruelty" that involves indifference to, rather than enjoyment of, suffering caused to others I call "brutal cruelty."

Now, cruelty of either kind, sadistic or brutal, can be manifested in what I call active or passive behavior. By "passive behavior" I mean to include acts of omission and negligence; by "active" I mean acts of commission. Thus a man who, without provocation, beats a dog into unconsciousness is actively cruel, whereas one who, through negligence, fails to feed his pet to the point where the dog's health is impoverished is passively cruel, not because of what he does but because of what he fails to do. Both active and passive cruelty have fuzzy borders. For example, a woman is not cruel if she occasionally fails to feed her cat. She *is* cruel if she fails to do so most of the time. But while there is no exact number of times, no fixed percentage, such that, once realized, cruelty is present, otherwise not, there are paradigms none the less.

We have, then, at least two kinds of cruelty (or two senses of the word "cruelty") and two different ways in which cruelty can be manifested. Theoretically, therefore, cruelty admits of at least four possible classifications: (1) active sadistic cruelty; (2) passive sadistic cruelty; (3) active brutal cruelty; and (4) passive brutal cruelty. Let us grant that all varieties of cruelty ought to be condemned and discouraged. The question that remains is, granting this, does anticruelty, in any or all of its forms, provide an adequate basis for our negative duties to animals? I do not believe it does. For cruelty, in all of its forms, necessarily involves reference to an individual's mental state—namely, whether one takes pleasure in causing or allowing another to suffer, or whether one is indifferent to doing this. Thus, if anticruelty were advanced as a basis for our negative duties to animals, it would follow that we fulfill our negative duties to them so long as we are not cruel to them—that is, so long as we do not enjoy, or are not indifferent to, causing or allowing them to suffer.

This is manifestly inadequate. How one feels about what one does is logically distinct from the moral assessment of what one does. More particularly, how one feels about the suffering one causes an animal is logically distinct from whether it is wrong to make the animal suffer. To make an animal suffer is not justified just on the grounds that one is not indifferent to its suffering, or just on the grounds that one does not enjoy making it suffer. In other words, to make an animal suffer is not justified just on the grounds that the one who makes it suffer is not cruel, in any or all of cruelty's various forms. So, while we can agree that cruelty is to be condemned and ought to be discouraged, we must not agree that the prohibition against cruelty provides a satisfactory basis for our negative duties to animals.[6]

Kindness

Kindness perhaps is an idea second only to cruelty in terms of its currency in discussions about our treatment of animals. "Be kind to animals," we are enjoined, and few, if any, would take exception to the spirit of this injunction. But, like the prohibition against cruelty, the prescription to be kind will not bear the weight some people want to place on it. It simply will not do the job of helping us determine our positive duties to animals.

Like "cruel," "kind" and its cognates are terms of moral appraisal we use to assess and describe a person's acts or character. A kind person is one who is inclined (disposed) to act with the intention of forwarding the interests of others, not for reasons of self-gain, but out of love, affection, or compassion for the individual whose interests are forwarded. Kind people, in a word, are not selfish, not ones who act to forward the interests of another only if or so long as doing so forwards their own interests.

What, then, does the injunction to be kind to animals mean? It means either that, when it comes to this or that individual act, we are to treat animals in such a way that our intention is to forward their interest, not from a selfish motive but out of love, affection, or compassion for them, *or* that we are to cultivate, through such individual actions, the disposition to treat animals in this way, for these reasons. And there is no denying, I think, the moral worth of the ideal the injunction to be kind, interpreted in either of these ways, places before us. And yet, for reasons in some cases not unlike those given against the view that the prohibition against cruelty can satisfactorily serve as the basis for our negative duties to animals, the injunction to treat animals kindly fails to provide us with a satisfactory basis for determining our positive duties.

My reasons for saying this are as follows. First, kindness, like cruelty, has conceptual connections with "the mind of the agent"— namely, with the agent's motives and intentions. And this invites the same observation in the case of kindness as was apposite in the earlier case of cruelty: the morality of what persons do (the rightness or wrongness of their actions) is logically distinct from, and should not be confused with, their "mental states," including the motives or intentions from which their acts proceed. Thus, while those who act kindly deserve our moral admiration, they deserve this not because they thereby do what is right (possibly they do; but possibly they do not); they deserve this because they exhibit their goodness as people. So, just as the evil that cruelty is must be kept distinct from judging a cruel act wrong, the good that kindness is must be kept distinct from judging a kind act right.

Second, the injunction to be kind to animals must fail to capture or account for the idea that we *owe* it to animals to treat them in certain ways, that treating them thus-and-so is something that is *due* them. The injunction in question cannot capture or account for this because kindness is not itself something we *owe* to anybody, is not *anyone's* due. To be the beneficiary of a kind act no doubt generally is to be blessed, but no one has a claim on anyone else's kindness. Thus, if sense can be made of the idea that we owe it to animals to treat them in certain ways and that they have valid claims against us,[7] we cannot look to the injunction that we be kind to animals as a principle that accounts, or even helps account, for this dimension of our duties to animals. For these reasons, then, the injunction to be kind to animals, like the prohibition not to be cruel to them, cannot serve as a principle we might use for determining what are our duties to animals.

Animal Rights

If our obligations to animals are not accounted for by either preventing cruelty or increasing kindness, where else are we to look? This is a question hotly debated by the philosophers whose work I cited earlier. Peter Singer, for example, by all accounts the most influential thinker in this area of philosophy, thinks that an adequate account can be gotten from the general theory called utilitarianism. I do not agree, however, and have challenged Singer's views on several different occasions.[8] I believe utilitarianism places too much value on consequences and not enough value on individuals. And I believe this deficiency in utilitarianism points to the need to postulate basic moral rights for animals as well as humans.

Now, to many, the idea that animals have rights will sound as silly as the proposal made some years back that animals be required to wear clothes when in public since, otherwise, parading around in their natural (unclothed) state, they violate well-established legislation outlawing public nudity. (I regret that I cannot recall or discover the name of the enterprising individual who put forth this proposal in the interests of public decency.) But silly-sounding ideas sometimes turn out to be true. The idea that blacks have rights no doubt sounded silly to persons accustomed to thinking of rights as the exclusive property of whites. The silly, extravagant, strange, or ludicrous sound of an idea sometimes tells us more about ourselves, about our prejudices and resistance to change, than about the truth contained in the idea itself. Such was true for those who, as it were, laughed off the idea that blacks have basic moral rights. And such is true, I believe, for those who react similarly to the idea of animals having rights.

I do not mean to suggest that the case for animal rights is simple. Far from it. If anything it is more difficult than the case for human rights, upon which it is parasitic. By this I mean that the case for animal rights must be built on, must be shown to be a rational extension of, the case for human rights. In the nature of the case, therefore, the principal arguments for postulating animal rights cannot be any stronger (and may in fact be weaker) than the principal arguments for postulating human rights. But just as the sound of an idea should be no reason to back away from it, so also the evident difficulty in making any headway with it should not make us not make the effort.

The main outline of the strongest case for human moral rights, I believe, in very broad outline, is as follows.[9] The world contains individuals (e.g., human beings) who not only are alive but have a life; these individuals are not mere things (objects), they are the subjects of a life; they have, in James Rachels's helpful phrase, autobiographies.[10] Moreover, these individuals have a life that is better or worse for them, logically independently of whether they are valued by anyone else (e.g., whether anyone else finds them useful). To put this last point differently, these individuals are valu*ers* whether valu*ed* by others or not. As such, these individuals have a different kind of value than those objects (things) that have value only if (and then only so long as) they are valued by someone else, the sort of value that, say, sticks and stones, pencils and tablets, tables and chairs would seem to have. Human beings in particular have a kind of value that is not reducible to, is not contingent upon, for example, how useful they are to others, how well liked, how skillful, how intelligent. This kind of value we might term inherent value to distinguish it from other sorts of value (e.g., instrumental).

Now, given that human beings have a special (inherent) kind of value, we can specify, in very general terms, what is involved in mistreating one another. Human beings are mistreated when we are treated as if we had value only if (and then only so long as) we answered the needs, desires, purposes, goals, and so on, of others, or, to put the point in Kantian terms, as if we had value merely as a means. But if we ask why, even granting that we humans have inherent value, it is wrong to mistreat us merely as a means, the most adequate answer appears to be that, as possessors of inherent value, we have *a moral right* to be treated in ways that are consistent with our having value of this kind—a moral right to have our status as valuers (and not mere things) in the world respected; such a right is violated whenever we are treated as if we had value only as a means. It is, as I said earlier, reasoning along these general lines which provides, I believe, the strongest argument for postulating moral rights in the case of human beings.

Can this argument be extended to include nonhuman animals? I believe it can, at least for many species of animals, including, not incidentally, many of those whose members are routinely used as "subjects" or "models" in scientific research. We have strong empirical grounds for believing that members of many species are not only alive, they have life; that they are not mere things (objects) but are subjects of a life, and this a life that is better or worse for them, logically independently of whether they are valued by anyone else (e.g., any human being); that, like us, they are valuers, logically independently of whether they are valued; that, like us, they have inherent, not just instrumental, value; and that, like us, therefore, they have a moral right to be treated in ways that are consistent with their having value of this kind, a right that is violated in their case, as in ours, if they are treated merely as a means.

Immediately someone will ask where to draw the line: Do frogs have a life? Are clams inherently valuable? Are paramecia valuers? Would that I (or anyone else) knew with certainty: We serve the cause of truth ill if we attempt to paper over these gray areas. But we serve the cause of morality ill if we act as if all areas are gray because some are, as if because it sometimes is uncertain whether someone is or is not bald, it therefore is uncertain whether Telly Savalas and Ringo Starr are bald. So, no, I do not believe that we know exactly where to draw the line that separates those individuals who have the necessary wherewithal to be valuers from those beings that do not. But that does not mean that we do not know what to say about many other cases, in particular, that we do not know what to say about the estimated[11] 400,000 dogs, 200,000 cats, 33,000 apes and monkeys, thousands of calves, sheep, ponies, horses; rabbits and other species in the millions—a total approaching 64 million in the United States alone, 200 million in the world at large, used in science just for the year 1978. We have very good empirical grounds to view these animals in ways that make the ascription of moral rights to them intelligible: for these animals not only are alive, they have a life; they are not mere objects to be valued, they are subjects that value; they do not have value, therefore, just to the extent that they are useful to us—they have value in their own right if humans do; and they have, therefore, a moral right to be treated in ways that respect their value, if it is true, as I believe it is, that humans have this right because we have value of the same kind. It is, as I have said, the moral rights of animals, not the injunction to be kind to them or the prohibition against cruelty, that must come to permeate our perception of their status in the world as fellow creatures and which must underpin the moral and legal constraints placed on how we may treat them. The full implications for our actions of this growing revolution in our thought are yet to be fully worked out, are yet even to be fully glimpsed. But that in time this revolution will require at least a vast reduction in research involving animals, that much is certain, and this, not because researchers are cruel people, nor because stopping it is a kindness (a favor) we can do for the animals, but because, as possessors of inherent value, animals have a moral right not to be treated merely as a means to human ends. The onus of justification—the burden to justify this use of this animal in this experiment—must always be borne by the researcher. The task before us all is earnestly to seek those principles by reference to which we might rationally answer this question of justification.

NOTES

1. Nicholas Wade, "Animal Rights: NIH Cat Sex Study Brings Grief to New York Museum," *Science* 194 (8 October 1976): 165.
2. These books include Peter Singer, *Animal Liberation* (New York: A New York Review Book, distributed by Random House, 1975; New York: Avon Books, 1977); Tom Regan and Peter Singer, eds., *Animal Rights and Human Obligations* (Englewood Cliffs, N.J.: Prentice-Hall, 1976); Stanley and Roslind Godlovitch and John Harris, eds., *Animals, Men, and Morals* (London: Gollancz; New York: Taplinger, 1972); D. A. Paterson and R. Ryder, eds., *Animals' Rights: A Symposium* (London: Centaur Press, 1979); and R. K. Morris and M. W. Fox, eds., *On The Fifth Day: Animal Rights and Human Ethics* (Washington, D.C.: Acropolis Press, 1978).
3. For a list of relevant essays, as well as a more comprehensive list of recent books, see Charles Magel and Tom Regan, "Animal Rights and Human Obligations: A Select Bibliography," *Inquiry* 22 (Summer 1979): 243–247; see bibliography, below.
4. The discussions of cruelty and kindness that follow form part of my essay "Cruelty, Kindness and Unnecessary Suffering," *Philosophy* 55:4 (Winter 1980): 532–541, and are reprinted here with the kind permission of that journal.
5. The full passage from Locke reads as follows: "One thing I have frequently observed in Children, that when they have got possession of any poor Creature, they are apt to use it ill: They often torment, and treat very roughly, young Birds, Butterflies, and such other poor Animals, which fall into their Hands, and that with a seeming kind of Pleasure. This I think should be watched in them, and if they incline to any such Cruelty, they should be taught the contrary Usage. For the Custom of Tormenting and Killing of Beasts, will, by Degrees, harden their Minds even towards Men; and they who delight in the Suffering and Destruction of Inferiour Creatures, will not be apt to be very compassionate, or benign to those of their own kind."(*John Locke, Some Thoughts Concerning Education, 5th ed. (London: printed for A. and C. Churchill, 1905). See also James Axtell, ed., The Educational Writings of John Locke (Cambridge: Cambridge University Press, 1968), sec. 116, pp. 225–226.*)
6. The general approach to our duties to animals suggested by this passage—namely, that our duties to animals are indirect duties to humankind—I label "the Kantian account" and subject it to criticism in my "Exploring the Idea of Animal Rights," in Paterson and Ryder, *Animals' Rights: A Symposium*. In an earlier examination of cruelty I failed to distinguish the brutal sense. See my "Animal Rights, Human Wrongs," *Environmental Ethics* 2, 2 (Summer 1980): 99–120 (essay 4, below). Discussions with Professor James Nickle have been very beneficial in this regard.

7. I argue this point in the essays cited in n. 6. I am especially indebted to Professor Joel Feinberg's work on this and related topics. See especially his "The Rights of Animals and Unborn Generations" in W. Blackstone, ed., *Philosophy and Environmental Crisis* (Athens: University of Georgia Press, 1974).

8. See in particular my "Utilitarianism, Vegetarianism, and Animal Rights," *Philosophy and Public Affairs* 9, 4 (Summer 1980): 305–324 (essay 2, above).

9. I have tried to develop this argument at greater length in different places. See "Animal Rights, Human Wrongs," "An Examination and Defense of One Argument Concerning Animal Rights" (essay 6, below), and "Exploring the Idea of Animal Rights."

10. James Rachels, "Euthanasia," in Tom Regan, ed., *Matters of Life and Death* (New York: Random House, 1980).

11. Patricia Curtis, "New Debate Over Experimenting with Animals," *The New York Times Magazine*, December 31, 1978, pp. 18–23. A condensed version appears in *Reader's Digest*, February 1980.

4
Animal Rights, Human Wrongs

The opening and concluding sections of "Animal Rights, Human Wrongs" are a far cry from the dispassionate, "ponderously prodding" style of the first essay, "The Moral Basis of Vegetarianism." The change reflects principally the different audiences for which the two essays were originally intended. "Animal Rights, Human Wrongs" is the main body of an address I was privileged to present as part of a series of lectures on "Problems and Directions of the Post-Abundant Society" at Muhlenberg College in March 1979. Dean Charles A. Bednar, who organized this innovative series, led me to believe that those who attended were unlikely to be familiar with how desperate is the plight of many animals in our trust, and I wanted to startle them into an awareness of the magnitude and moral gravity of the situation. Thus I chose to begin with particular cases—vivid, tragic cases—to illustrate that the questions I would be discussing were not "other worldly" but were eminently "practical" in their implications.

Some of the ideas addressed in the lecture—for example, "the cruelty account" and the defects of utilitarianism—were explored in previous essays, and there is some repetition here. But there is also some further refinement, I think, especially regarding the role that animal rights plays in our critical assessment of how animals are treated, whether they are domestic animals (chickens, hogs, veal calves), animals used in science (rats, dogs, rabbits), or animals trapped or otherwise killed in the wild (chimpanzees, elephants, whales). If these animals have rights, then we cannot justify what we do to them *just* on the grounds that we happen to benefit, whether the benefits be gastronomic (they taste good), medical (we live longer or healthier lives as a result of using them for scientific purposes), or commercial (they are a source of revenue). We do not recognize such appeals as adequate justifications for harming human beings, and we cannot count them as adequate in the case of animals either, *if* they have rights. A sustained defense of the position that they do have rights, if humans do, is offered in the following essay.

J. Baird Callicott criticizes the general approach to our treatment of animals which characterizes this essay, particularly the "lumping together" of wild and domesticated animals. See his "Animal Liberation: A Triangular Affair," *Environmental Ethics* 2, 4 (Winter 1980): 311−338. The references cited in the introductions to essays 1 and 2 also are relevant to the issues discussed in "Animal Rights, Human Wrongs."

"Animal Rights, Human Wrongs" originally appeared in *Environmental Ethics* 2, 2 (1980): 99−120. A somewhat different version appears in H. Miller and W. Williams, eds., *Ethics and Animals* (Crescent Manor: Humana Press, 1982) and, in a Polish translation, in *Etyka* 18, 1980. The former version is the one reproduced here; but since there is significant overlap between that version and the one that appears in *Ethics and Animals*, it is a pleasure to acknowledge permission to reprint from Humana Press.

At this moment workers on board the mother ship of a whaling fleet are disassembling the carcass of a whale. Though the species is officially protected by agreement of the member nations of the International Whaling Commission, it is not too fanciful to imagine the crew butchering a great blue whale, the largest creature ever known to have lived on the earth—larger than thirty elephants, larger even than three of the largest dinosaurs laid end to end. A good catch, this leviathan of the deep. And, increasingly, a rare one. For the great blue, like hundreds of other animal species, is endangered, may, in fact, already be beyond the point of recovery.

But the crew has other things on their mind. It will take hours of hard work to butcher the huge carcass, a process now carried out at sea. Nor is butchering at sea the only thing in whaling that has changed. The fabled days of a real hunt, of an individual Ahab pitted against a treacherous whale, must remain the work of fiction now. Whaling is applied technology, from the use of the most sophisticated sonar to on-board refrigeration, from tracking helicopters to explosive harpoons, the latter a technological advance that expedites a whale's death. Average time to die: sometimes as long as twenty minutes; usually three to five. Here is one man's account of a whale's demise:

> The gun roars. The harpoon hurls through the air and the whale-line follows. There is a momentary silence, and then the muffled explosion as the time fuse functions and fragments the grenade. . . . There is now a fight between the mammal and the crew of the catching vessel—a fight to the death. It is a struggle that can have only one result. . . . Deep in the whale's vast body is the mortal wound, and even if it could shake off the harpoon it would be doomed. . . . A second harpoon buries itself just behind the dorsal fin . . . There is another dull explosion in the whale's vitals. Then comes a series of convulsions—a last despairing struggle. The whale spouts blood, keels slowly over and floats belly upward. It is dead.[1]

For what? To what end? Why is this being done to the last remaining members of an irreplaceable species, certainly until recently, possibly at this very moment, by supposedly civilized men? For candle wax. For soap and oil. For pet food, margarine, fertilizer. For perfume.

In Thailand, at this moment, another sort of hunt, less technologically advanced, is in progress. The Thai hunter has hiked two miles through thick vegetation and now, with his keen vision, spots a female gibbon and her infant, sleeping high in a tree. Jean-Yves Domalain describes what follows:

> Down below, the hunter rams the double charge of gun-powder down the barrel with a thin iron rod, then the lead shot. The spark flashes from two flints, and the gun goes off in a cloud of white smoke. . . . Overhead there is an uproar. The female gibbon, mortally wounded, clings to life. She still has enough strength to make two gigantic leaps, her baby still clinging to the long hair of her left thigh. At the third leap she misses the branch she was aiming for, and in a final desperate effort manages to grasp a lower one; but her strength is ebbing away and she is unable to pull herself up. Slowly her fingers begin to loosen her grip. Death is there, staining her pale fur. The youngster flattens himself in terror against her bloodstained flank. Then comes the giddy plunge of a hundred feet or more, broken by a terrible rebound off a tree trunk.[2]

The object of this hunt is not to kill the female gibbon, but to capture the baby. Unfortunately, in this case the infant's neck is broken by the fall, so the shots were wasted. The hunter will have to move on, seeking other prospects.

We are not dealing in fantasies when we consider the day's work of the Thai hunter. Domalain makes it clear that both the method of capture (killing the mother to get the infant) and the results just seen (the death of both) are the rule rather than the exception in the case of gibbons. And chimpanzees. And tigers. And orangutans. And lions. Some estimate that for every one animal captured alive, ten have been killed. Domalain further states that for every ten captured only two will live on beyond a few months. The mortality rate stemming from hunts that aim to bring animals back alive thus is considerable.

Nor do we romanticize when we regard the female gibbon's weakening grip, the infant's alarmed clutching, the bonds of surprise and terror that unite them as they begin their final descent. And for what? To what end? Why is this scene played out again and again? So that pet stores might sell "exotic animals." So that roadside zoos might offer "new attractions." So that the world's scientists might have "subjects" for their experiments.

Not far from here, perhaps at this moment, a rabbit makes a futile effort to escape from a restraining device, called a stock, which holds the creature in place by clamping down around its neck. Immediately the reader thinks of trapping in the wild—that the stock must be a sort of trap, like the infamous leg-hold trap—but this is not so. The stock is a handmaiden of science, and the rabbit confined by it is not in the wild but in a research laboratory. If we look closely, we will see that one of the rabbit's eyes is ulcerated. It is badly inflamed, an open, running sore. After some hours the sore increases in size until barely half the eye is visible. In a few days the eye will become permanently blind. Sometimes the eye is literally burned out of its socket.

This rabbit is a research subject in what is known as the Draize test, named after its inventor. This rabbit, and hundreds like it, is being used because rabbits happen not to have tear ducts and so cannot flush irritants from their eyes. Nor can they dilute them. The Draize test proceeds routinely as follows: concentrated solutions of a substance are made to drip into one of the rabbit's eyes; the other eye, a sort of control, is left untroubled. Swelling, redness, destruction of iris or cornea, loss of vision are measured and the substance's eye-irritancy is thereby scientifically established.

What is this substance which in concentrated form invades the rabbit's eye? Probably a cosmetic, a new variety of toothpaste, shampoo, mouthwash, talcum, hand lotion, eye cosmetic, face cream, hair conditioner, perfume, cologne. Why? To what end? In the name of what purpose does this unanesthetized rabbit endure the slow burning destruction of its eye? So that a researcher might establish the eye-irritancy of mouthwash and talc, toothpaste and cologne.[3]

A final individual bids for our attention at this moment. A bobbie calf is a male calf born in a dairy herd. Since the calf cannot give milk, something must be done with it. A common practice is to sell it as a source of veal, as in veal Parmigiana. To make this commercially profitable the calf must be raised in highly unnatural conditions. Otherwise the youngster would romp and play, as is its wont; equally bad, it would forage and consume roughage. From a businessman's point of view, this is detrimental to the product. The romping produces muscle, which makes for tough meat, and the roughage will contain natural sources of iron, which will turn the calf's flesh red. But studies show that consumers have a decided preference for pale veal. So the calf is kept permanently indoors, in a stall too narrow for it to turn around, frequently tethered to confine it further, its short life lived mostly in the dark on a floor of wood slats, its only contact with other living beings coming when it is fed and when, at the end, it is transported to the slaughterhouse.

Envision then the tethered calf, unable to turn around, unable to sit down without hunching up, devoid of compansionship, its natural urges to romp and forage denied, fed a wholly liquid diet deliberately deficient in iron so as not to compromise its pale flesh but to keep it anemic. For what? To what end? In the name of what purpose does the calf live so? So that humans might have pale veal![4]

Multiply these cases by the hundreds, multiply them by the thousands, and we approach, perhaps, the magnitude of the death and suffering animals are enduring, at this moment, at the hands of human beings. The numbers are like distances in astronomy. We can write them down, compare them, add and subtract them, but, like light years stacked on light years, we lack the intellectual or imaginative wherewithal to hold them in steady focus. Item: two million whales killed in the last fifty years. Item: in the mid-nineteenth century there were upwards of two billion passenger pigeons in the United States; now there are none. Item: when white settlers set foot on North America, there were sixty million buffalo; now the largest wild herd numbers six hundred.

Extinct or endangered species aside, consider these figures for legally imported wildlife brought into the United States, in one year (1970) alone, to supply the needs of the pet industry, zoos, and scientific researchers.

101,302 mammals, 85,151 of which were primates (mainly monkeys)

687,901 wild birds, not including canaries, parrots, and parakeets, millions of which are annually imported

572,670 amphibians (frogs, toads, salamanders)

2,109,571 reptiles[5]

In the United States alone for the year 1978, 400,000 dogs, 200,000 cats, 33,000 apes and monkeys, thousands of calves, sheep, ponies, horses, were used in research as well as rabbits, hamsters, guinea pigs, rats, birds, mice by the millions. Altogether an estimated 64 million animals were used in research. Worldwide, educated estimates place the figure at about 200 million.[6]

As for slaughter, incomplete data suggest that, worldwide, the number of animals killed for food exceeds hundreds of millions for individual species, involving upwards of 100 million cattle, 100 million sheep, 200 million pigs, 26 million calves, and, in the United States alone, 3 billion chickens.[7]

But numbers prove nothing. They neither establish that something is right nor that it is wrong. They merely confirm what we know already. The use of animals as a primary food source and as subjects in scientific research knows no geographical boundaries. The extinction of unique species is not perpetrated by only a few political ideologies. Aside from economic considerations, and excluding the privileged status that pet animals may have as honorary members of the family, few things are regarded so cheaply as an animal's life. Few things now call forth less collective compassion of humankind than the great suffering animals endure in the name of human interests.

But these numbers serve another function. They serve as an index of the complexity of any questioning of those activities that involve the pain or destruction of animals. Questions about morality here are not likely to have simple answers. They require patient examination, due attention to competing forces, an eye for subtlety and nuance. Difficult questions are like knots; they are not unraveled just by pulling hard on one idea. For example, there is no reason to believe that such ideas as "all life is sacred," or "we ought to reverence all life," or "all forms of life are good" will dissolve the complexity before us. For these ideas, simply stated, leave unanswered crucial questions that arise when the interests of one form of life come into conflict with those of another. What is needed is not a simple declaration that all life is sacred, and so on. What is wanted is some rational way to resolve such conflicts. What is wanted are moral principles that resolve the conflict equitably.

Now, these moral principles will not tell us, for example, how the population of whales will be affected if whaling is stopped or how that will affect the population of tuna. By themselves, that is, moral principles will not tell us *the facts* about whaling practices, nor will they give us a means of predicting what the facts will be. What these principles *will* tell us is what sort of facts to look for. In other words, they will tell us what facts are *morally relevant* to reaching a rational decision. The task of identifying what these principles are is one of the distinctive tasks of moral philosophy. This task occupies most of my attention in what follows. But I also want to bring my results back to the rabbit, the calf, the whale, and the gibbon with which we began.

The Kantian Account

It is a commonplace to say that morality places some limits on how animals may be treated. We are not to kick dogs, set fire to cats' tails, torment hamsters or parakeets. Philosophically, the issue is not so much *whether* but *why* these acts are wrong.

An answer favored by many philosophers, including Thomas Aquinas and Immanuel Kant, is that people who treat animals in these ways develop a habit that, in time, inclines them to treat humans similarly.[8] People who torment animals will, or are likely to, torment people. It is this spillover effect that makes mistreating animals wrong. We are not concerned directly with the ill-treatment that the animals themselves receive. Rather, our concern is that this bodes ill for humankind. So, on this Kantian account, the moral principle runs something like this: don't treat animals in ways that will lead you to mistreat human beings.

One need have no quarrel with this principle itself. The real quarrel lies with the grounds on which this principle is allegedly based. Peter Singer argues that there is a close parallel between this view and those of the racist and sexist, a view that, following Richard Ryder, he denominates speciesism.[9] The racist believes that the interests of others matter only if they happen to be members of his own race. The speciesist believes that the interests of others matter only if they happen to be members of his own species. Racism has been unmasked for the prejudice that it is. The color of one's skin cannot be used to determine the relevance of an individual's interests. Singer and Ryder both argue that neither can the number of one's legs, whether one walks upright or on all fours, lives in the trees, the sea, or the suburbs. Here they recall Bentham.[10] There is, they argue forcefully, no rational, unprejudiced way to exclude the interests of nonhuman animals just because they are not the interests of human beings. Because the Kantian account would have us think otherwise, we are right to reject it.

The Cruelty Account

A second view about constraints on how animals may be treated involves the idea of cruelty. The reason we are not to kick dogs is that we are not to be cruel to animals and kicking dogs is cruel. It is the prohibition against cruelty that covers and conveniently sums up our negative duties to animals, duties concerning how animals are *not* to be treated.

The prohibition against cruelty can be given a distinctively Kantian twist. This happens when the grounds given are that cruelty to animals leads people to be cruel to other people. John Locke suggests, but does not clearly endorse, this view:

> One thing I have frequently observed in Children, that when they have got possession of any poor Creature, they are apt to use it ill: They often *torment*, and treat very roughly, young Birds, Butterflies, and such other poor Animals, which fall into their Hands, and that with a seeming kind of Pleasure. This I think should be watched in them, and if they incline to any such *Cruelty*, they should be taught the contrary Usage. For the Custom of Tormenting and Killing of Beasts, will, by Degrees, harden their Minds even towards Men; and they who delight in the Suffering and Destruction of Inferior Creatures, will not be apt to be very compassionate, or benign to those of their own kind.[11]

Locke's position suggests the speciesism that characterizes the Kantian account and will not do for the same reasons. But Locke's understanding of what cruelty is—tormenting a sentient creature or causing it to suffer, "with a seeming kind of Pleasure"—seems correct and has important implications. Many thinkers, including many persons active in the humane movement, champion the prohibition against cruelty to animals because it is wrong to be cruel to the animals themselves. This way of grounding the prohibition against cruelty, which I call "the cruelty account," deserves our critical attention.

It is difficult to overestimate the importance the idea of preventing cruelty has played, and continues to play, in the movement to secure better treatment for animals. Entire societies are devoted to this cause, the Society for the Prevention of Cruelty to Animals (SPCA) in the United States and the Royal Society for the Prevention of Cruelty to Animals (RSPCA) in Great Britain being perhaps the best-known examples. I do not wish to deny the importance of preventing cruelty nor to deprecate the crusading work done by these organizations, but I must conclude that to stake so much on the prevention of cruelty both clouds the fundamental moral issues and runs a serious risk of being counterproductive.

Cruel is a term of moral appraisal used to refer either to the character of a person or to an individual action. Persons are cruel who are inclined to delight in or, in Locke's phrase, to take "a seeming kind of Pleasure" in causing pain. An individual action is cruel if one takes pleasure in making another suffer. It is clear that someone's being cruel is distinct from someone's causing pain. Surgeons cause pain. Dentists cause pain. Wrestlers, boxers, football players cause pain. But it does not follow that they are cruel people or that their individual actions are cruel. To establish cruelty we need to know more than that someone caused pain; we also need to know the state of mind of the agent, whether he/she took "a seeming kind of Pleasure" in the pain inflicted. It is faulty to reason in this way:

> Those who are cruel cause pain. Surgeons (football players, etc.) cause pain. Therefore, surgeons (football players, etc.) are cruel.

But just as clearly, it is faulty to reason in the following way:

> Those who are cruel cause pain. Those who experiment on animals (or kill whales, or raise veal calves in isolation, etc.) cause pain. Therefore, those who treat animals in these ways are cruel.

Those who are inclined to march under the banner of anticruelty must soon recognize the speciousness of this line of reasoning, if their thought, however well intentioned, is not to cloud the issues.

Once cruelty is understood in the way Locke saw that it should be, we can see why more understanding is needed to object to how animals are treated. Take the use of animals in the Draize test. Increasingly people want to object morally to this, to say it is wrong. If this required establishing cruelty, however, the weight of the evidence would be on the side of the experimenters and against the objectors, for there is no adequate evidence for believing that people who administer the Draize test are cruel people or that they are cruel when they administer this test. Do they take "a seeming kind of Pleasure" in causing the animals pain? That they cause *pain* to the animals is certain. But causing pain does not establish cruelty. Except for a few sadists in the scientific community, there is good reason to believe that researchers are no more cruel than are most persons.

Does this mean that using animals in the Draize test is right? Precisely not. Rather, to ask whether this is right is logically distinct from, and should not be confused with, asking whether someone is cruel.

Cruelty has to do with a person's state of mind. The moral rightness or wrongness of a person's actions is different. Persons can do what is right or wrong whatever their state of mind. Researchers using the Draize test can be doing what is wrong, whether or not they enjoy causing animals to suffer. If they do enjoy this, we shall certainly think less of them as persons. But even if they enjoy the pain it will not follow that the pain is unjustified, any more than it will follow that the pain is justified if they feel sorry for the animals or feel nothing at all. The more we are able to keep in view how the morality of what a person does is distinct from his/her state of mind, distinct from the presence or absence of taking pleasure in causing pain, the better the chances will be for significant dialogue between those who support and those who oppose continued routine use of animals for scientific purposes.

To charge those who favor their continued use with cruelty *can* only serve to call forth all their defenses, because the charge will be taken as a denunciation of *what they are* (evil people) rather than of *what they do*. It will also give them an easy way out. After all, *they* are in a privileged position to know their own mental states; *they* can take a sober moment and see whether in fact they do take a "seeming kind of Pleasure" in causing pain. If, as will usually be the case, they find that they honestly do not, then they can reply that they are not cruel (evil) people. So we see now where the well-intentioned efforts of those defending animals can be and often are counterproductive. If it is cruelty researchers are charged with, and they are not cruel, then they can come away with a feeling that their hands are clean. They win, and the litany of accusations about cruelty is so much water off their backs. It is no good trying to improve the lot of animals by trying to convince persons who are not cruel that they are.

Some will complain that my argument is "too picky." They might say that cruelty has been interpreted too narrowly: what is meant is treating animals badly in ways they do not deserve, harming or wronging them. In practice this is what anticruelty charges often come to. But then this is the way the charges should be made, lest they be misunderstood or be counterproductive. To ask for more care in the charges leveled is not to strain at gnats. It is to begin to make the charges more difficult to answer. Perhaps a name like "The Society for the Prevention of Maltreatment of Animals" is not as euphonious as "The Anti-Cruelty Society," but a lack of euphony is a price those laboring for animal welfare should gladly pay.

The Utilitarian Account

Utilitarians give a different account of the constraints regarding how animals ought to be treated. The utilitarian account, or one version of it, involves two principles.[12] The first is a principle of equality. This principle declares that the desires, needs, hopes, and so on, of different individuals, when these are of equal importance *to* these individuals, *are* of equal importance or value no matter who the individuals are, prince or pauper, genius or moron, white or black, male or female, *human or animal*. This equality of interests principle seems to provide a philosophical basis for avoiding the grossest forms of prejudice, including racism, sexism, and, following Ryder and Singer, speciesism. Whether it succeeds is an issue that we shall take up below.

The second principle is that of utility itself. Roughly speaking, according to this principle, we are to act so as to bring about the greatest possible balance of good over evil, for example, the greatest possible balance of satisfaction over dissatisfaction, taking the interests of everyone affected into account *and* counting equal interests equally. Now, since animals have interests, *their* interests must be taken into account, and because their interests are frequently as important to them as comparable interests are to human beings, *their* interests must be given the same weight as comparable human interests. It is because kicking dogs and setting fire to cats' tails run counter to the principles of equality and utility that, on this utilitarian account, they are wrong.

Granted, this is a very rough sketch; nonetheless, it enables us to understand the main features of the utilitarian account, and also to find points of resemblance and contrast between it and the other accounts so far described. Like the Kantian account, but unlike the cruelty account, the utilitarian account emphasizes results or consequences, but unlike the Kantian account, and resembling the cruelty account, the utilitarian account recognizes the moral status of animals in their own right. We are not to measure morality by the speciesist yardstick of human interest alone. Finally, unlike the cruelty account, but in concert with the Kantian, the utilitarian does not conflate the morality of an act with the mental state of the agent. The utilitarian can be as opposed to cruelty as anyone else, but within the utilitarian theory right and wrong are determined by consequences, not by feelings and intentions: the ordinary moral constraints placed on how we may treat animals are accounted for because they are necessary if we are not to violate the equality of interests principle *or* if we are to succeed in bringing about the greatest possible balance of good over bad.

The utilitarian account has much to recommend it. How far can it take us in challenging the way in which animals are routinely treated, for example, as subjects in scientific research? Peter Singer, a utilitarian whose work has well-deserved influence, holds that utilitarianism leads to far-reaching consequences here. Singer argues that we become vegetarians *and* that we oppose much (even if not quite all) research involving animal subjects. Singer's main argument is that the intensive rearing of animals as well as their routine use in experimentation violates the equality of interests principle. The animals involved, we have reason to believe, have an interest in not being made to suffer, and this interest, we have further reason to believe, is as important to them as is the comparable interest in the case of human beings. This being so, Singer contends, it is wrong to do to animals what we would not do to humans. It cannot be right to raise animals intensively or use them in research if we would morally oppose doing these things to human beings. We do condemn cannibalism and the coerced use of humans in research and we must, Singer argues, morally condemn the comparable treatment of animals. We have a moral obligation to become vegetarians and oppose much, if not quite all, use of animals in science.

As clear and powerful as this argument is, I do not believe that Singer succeeds in making a fully convincing case. He shows that the treatment of animals is different from that of human beings, but not that this differential treatment violates either the equality of interests principle or the principle of utility. Consider the equality of interests principle first. We can count equal interests equally, no matter whose interests they are, and still treat individuals quite differently. For example, I might correctly regard my son's and my neighbor's son's interests in receiving a medical education as being equal and yet help only my son. I treat them differently but I do *not* necessarily count their equal interests differently, and neither do I thereby do anything that is in any obvious sense morally reprehensible. I have duties to my son which I do not have to the children of others.

The general point is this: the differential treatment of individuals with equal interests does not by itself violate the equality of interests principle. Singer has to give an *argument* that shows *more* than that humans and animals are treated differently. What argument does he give and how adequate is it? Singer proceeds by asking whether we would do to humans what we allow to be done to animals.[13] For example, would a researcher use an orphaned, profoundly retarded human baby in the sort of painful experiment in which he is willing to use a more intellectually and emotionally developed animal? If the researcher says no, Singer charges him with speciesism, with violating the equality of interests principle. The animal's interest in avoiding pain is just as important to it as is the infant's interest to him/her.

This argument begs the question. It assumes that by treating the involved individuals differently, we count their equal interests differently. As I have explained, however, this is not always true. Whether it is true in any particular case, therefore, is something that must be established, not simply assumed on the basis of differential treatment. Singer, I believe, assumes just this, and thus begs the question.

Singer's argument has a further deficiency, which involves the principle of utility. First, Singer does not show that the differential treatment of animals runs counter to the utilitarian objective of bringing about the greatest possible balance of good over evil. To show this Singer would have to give an elaborate, detailed description, not only of how animals are treated, a part of the task that he does complete with great skill, but an analysis of what, all considered, are the consequences for everyone involved. He would have to inquire how the world's economy depends on present levels of productivity in the animal industry, how many people's lives are directly and indirectly involved with the maintenance or growth of this industry, and so forth. Even more, he would have to show in detail what would probably be the consequences of a collapse or slowdown of the animal industry's productivity.

Second, Singer needs to make a compelling case for the view that *not* raising animals intensively or *not* using them routinely in research leads to better consequences, all considered, than those that now result from treating animals in these ways. Singer is required to show that better consequences *would* result, or at least that it is *very probable* that they would. Showing that it is possible or conceivable that they might is insufficient. It comes as a disappointment, therefore, that we do not find anything approaching this kind of required empirical data. What we find, instead, are passages where he bemoans (rightly, I believe) that animals are fed protein-rich grains that could be fed to malnourished human beings.[14] The point, however, is not whether these grains *could* be fed to the malnourished; it is whether we have solid empirical grounds for believing that they *would* be made available to and eaten by these people, if they were not fed to animals, *and* that the consequences resulting from this shift would be better, all considered. I hope I am not unfair to Singer in observing that these calculations are missing, not only here, but, to my knowledge, throughout the body of his published writings.

This, then, is the first thing to note regarding Singer and the principle of utility: *he fails to show, with reference to this principle, that it is wrong* to treat animals as they are now being treated in modern farming and scientific research. The second thing to note is that, for all we know and so long as we rely on the principle of utility, the present treatment of animals might actually be justified. The grounds for thinking so are as follows.

On the face of it, utilitarianism seems to be the fairest, least prejudicial view available. Everyone's interests count, and no one's counts for more or less than the equal interests of anyone else. The trouble, as we have seen, is that there is no necessary connection, no preestablished harmony between respect for the equality of interests principle *and* promoting the utilitarian objective of maximizing the balance of good over bad. On the contrary, the principle of utility might be used to justify the most radical kinds of differential treatment between individuals or groups of individuals, and thus it might justify forms of racism and sexism, for these prejudices can take different forms and find expression in different ways. One form consists in not even taking the interests of a given race or sex into account at all; another takes these interests into account but does not count them equally with those of the equal interests of the favored group. Another does take their interests into account equally, but adopts laws and policies, engages in practices and customs that give greater opportunities to the members of the favored group, because doing so promotes the greatest balance of good over evil, all considered.

Thus, forms of racism or sexism, which seem to be eliminated by the utilitarian principle of equality of interests, could well be resurrected and justified by the principle of utility. If a utilitarian here replies that denying certain humans an equal opportunity to satisfy or promote their equal interests on racial or sexual grounds must violate the equality of interests principle and so, on his position, is wrong, we must remind him that differential treatment is not the same as, and does not entail, violating the equality of interests principle. It is quite possible, for example, to count the equal interests of blacks and whites the same (and thus to honor the equality principle) and still discriminate between races when it comes to what members of each race are permitted to do to pursue those interests, on the grounds that such discrimination promotes the utilitarian objective. So, utilitarianism, despite initial appearances, does not provide us with solid grounds on which to exclude all forms of racism or sexism.

Similarly with speciesism. The same kind of argument can show a possible utilitarian justification of an analogous speciesism. We count the equal interests of animals and humans equally; it just so happens that the consequences of treating animals in ways that humans are not treated, such as intensively raising animals, but not humans, are better, all considered, than are other arrangements. Thus, utilitarianism might provide a basis for speciesist practices. Whether it *actually* does depends on whether the consequences are better, all considered, if animals continue to be treated as they are. Since Singer fails to provide us with empirical data showing that the consequences would be better if we changed, it follows that, for all we know, the present speciesist way of treating animals might actually be justified, given his version of utilitarianism.

Animal Rights

Our results to this point are mainly negative. I have thus far argued (1) that the moral principles we seek cannot refer to the agent's state of mind, to whether the agent takes a "seeming kind of Pleasure" in causing animal suffering. (2) These principles cannot refer only to consequences that harm or benefit human beings, since this prejudicially leaves out of account the harms and benefits to the animals themselves. (3) These principles cannot refer only to the utilitarian objective of maximizing the balance of good over evil, even if animal harms and benefits are taken into account. What is wanted, then, is an account that avoids each of these shortcomings. This account is to be found, I believe, by postulating the existence of animal rights. Indeed, I believe that only if we postulate human rights can we provide a theory that adequately guards humans against the abuses that utilitarianism might permit.

Various analyses of the concept of a right have been proposed. We will bypass the nooks and crannies of these competing analyses so as to focus attention on the role that moral rights play in our thinking about the status of the individual, relative to the interests of the group. Here the truth seems to lie where Ronald Dworkin sees it: the rights of the individual trump the goals of the group.[15]

What does this mean? It means that the moral rights of the individual place a justifiable limit on what the group can do to the individual. Suppose a group of people stand to gain enjoyment by arranging for others to be harmed. Imagine, for example, the Romans enjoying how the Christians go up against lions. Such a group does wrong because they allow their interests to override the individual's moral rights. This does not mean that there are no circumstances in which an individual's rights must give way to the collective interest. Imagine that Bert has inadvertently swallowed the microfilmed code that we must have to prevent a massive nuclear explosion in New Zealand. Bert sits safely in Tucson, Arizona. We explain the situation but Bert refuses to consent to our request that we operate, retrieve the code, and prevent the explosion. He cites his right to determine what is to be done to his body. In such a case it is not implausible to say that Bert's right must give way to the collective interests of others.

Individual rights then normally, but not always, trump collective interests. To give a precise statement of the conditions that determine which ought to prevail is very difficult indeed, but the following conditions, which deal only with the right not to be harmed, at least seem to incorporate necessary conditions for overriding this right.[16]

An individual's right not to be harmed can justifiably be overridden only if—

> a. we have very good reason to believe that overriding the individual's right by itself will prevent, and is the only realistic way to prevent, vastly greater harm to other innocent individuals; or
>
> b. we have very good reason to believe that allowing the individual to be harmed is a necessary link in a chain of events that collectively will prevent vastly greater harm to innocent individuals, *and* we have very good reason to believe that this chain of events is the only realistic way to prevent this vastly greater harm; or
>
> c. we have very good reason to believe that it is only if we override the individual's right that we can have a reasonable hope of preventing vastly greater harm to other innocent individuals.

There is much that is vague in these conditions, for example, "vastly greater harm," "innocent individuals," "reasonable hope." At present, however, we will have to make do with them as they stand.

Even so we can see that these conditions attempt to do justice to the complexity of conflicts of interest. In particular, they attempt to explain how, in a principled way, we might justify overriding an individual's right not to be harmed even though *just* doing this will not guarantee the prevention of vastly greater harm. Condition (*b*) brings this out—harming an individual is only one part of a more complex series of events which we have very good reason to believe will prevent vastly greater harm, or because—as (*c*) brings out—we simply do not know how things will turn out, but do have very good reason to believe that we have no reasonable hope of preventing some catastrophe unless we allow an individual to be harmed. Possibly some will find these conditions too liberal. Condition (*c*) in particular might seem too lenient. Even (*b*) might go too far. I am not certain what to say here and beg to leave this issue unresolved, except to say that the case for not harming animals is proportionately greater the more one is inclined to restrict the above set just to condition (*a*). For reasons that will become clearer, however, even the more liberal view, that harm can be justified if one of the three conditions is met, is sufficient to make a strong case against our routine abuse of animals.

These conditions share an extremely important feature. Each specifies what we must know or have good reason to believe if we are justified in overriding an individual's right not to be harmed. Each requires anyone who would harm an individual to show that this does not involve violating the individual's right. Part of the importance of the question, whether animals have rights, specifically, the right not to be harmed, now comes into clear focus. *If* they have this right, then it will be violated whenever animals are harmed and condition (*a*), or (*b*), or (*c*) is not satisfied. Moreover, the onus of justification is always on those who harm animals to explain how they are not violating the right of animals not to be harmed, if animals have this right. So, the question continues to press itself upon us. Do animals have the right not to be harmed?

This is not an easy question to answer. One is reminded of Bentham's observation that the idea of moral rights is "nonsense on stilts." Bentham meant this in the case of *human* moral rights. One can only speculate regarding what he might have thought concerning the moral rights of *animals*! So, how is one to proceed? The circuitous path we must cautiously travel, I think, is in broad outline as follows.[17]

We begin by asking about our reasons for thinking that human beings have the moral right not to be harmed; then we go on to ask whether, given these reasons, a case can be made for saying that animals have this right as well. Let us go back to the idea that individual human beings have this right and that, except in extreme cases, this right trumps collective interest. Why? What is there about being a human being to which we can point and say, "*That's* why you must not harm the individual even if the group benefits?"

The heart of the answer lies, I believe, in thinking that human beings have a certain kind of value: inherent value. By this I mean that each human being has value logically independently of whether he/she is valued by anyone else (or, what perhaps comes to the same thing, whether he/she is the object of anyone else's interest).[18] The view that human beings have inherent value implies that the kind of value properly attributable to them is not exclusively instrumental. Humans have value not just because, and not just so long as, they are good for something. They have value distinct from their utility and skill.

If this is true, we can explain, in general terms reminiscent of Kant, what is involved in mistreating human beings. Humans are mistreated if they are treated as valuable only if they forward the interests of other beings. To treat a human being thus is to show a lack of proper respect for the sort of value humans have. In Kant's terms, what has value in itself must always be treated as an end, never merely as a means. But this is precisely what we are doing if we harm an individual so that others might gain pleasure or profit; we are treating the individual merely as a means, as valuable only to the extent he/she contributes to the collective interest.

Now, *if* we accept the postulate that human beings have inherent value, we can press on and ask how rights enter the picture. They enter in being grounded in inherent value. In other words, it is individuals who have inherent value who have moral rights, and it is *because* they have value of this kind that they have a moral right not to be treated in ways that deny their having this kind of value. Rather than rights being connected with *the value of consequences* that affect individuals for good or ill, rather than rights being justified by the utility of recognizing them, rights are based on *the value of individuals*. In the case of the right not to be harmed, then, what we can say is that individuals who have inherent value have the right not to be harmed, which precludes treating them merely as a means. This would fail to treat these individuals with that respect to which, because of the kind of value they have, they are entitled.

Now, certainly the foregoing is not a definitive account of the view that individuals having inherent value have basic moral rights, in particular the right not to be harmed. One omission is especially conspicuous. What is there about being a human being that underlies this inherent value? Any answer is controversial, and a sustained defense of the answer proposed here is not possible.[19] But here is the answer I would give: human beings not only are alive; *they have a life*.[20] What is more, we are the subjects of a life that is better or worse for us, logically independently of anyone else's valuing us or finding us useful.

I do not mean that others cannot contribute to or detract from the value of our lives. On the contrary, the great goods of life (love, friendship, and, in general, fellow feeling) and its great evils (hatred, enmity, loneliness, alienation) all involve our relationships with other persons. What I mean, rather, is that our being *the subject* of a life that is better or worse for us does not depend logically on what others do or do not do. This fact, I believe, provides the illumination we seek. Humans have inherent value because we are ourselves the subjects of a life that is more or less valuable to us. In sum:

> Human beings have inherent value because, logically independently of the interest of others, each individual is the subject of a life that is better or worse for that individual. Because of the type of value that human beings have, it is wrong (a sign of disrespect and a violation of rights) to treat humans as if they had value merely as a means (e.g., to use humans merely to advance the pleasures of the group). In particular, to harm human beings for the sake of the profit or pleasure of any group is to violate their right not to be harmed.

The question now arises whether this same line of argument can be developed in the case of animals. It can, at least in the case of those animals who are the subjects of a life that is better or worse for them, logically independently of whether they are valued by anyone else. And there can be no rational doubt that there *are* numerous species of animals of which this is true, including the great blue whale, gibbons, and the others with which we began. They too have a distinctive kind of value in their own right, if we do; therefore, they too have a right not to be treated in ways that fail to respect this value, if we do. And, like humans, this right of theirs will be overridden unjustifiably if they are harmed merely to advance the profits or pleasures of others.

Conclusion

Two final philosophical points are in order, before I bring the results of my argument to bear on how animals are treated in the world at large. First, it is important to realize that I have not *proven* that animals have rights, or even that *human* beings have rights. Rather, I have argued that if humans have rights, so do many animals. More particularly, I have argued for what appears to be the most promising line of argument for explaining human rights, the view that we have inherent value, and that this can rationally be extended to animals of some kinds. So, while I admit that I have not proven that animals (or humans) have rights, I hope at least to have made clear the direction in which future argument ought to proceed. Erecting pointers, to be sure, is not the same as constructing proofs, but pointers are the best I can do here.

Second, the history of moral philosophy teaches us that utilitarianism dies hard. Just when one thinks it has been forced off the stage for good, one finds it loitering in the wings, awaiting yet another curtain call. The utilitarian can be counted on to say that there is nothing introduced by the idea of rights for which he cannot account.[21] One has only to see that the utilitarian objective is promoted if we recognize a strict obligation not to harm individuals except in extreme cases, *and* that, furthermore, utility is promoted by saying that individuals have the right not to be harmed, this invocation of a right functioning as an especially forceful way of conveying the idea that we ought not to harm individuals.

I am not convinced by this attempt to resurrect utilitarianism, and here I raise my final and most fundamental objection to it. The utilitarian is in no position to say that he knows that the utilitarian objective is promoted by talk of individuals having rights. But even if it is true that talk of rights helps promote the utilitarian objective, and for this reason such talk ought to be encouraged and honored, there can only be a *contingent* connection between respecting any right, such as the right not to be harmed, and forwarding the utilitarian objective. The most that the utilitarian can say is that recognizing the right not to be harmed *as a matter of fact* fits in with forwarding his goal of maximizing the balance of good over evil.[22] The utilitarian must also accept that things could have been (and could become) otherwise. He must accept the possibility that it could have been or might become all right to harm individuals if this ever happened to forward the utilitarian objective. But neither the wrong of harming individuals nor the right not to be harmed can change in the ways utilitarian theory implies they can. They are not contingent upon *utility*. Neither depends on the value of consequences. Instead, each depends on *the value of individuals*.

Let us put this in perspective before applying it. Earlier we said that before making an informed judgment about the morality of whaling or the use of the Draize test we must use both facts and moral principles. Otherwise, we cannot know which facts are morally relevant; and without this preliminary knowledge, we do not know what moral judgments to make. To determine what these principles are, we said, is one of the distinctive tasks of moral philosophy. Three positions were examined and found wanting: the Kantian account, the cruelty account, and the utilitarian account. We then considered an account ascribing rights to animals, a position that meets the objections that were fatal to the views examined earlier. Unlike the Kantian account, the rights account insists upon the moral status of animals in their own right; unlike the cruelty account, the rights account does not confuse the morality of acts with the mental states of agents; and unlike utilitarianism, this account closes the door to the justification of prejudices that merely happen to bring about the best consequences and emphasizes the value of individuals as distinct from the value of consequences. This emphasis on the value of individuals becomes prominent now as we turn at last to the task of applying the rights account to the whale, the veal calf, and the others.

It would be grotesque to suggest that the whale, the rabbit, the gibbon, the bobbie calf, the millions of animals brought so much pain and death at the hands of humans are not harmed, for harm is not restricted to human beings. They are harmed, harmed in a literal, not a metaphorical sense. They are made to endure what is detrimental to their welfare, even death. Those who would harm them, therefore, must justify doing so. Thus, members of the whaling industry, the cosmetics industry, the farming industry, the network of hunters-exporters-importers must justify the harm they bring animals in a way that is consistent with recognizing the animals' right not to be harmed. To produce such a justification it is not enough to argue that people profit, satisfy their curiosity, or derive pleasure from allowing animals to be treated in these ways. These facts are not the morally relevant ones. Rather, what must be shown is that overriding the right of animals not to be harmed is justified because of further facts. For example, because we have very good reason to believe that overriding the individual's right prevents, and is the only realistic way to prevent, vastly greater harm to other innocent individuals.

Let us ask the whaling industry whether they have so justified their trade. Have they made their case in terms of the morally relevant facts? Our answer must be: No! And the cosmetic industry? No! The farmers who raise veal calves? No! The retailer of exotic animals? No! A thousand times we must say: No! I do not say that they cannot possibly justify what they do. The individual's right not to be harmed, we have argued, almost always trumps the interests of the group, but it is possible that such a right must sometimes give way. Possibly the rights of animals must sometimes give way to human interests. It would be a mistake to rule this possibility out. Nevertheless, the onus of justification must be borne by those who cause the harm to show that they do not violate the rights of the individuals involved.

We allow then that it is *possible* that harming animals might be justified; but we also maintain that those harming animals typically fail to show that the harm caused is *actually* justified. A further question we must ask ourselves is what, morally speaking, we ought to do in such a situation? Reflection on comparable situations involving human beings will help make the answer clear.

Consider racism and sexism. Imagine that slavery is an institution of the day and that it is built on racist or sexist lines. Blacks or women are assigned the rank of slave. Suppose we are told that in extreme circumstances even slavery might conceivably be justified, and that we ought not to object to it or try to bring it down, even though no one has shown that it is actually justified in the present case. Well, I do not believe for a moment that we would accept such an attempt to dissuade us from toppling the institution of slavery. Not for a moment would we accept the general principle involved here, that an institution actually is justified because it might conceivably be justified. We would accept the quite different principle that we are morally obligated to oppose any practice that appears to violate rights unless we are shown that it really does not do so. To be satisfied with anything less is to cheapen the value attributable to the victims of the practice.

Exactly the same line of reasoning applies in the case where animals are regarded as so many dispensable commodities, models, subjects, and the like. We ought not to back away from bringing these industries and related practices to a halt just because it is *possible* that the harm caused to the animals *might* be justified. If we do, we fail to mean it when we say that animals are not mere things, that they are the subjects of a life that is better or worse for them, that they have inherent value. As in the comparable case involving harm to human beings, our duty is to act, to do all that we can to put an end to the harm animals are made to endure. That the animals themselves cannot speak out on their own behalf, that they cannot organize, petition, march, exert political pressure, or raise our level of consciousness—all this does not weaken our obligation to act on their behalf. If anything, their impotence makes our obligation the greater.[23]

We can hear, if we will but listen, the muffled detonation of the explosive harpoon, the sharp crack of the Thai hunter's rifle, the drip of the liquid as it strikes the rabbit's eye, the bobbie calf's forlorn sigh. We can see, if we will but look, the last convulsive gasps of the great blue whale, the dazed terror of the gibbons' eyes, the frenzied activity of the rabbit's feet, the stark immobility of the bobbie calf. But not at this moment only. Tomorrow, other whales, other rabbits will be made to suffer; tomorrow, other gibbons, other calves will be killed, and others the day after. And others, stretching into the future. All this we know with certainty. All this and more, incalculably more, *will* go on, if we do not act today, as act we must. Our respect for the value and rights of the animals cannot be satisfied with anything less.

NOTES

1. Captain W. R. D. McLaughlin, *Call to the South* (London: Harrap and Co., n.d.), quoted in Muriel the Lady Dowding, "Furs and Cosmetics: Too High a Price?" in Stanley and Roslind Godlovitch, and John Harris, eds. *Animals, Men, and Morals* (London: Gollancz; New York: Taplinger, 1972), p. 35.

2. Jean-Yves Domalain, *The Animal Connection: The Confessions of an Ex-Wild Animal Trafficker* (New York: William Morrow, 1977), p. 21. For additional information on endangered species, see Cleveland Amory, *Man Kind? Our Incredible War on Wildlife* (New York: Harper and Row, 1974) and Lewis Regenstein, *The Politics of Extinction* (New York: Macmillan, 1975).

3. Especially important sources on the use of animals in research are Richard Ryder, *Victims of Science* (London: Davis-Poynter, 1975); Hans Ruesch, *Slaughter of the Innocent* (New York: Bantam Books, 1978); John Vyvyan, *The Dark Face of Science* (London: Michael Joseph, 1971); and E. A. Westacott, *A Century of Vivisection and Anti-Vivisection* (London: Daniel, 1949).

4. For information on modern factory farming methods, see Ruth Harrison, *Animal Machines* (London: Stuart, 1964) and Peter Singer, *Animal Liberation*

(New York: A New York Review Book, distributed by Random House, 1975; New York: Avon Books, 1977).

5. As quoted in Regenstein, *Politics of Extinction*, p. 121.

6. These figures are suggested by Ryder. See also his "Experiments on Animals" reprinted in Tom Regan and Peter Singer, eds., *Animal Rights and Human Obligations* (Englewood Cliffs, N.J.: Prentice-Hall, 1976).

7. These figures are based on estimates furnished for the year 1968 by the United Nations Food and Agriculture Organization and quoted in Nathaniel Altman, *Eating for Life: A Book About Vegetarianism* (London: Theosophical Publishing House, 1973), p. 59.

8. Relevant selections from both Saint Thomas and Kant are included in Regan and Singer, eds., *Animal Rights and Human Obligations*. What I call the Kantian account is criticized further in my "Exploring the Idea of Animal Rights" in D. Paterson and R. Ryder, eds., *Animals' Rights: A Symposium* (London: Centaur Press, 1979). Kant's views are criticized at length by Elizabeth Pybus and Alexander Broadie, "Kant's Treatment of Animals," *Philosophy* 49 (1974): 375–383. I defend Kant against their objections in my "Broadie and Pybus on Kant," *Philosophy* 51 (1976): 471–472. Broadie and Pybus reply in their "Kant on the Maltreatment of Animals," *Philosophy* 53 (1978): 560–561.

9. Singer, *Animal Liberation*, and Ryder, *Victims of Science*.

10. The famous passage from Bentham reads as follows (from *The Principles of Morals and Legislation* [1789], chap. 17, sec. 1, reprinted in Regan and Singer, *Animal Rights and Human Obligations*, p. 130: "The day has been, I grieve to say in many places it is not yet past, in which the greater part of the species, under the denomination of slaves, have been treated by the law exactly upon the same footing as, in England for example, the inferior races of animals are still. The day may come, when the rest of the animal creation may acquire those rights which never could have been withholden from them but by the hand of tyranny. The French have already discovered that the blackness of the skin is no reason why a human being should be abandoned without redress to the caprice of a tormentor. It may come one day to be recognized, that the number of the legs, the villosity of the skin, or the termination of the os sacrum, are reasons equally insufficient for abandoning a sensitive being to the same fate. What else is it that should trace the insuperable line? Is it the faculty of reason, or, perhaps, the faculty of discourse? But a full-grown horse or dog is beyond comparison a more rational, as well as a more conversable animal, than an infant of a day, or a week, or even a month, old. But suppose the case were otherwise, what would it avail? The question is not, Can they reason? nor, Can they talk? but, *Can they suffer?* "

11. John Locke, *Some Thoughts Concerning Education*, 5th ed. (London: printed for A. and C Churchill, 1905). See also James Axfell, ed., *The Educational Writings of John Locke* (Cambridge: Cambridge University Press, 1968), sec. 116, pp. 225–226.

12. The utilitarian position I consider is the one associated with Bentham and forcefully presented by Peter Singer. That Singer is a utilitarian is made unmistakably clear in his "The Fable of the Fox and the Unliberated Animals" *Ethics* 88 (1978):119–125. (A more complete examination of Singer's position is offered in essay 2, above).

13. See Singer, *Animal Liberation*, esp. pp. 78–83.

14. Ibid., essay 4.

15. Ronald Dworkin, *Taking Rights Seriously* (Cambridge: Harvard University Press, 1977).

16. The present statement of these conditions deviates somewhat from my earlier effort in "The Moral Basis of Vegetarianism," *Canadian Journal of Philosophy* 5 (1975):181–214 (essay 1 above). I believe the inclusion of conditions (*b*) and (*c*) marks an improvement over the earlier formulation. A fuller statement, however, has to include more than simply the idea of *preventing* vastly greater harm; for example, *reducing* already existing harm also has a place.

17. See my "An Examination and Defense of One Argument Concerning Animal Rights," *Inquiry* 22 (1979):189–219 (essay 6, below).

18. Whether sense can be made of including irreversibly comatose human beings in the class of beings having inherent value is a troublesome question indeed. I consider this issue, perhaps not very adequately, in essay 6, below.

19. I do not believe it is absurd to think of natural objects that lack consciousness, or collections of such objects, as having inherent value, in the sense in which I use this expression. An *x* has inherent value if it has value logically independently of anyone's valuing *x*. I do not say this is easy to clarify or to defend, and it may be wrongheaded. At present, however, I believe it is a view that must be held, if we are to develop an environmental ethic, as distinct from an ethic for the use of the environment. (This point is pursued at length in essays 8 and 9 below.)

20. The distinction between being alive and having a life is one James Rachels frequently makes. See, for example, his "Euthanasia" in Tom Regan, ed., *Matters of Life and Death* (New York: Random House, 1980). Rachels does not, so far as I am aware, relate this distinction to the idea of inherent value.

21. It is possible that Mill meant to give rights a utilitarian basis. On this see David Lyons, "Human Rights and the General Welfare," *Philosophy and Public Affairs* 6 (1977): 113–129, reprinted in David Lyons, ed., *Rights* (Belmont, Ca.: Wadsworth, 1979). The principal objection to this enterprise is the third objection I raise against utilitarianism here.

22. I do not believe utilitarianism is alone in implying that the duty not to harm an individual (or the individual's right not to be harmed) are *contingent* moral truths, which *might* have been otherwise (or *might* become otherwise). Certain aspects of Kant's theory as well as ethical egoism arguably imply this as well. This is absolutely fatal to these theories, a point I argue in my

"Utilitarianism, Vegetarianism, and Animal Rights," *Philosophy and Public Affairs* 9, 4 (1980):306–324 (essay 2, above).

23. For a more complete list of recent philosophical work relating to the topics discussed in the present essay, see Charles Magel and Tom Regan, "Animal Rights and Human Obligations: A Select Bibliography," *Inquiry* 22 (1979): 243–247 (reproduced below).

5
Why Whaling Is Wrong

In April 1980 the International Whaling Commission (IWC) sponsored a Conference on Cetacean Behavior and Intelligence and the Ethics of Killing Cetaceans. The conference, ably organized by Ray Gambell, was precedent setting. The IWC was not bound by the outcome of the Washington meeting; the precedent set was that the conference was held at all. It marked the first time the IWC officially sponsored a conference that included the ethical dimensions of whaling.

My submission to the conference sought clearly to distinguish between (1) objections to whaling based on *the painful methods* used to kill whales and (2) objections based on *the killing* of whales, whatever the method used. Both types of objection, I argue, can be lodged against the whaling industry, and both can be sustained. The moral case against commercial whaling is thus very strong indeed.

In insisting on the wrong done to animals (in this case, whales), when they are killed, I reaffirm a theme that has characterized my work from "The Moral Basis of Vegetarianism" onward. Theoretical questions, which figure prominently in most of the other essays in this volume, largely go unasked in "Why Whaling is Wrong." It is appropriate to note, however, that no philosophical account of our duties to animals can be adequate if it fails to illuminate why killing a creature such as a whale, except in quite exceptional circumstances, is wrong, independently of the means used—though the use of painful methods obviously can aggravate the moral wrong that is done. Utilitarians, I believe, are hard pressed indeed to present a plausible account of why the painless killing of whales and similar creatures is wrong, a fatal defect of their theory, in my view.

James E. Scarff's paper, "Ethical Issues in Whale and Small Cetacean Management," *Environmental Ethics* 2, 2 (1980): 241–280, which includes extensive bibliographical material, is "must" reading for those interested in the ethics of whaling. Singer discusses the utilitarian position on the killing of whales and relevantly similar creatures in "Animals and the Value of Life," in Tom Regan, ed., *Matters of Life and Death* (New York: Random House, paperback; Philadelphia: Temple University Press, clothbound, 1980), pp. 244–246 and in *Practical Ethics* (Cambridge: Clarendon Press, 1980), pp. 93ff. Also relevant is L. W. Sumner, "A Matter of Life and Death," *Nous* 10, 2 (1976): 145–171.

Four provocative essays that touch on wild and endangered species are J. Baird Callicott, "Animal Liberation: A Triangular Affair," *Environmental Ethics* 2, 4 (Winter 1980): 311–338; Stephen Clark, "The Rights of Wild Things," *Inquiry* 22, 1–2 (1978): 171–188; Alastaire Gunn, "Why Should We Care About Rare Species?" *Environmental Ethics* 2, 1 (1980): 17–37; and Peter Singer, "Not for Humans Only: The Place of Nonhumans in Environmental Ethics," *Ethics and Problems of the 21st Century*, K. E. Goodpaster and K. M. Sayre, eds. (Notre Dame: University of Notre Dame Press, 1980), pp. 191–206.

The proceedings of the IWC Conference are forthcoming in *Cetaceans, Brains, and Ethics*, Phoebe Wray, ed. (Washington: Center for Action on Endangered Species). When my time came to address the Conference, I chose to reply to some of those who went before me on the program, rather than to read my submission, which had been distributed. These remarks, titled "A Critique of the Defense of Whaling," are included in the *Proceedings*. "Why Whaling is Wrong" thus appears in print here for the first time.

To investigate the ethics of whaling[1] involves, but is not limited to, two questions. First, does whaling cause significant pain, and, if so, is this wrong? Second, is it wrong to kill whales? It is extremely important to emphasize that both questions must be addressed *and* that they really pose distinct moral issues. Both must be addressed because to cause significant pain and to kill are acts that stand in need of special moral justification, acts that, in the absence of such justification, must be condemned as wrong. And they pose distinct moral issues because the immorality of the one is not reducible to the immorality of the other—in particular, the immorality of killing is not just a matter of how much, or how little, pain is caused. Imagine, if you will, that John kills Jane painlessly: A lethal dose of poison is skillfully administered while Jane sleeps, and she suffers not, neither physically nor mentally. Well, we would not say that, since Jane does not suffer, what John has done is therefore quite all right. In the absence of special circumstances (e.g., perhaps Jane was terminally ill, had written a living will, and the like) what John does *clearly* is wrong. Just as clearly, then, the wrongness of killing does not turn only on how much pain is caused.

So we have two different, important questions that must be asked, when we turn to consider the ethics of whaling, one dealing with the suffering whaling causes whales, the other concerning the morality of killing whales, period. Both questions are examined in what follows. But first let us remind ourselves of some well established, relevant facts about whales.[2]

1. Whales are mammals. Infants are fed and cared for by their mothers, and the bond between mother and child appears to persist beyond the period of lactation.

2. Whales are social animals. They live in groups and relate to each other as individuals. Some species are thought to be monogamous, keeping the same mate throughout life. As Lewis Regenstein has noted: "There are numerous recorded incidents in which a whale has been harpooned or captured and taken to shore, and its mate or family has followed it or waited offshore for its return for days, even weeks at a time" (Regenstein, 1975). Farley Mowat has described one such incident (Mowat, 1974).

3. Whales have exceptionally large brains, both in absolute terms and in proportion to body weight (Jacobs, 1974; Morgane, 1974). The

area of the cetacean brain which corresponds to that part of the human brain controlling emotions and affective states is well developed. This is not unusual in social mammals, and suggests that whales may have a complex and deeply felt emotional life. It may be objected that to think of whales in this way involves unscientific anthropomorphizing. This is not so. There is good scientific evidence to back up the ascription of a sophisticated emotional life to whales. As the Federation of American Scientists (FAS) Public Interest Report, speaking on behalf of 7,000 American scientists, said recently: "There is a good deal to be said for emphathizing with whales" (FAS, 1977).

4. Whales appear to be capable of enjoying life. The playfulness and sense of humour of the small whales (orcas and dolphins) has made them popular attractions in captivity. Similar playful behavior has been observed with the great whales in the wild (Payne, 1972).

5. The nervous system of whales and the parts of the brain relating to the perception of pain are essentially similar to our own. There are no grounds for denying that whales feel physical pain much as we do (Singer, 1975).

6. Whaling kills whales. This means that it kills intelligent social mammals, capable of enjoying life. It also means that it may cause feelings akin to grief in mothers deprived of their young, or young deprived of their mothers, or in adults deprived of their lifetime mate, or in members of a group deprived of one of their number.

7. The method of killing is often neither quick nor painless . . . . According to an IWC study, the average length of time it takes a whale to die is between two and five minutes, and in some cases death does not occur until twenty-five minutes after the first harpoon explodes inside the whale's body. The IWC is hardly likely to overestimate the length of time it takes a whale to die. Others have suggested that death can take much longer still, as long as several hours. In any case it is indisputable that it is sometimes necessary to use a second harpoon to kill a whale, and the second harpoon will not be fired until several minutes after the first one has hit.

In view of these facts, there can be no doubt *either* that whales can experience pain *or* that they are caused significant pain by present-day whaling techniques. Even those with the strongest vested interest in the survival of the whaling industry, therefore, if they are rational, must accept this much. But even those who are most opposed to this industry must, if they are rational, also acknowledtge that causing pain, even causing significant pain, is not always wrong. Surgeons cause significant pain. So do wrestlers. So do physical therapists. But it does not follow from this that what these persons do is wrong. Similarly, therefore, one cannot infer that whaling is wrong *just* because whales are made to suffer significant pain.

But while there is no strict entailment between someone's causing significant pain and their acting immorally, it must be conceded that because an activity causes significant pain is always a moral point against it. That is, those involved in such an activity cannot be rational and at the same time say, "What's all the fuss about pain?" On the contrary, because significant pain is caused makes it rationally incumbent on those involved in the activity to justify that activity—to show, that is, that there are other, more stringent moral demands that justify this pain-causing activity. Not to see the need to offer such a justification is to fail to recognize a requirement of rationality.

How might such a justification be given? This is a very difficult question, one that cannot receive a full airing here. At least this much is clear, however. We cannot justify causing others significant pain, as a result of our pursuing certain ends, if we can achieve these ends without causing significant pain. For if these ends can be achieved without causing significant pain, then the pain caused surely is gratuitous (unnecessary). And if the pain caused is gratuitous, then causing it is wrong. Thus, for example, I could not justify burning people alive as a source of heat for my home, even assuming that doing so would help me achieve the end I seek (warmth); and I could not justify doing this for the very good reason, among others, that there exist other alternatives that I could make use of to achieve this end, alternatives that would not cause anyone any significant pain.

Now, the preceding is relevant to assessing the morality of whaling, when we make this assessment just in terms of the significant pain whales are caused. For it there are alternative ways of achieving the ends whaling seeks; and if these ends can be achieved without causing significant pain; then the pain whales are made to endure is unnecessary—is gratuitous; and if that is so, then the activity that causes it, whaling, stands morally condemned, and rightly so.

So let us ask about the ends sought by the whaling industry, and whether these ends might be achieved in ways that do not cause significant pain. As for the ends, the relevant ones appear to be these: To produce products, or ingredients for products, that can compete successfully in the marketplace. But with respect to these products, there can be no doubt that other, equally good alternatives exist that contain no ingredients obtained from whales. Thus, the door is shut on the argument that there are products, intended for a certain range of purposes, that can be made *only* if ingredients from whales are used. And, with respect to the question of producing *marketable* products (ones that will turn a profit) that do not include ingredients from whales, there again can be no doubt that this can be done. One has only to point to the economic success of manufacturers who do not use ingredients from whales, but who compete successfully with manufacturers who do use such ingredients, to show that including ingredients from whales is not essential to achieving the economic ends of the whaling industry. Thus, both with respect to products and economic aspirations, there is no demonstrable need for using the ingredients of whales; in both cases, other, viable alternatives exist. Thus, since the ends of the whaling industry can be achieved by means that do not cause significant pain, the pain caused by that industry is gratuitous, and the activity that causes it, whaling, is, viewed from this vantage point, morally unjustified.

This, then, is our finding about the whaling industry, when viewed solely in terms of one moral parameter—the one that focuses attention on the idea of causing significant pain. But there is a second relevant moral parameter, the other one mentioned at the outset. This concerns the wrongness of killing, an issue that, as we know, is not reducible to causing significant pain, since a particular act of killing might be wrong even though no pain is caused. (Recall the example of John's killing Jane, cited earlier). So let us now turn our attention to this second moral parameter, seek to gain some insight into what makes killing wrong, and then try to apply this insight to the particular issue of the ethics of whaling.

Now, clearly, if killing *any* living thing is wrong, then killing whales is wrong. But it is extremely doubtful that a compelling argument can be given for the view that it is wrong to kill any living thing, from bacterium to cancer cell, from amoeba to paramecium. In any event, the question, whether it is wrong to kill whales, does not depend on so universal an interpretation of the wrongness of killing. Rather, it depends on our thinking through why it is wrong to kill in those cases where the immorality of killing is clearest to us—namely, in those cases where human beings are killed.

Why is killing wrong in these cases? In general, it is wrong because death is a great evil. And death is a great evil because it marks the loss of what is necessary for all of life's other goods: It marks the cessation of life itself. Granted, there may be extreme cases where death may be a merciful release from a life of agony. Nevertheless, we are agreed that, in general, continued life is in the interests of a human being, while death is contrary to these interests. And it is because it runs contrary to these interests, because it is the reverse of what is beneficial, that death is the great harm that it is, whether it is caused by painful means or not. For what is harmful is not the same as, and does not necessarily involve, suffering or pain.

But it is not only the killing of a *human being* that can be wrong. On the contrary, any time killing an individual *harms that individual*, we can intelligibly view that killing as wrong; and killing that individual *will* be wrong, unless it can be shown that it is justified by appeal to other, more stringent moral demands—for example, unless the killing is done in self-defense or to protect the innocent. We return to this question of justification in a moment. First, though, it is essential to see that the wrongness of killing is not restricted only to the killing of human beings but encompasses all those individuals, whether human or not, for whom death is harmful. The questions that remain, then, are (*a*) How may we rationally decide which individuals these are? and (*b*) Does reason constrain us to include whales?

As for (*a*), the answer is implied in the preceding. For since the death of an individual is harmful to that individual if that individual can be harmed or benefited, and since individuals can be harmed or benefited if they have interests, it follows that death is harmful to those individuals who have interests. This being so, our answer to (*b*) must turn on how reason constrains us to answer the question, Do whales have interests? And once the question is posed in this way, there is no rational way to avoid an affirmative answer. Whales are intelligent, social creatures, with remarkable sensory powers; they give behavioral evidence of memory and desire; they can feel pain, both physical and psychological; they can take pleasure in various activities. All these facts and the others summarized earlier, support our finding that certain things are in their interests while others are not; that they are a sort of individual that can be benefited or harmed; that what transpires in their life *matters to them* individually, makes a difference to the quality of *their* life, *as experienced by them*. Thus is it that death, for them, is harmful because it deprives them of what is necessary for all of their life's goods: it deprives them of life itself. And thus is it that killing them is, in the absence of a compelling justification, wrong.

There are numerous ways by which some might endeavor to avoid this conclusion. None, however, is rationally successful. For example, one cannot avoid it by arguing that death is harmful only to human beings, since one will then have to specify what it is about being human that makes a human's death harmful, and, in doing this, the notion of what is in an individual's interests will arise, a notion that, as has just been argued, is not bound in its application only to *Homo sapiens*. Nor can it credibly be argued that death is not an evil, not a harm, since our practice belies this denial. Nor, to give a final example, can the preceding argument be reduced to absurdity on the grounds that it commits one to viewing the killing of any living thing, including, say, cancer cells, as wrong because harmful. This objection misfires because there is no rational basis for believing that anything we do to cancer cells matters to these cells themselves, or that it makes a difference to the quality of their life as experienced by them, or, in short, that they can be benefited or harmed by what we do to them. So, no, the argument that would provide a basis for including whales within the class of beings it is wrong to kill does not commit us to including all living things within that class.

But unless we subscribe to a form of absolute pacifism, we must agree that not all killing is wrong, just as, earlier, it was agreed that it is not always wrong to cause pain. And just as, in that earlier case, we were obliged to ask about the justifiability of causing pain, so here, too, we must ask about when, if ever, killing can be justified. That we will not be able to examine this question in much detail will come as no surprise. Nevertheless, enough can be said to provide a very strong case against the killing of whales.

The general principle involved is this: That it is wrong to engage in any activity that kills individuals, where these individuals are harmed by being killed, if the ends of this activity can be achieved without killing such individuals. And the reason such an activity stands condemned on moral grounds is that the killing it causes clearly is gratuitous—unnecessary. The previous example, about using human beings as a source of heat, can be used to illustrate this principle. For it is wrong to use humans to heat my home, whether they are caused pain or not; and it is wrong to do this, first, because to do so is to harm them, and, second, because it is possible for me to achieve the ends I seek (warmth) without killing any living thing that is harmed by my killing. Such gratuitous killing of individuals who are harmed when killed is wrong, if anything is.

The application of this general principle to the case of whaling is straightforward. The question to be asked is whether the ends of whaling can be achieved without killing whales. Those ends, again, or at least the relevant ones, are to produce products that can compete successfully in the marketplace. And those ends, for reasons already given, *can* be achieved without killing whales. Thus, inasmuch as whales are harmed when killed; and inasmuch as we cannot be justified in killing such individuals if we can achieve our ends without killing them; it follows that killing whales is morally unjustified—is wrong. And it follows that this is wrong independently of how much, or how little, pain the whales suffer when they are killed. For a painless killing, from the point of view of what a whale loses when killed, is just as harmful, just as great a loss to the whale, as a painful one. Granted, that the whale is made to suffer compounds the wrong; but the wrong involved in killing it is a separate, a distinct wrong, based on the harm that is done, not the pain that is felt. Even were the day to come, therefore, where we had the technological means to kill a whale instantaneously, painlessly, that would not cancel the immorality of the killing. It would remove the wrong of causing gratuitous suffering. It would make whaling *less* wrong. But a less wrong does not make a right.

Three final points. First, those who argue morally against many of the customary ways in which animals are treated, including objecting to whaling, sometimes are accused of caring too much for animals and of not caring enough for human beings. But this is to misunderstand the thrust of efforts to improve the lot of animals. To be "for" animals is not necessarily to be "against" humanity. On the contrary, the very same principles one would urge to improve the treatment of animals are those one ought to urge to improve the lot of human beings. For it cannot be right, for example, to engage in activities that cause the gratuitous pain or death of *human* beings, if it is wrong to cause the gratuitous pain or death of animals. Thus, the principles involved in the effort to secure more enlightened treatment of animals are not—and, indeed, cannot be—prejudicial to the interests of human beings.

Second, the cessation of whaling, as we know it, will inevitably involve some degree of economic dislocation. People will lose jobs. Owners will lose capital. Investors will lose money. It is not contrary to the dictates of morality to urge that steps be taken to ease the burdens persons must shoulder in a time of transition. Those nations affected, for example, ought to take the necessary steps to provide displaced workers with an opportunity to acquire training or skills that qualify them for a new line of work. And arrangements should be made, so far as this is practicable, to equalize the financial contributions that affected parties will have to make to pay for the costs of transition. Obviously this will be complicated. But just as obviously morality would not look with disfavor on efforts to ease the pain of moral progress.

Third, and finally, much emphasis is placed on the idea of cruelty, when the treatment of animals is discussed. Not infrequently those in the so-called "pro" animal camp charge those in the so-called "con" animal camp (for instance, factory farmers, scientists who use animals in painful research, whalers) with cruelty. This is regrettable for several reasons, paramount among them being that it rests on, and helps perpetuate, a pernicious confusion. "Cruel" is a term that applies to a person's character or individual actions, and it is correctly applied only if persons' acts are accompanied by a certain mental state—in particular, if they enjoy causing pain to, or harming, others. It should be clear to anyone that persons are not cruel just because they cause pain. And this should be clear because we do not think that surgeons and physical therapists, for example, must be cruel because they cause pain. Similarly, therefore, it simply is not true that whalers are cruel people because they cause pain. Indeed, there is very little reason to believe that whalers, as a class, are any more cruel than the general lot of humanity. It is, therefore, long past time that others stopped charging whalers with cruelty, just as it is long past time that whalers stopped whaling. For though whaling is wrong, for the reasons given, it is not true that whalers must be cruel or evil people.

NOTES

1. I use "whaling" here and throughout this essay as a shorthand way to refer to those involved in the whaling industry or others who kill whales to turn an economic profit.

2. The seven points that follow are quoted from Peter Singer's submission to the Australian government's Inquiry into Whales and Whaling. I am grateful to Professor Singer for making this material available to me and strongly recommend that those interested in the ethics of whaling consult his submission. The sources cited by Singer are the following: Federation of American Scientists, *Report*, October 1977. Jacobs, Myron, "The Whale Brain, Input and Behavior" in MacIntyre, Joan, *Mind in the Waters* (New York: Charles Scribner's Sons, 1974). Morgane, Peter, "The Whale Brain: Anatomical Basis of Intelligence," in MacIntyre, *Mind in the Waters*. Mowat, Farley, "The Trapped Whale," in MacIntyre, *Mind in the Waters*. Payne, Robert, "Swimming with Patagonia's Right Whales," *National Geographic*, October 1972. Regan, Tom, and Peter Singer, eds., *Animal Rights and Human Obligations* (Englewood Cliffs, N.J.: Prentice-Hall, 1976). Regenstein, Lewis, *The Politics of Extinction* (New York: Macmillan, 1975). Singer, Peter, "Animal Liberation," *New York Review of Books*, April 5, 1973. Singer, Peter, "All Animals are Equal," *Philosophic Exchange* 1:5 (Summer 1974): 103–115. Singer, Peter, *Animal Liberation* (New York: A New York Review Book, distributed by Random House, 1975; New York: Avon Books, 1977).

6

An Examination and Defense of One Argument Concerning Animal Rights

"An Examination and Defense of One Argument Concerning Animal Rights" is one of eleven essays published in a special double issue of the Norwegian journal *Inquiry* (22, 1−2 [1979]) under the forceful editorship of Alastair Hannay. Such an event would have been unthinkable twenty, even ten years ago, and it is a symptom of the growing intellectual respectability of exploring the moral status of animals that not only *Inquiry*, but three other journals have devoted the whole, or the lion's share, of an issue to this topic—the American journal *Ethics* (88, 2 [January 1978]), the English journal *Philosophy* (53, 206 [October 1978]) and the Polish journal *Etyka* 18, 1980. When, in 1973, Peter Singer and I decided to collect the relevant material on animal rights and human obligations, the problem was not too much, but too little good material from which to choose. That situation has changed, and changed radically, in less than ten years. There is now a steady flow of quality papers in the professional journals, in no small measure owing to the timely birth of *Environmental Ethics*, and each year brings the publication of another relevant book or two, each in its own way elevating the level of debate. Though not all who write on the topics involved are on the side of "animal rights" or "animal liberation," enough now are that we may safely put to rest the stereotypical picture of "little old ladies in tennis shoes." While granting that one can lose perspective about such things, even an outsider to the recent turn of events might begin to wonder whether we are not now on the cutting edge of a significant development in our moral and cultural evolution.

Unlike the previous essays in this collection, my contribution to the *Inquiry* volume, reprinted here with the permission of that journal, focuses exclusively on the question of animal rights and represents my most extensive treatment of this difficult topic published to date. What the argument seeks to show, to put it as simply as possible, is that higher animals cannot be denied basic moral rights if humans, including the mentally enfeebled, are said to have them, whereas these humans will lack them if these animals are denied them. Both aspects of the argument are conditional. It is not argued that animals *have* basic moral rights, for example, only that they do, *if* these humans do.

Even this conditional argument would be disputed by some. The Australian philosopher H. J. McCloskey, for example, denies that animals can possibly have rights ("Rights," *Philosophical Quarterly* 15, 1 (1965): 115−127). McCloskey's arguments go unaddressed in the essay below (for a reply, see my "McCloskey on Why Animals Cannot Have Rights," *Philosophical Quarterly* 26, 104 [1976]: 251−257). The views of R. G. Frey, a defender of McCloskey, however, are considered. For an earlier exchange between Frey and myself, see his "Interests and Animal Rights," *Philosophical Quarterly* 27, 108 (1977): 254−259, and my "Frey on Interests and Animal Rights," *Philosophical Quarterly* 27, 109 (1977): 335−337.

A central focus of this sixth essay is the identification of the most reasonable criterion of right possession, and it is the discussion of this issue which signals, not a break with the major trends of "The Moral Basis of Vegetarianism" and later works, but a clearer understanding of what must be argued if the rights of animals are to find a secure foundation. Of particular significance is my attempt to supplant sentiency (the capacity for feeling pleasure and pain) as the most adequate criterion of right possession, since, though sentiency is a morally relevant capacity it seems to be neither the only one nor the most fundamental. In some ways this may seem to depart from some earlier work (e.g., my "Exploring the Idea of Animal Rights" in David Paterson and Richard D. Ryder, eds., *Animals' Rights—A Symposium* (London: Centaur Press, 1979). But a closer reading will reveal that nowhere in my own work is sentience ever unqualifiedly set forth as necessary for having moral rights or, as in Singer's view, moral standing (cf. *Animal Liberation* [New York: A New York Review Book, distributed by

Random House, 1975; New York, Avon Books, 1977], pp. 8—9). In place of sentiency I here recommend the possession of inherent value as necessary and sufficient for possession of basic moral rights, a move that proves to be important for essays 8 and 9 (below) since, given this concept of value, nonconscious things (e.g., trees) *might* have inherent value. Conceptually, that is, inherent value is not tied *necessarily* only to those beings who are conscious, even if it should happen to be true that it is shared by all those who are.

In retrospect I believe that what I am groping for in this essay is a way to express the difference between (1) the value of individuals and (2) the value of mental states or states of affairs. The former kind of value I call "inherent value," the latter is customarily referred to as "intrinsic value." Utilitarianism, my major theoretical nemesis, can accept value only of the latter kind (e.g., pleasure or preference satisfaction). A rights-based theory can accept values of both kinds. Though this point is not made clear in the essay that follows, its analysis begins to scratch at the surface of the deepest difference separating utilitarianism from rights-based theories. Fundamentally, that difference concerns whether *individuals* have value. If not, there can be no basic moral rights. If so, then basic rights have the foundation they require. To argue that inherent value is a better (i.e., rationally preferable) criterion for right possession than is sentience is thus fraught with enormously important theoretical implications. Fundamentally this is where the theoretical action is. The references given in the introductions to the previous essays, especially essays 1 and 2, also are relevant here.

Certainly the most common and, in the words of one of its critics,[1] "the most important" type of argument advanced in support of the view that some animals have rights has its basis in reflection upon the attribution of rights to certain human beings. The humans in question are babies and the mentally enfeebled, including the severely mentally enfeebled. Proponents of the type of argument I have in mind may argue *either* that (1) certain animals *have* certain rights because these humans *have* these rights *or* that (2) *if* these humans have certain rights, *then* certain animals have these rights also. The former alternative represents what might be termed the stronger argument for animal rights; the latter, the weaker argument. They differ in that proponents of the stronger argument must include a defense of the view that the humans in question do have certain rights, whereas the weaker version leaves this an open question and argues only that if they do, then we cannot avoid attributing these same rights to certain animals. It is the weaker argument that occupies my attention throughout.

   In an important review of some of the recent literature on animal rights Jan Narveson[2] refers to arguments for animal rights that are grounded in considerations about the rights of babies and the mentally enfeebled as "argument(s) from marginal cases" because, he says, these arguments involve making an appeal to "nonparadigmatic"—that is, "marginal"—"human beings." I follow Narveson's usage and, in fact, refer to all "nonparadigmatic humans" as "marginal humans." By this I do not mean to suggest, any more than Narveson, that, say, mentally enfeebled humans are not human beings. They are. All that I mean to convey, and all I think Narveson intends, is that these humans are nonparadigmatic in the sense that they do not possess those attributes (e.g., rationality) that are paradigmatic of being human.

   The argument that occupies my attention, therefore, might be christened "the weaker version of the argument from marginal cases." Since this is rather a mouthful, I normally refer to the argument simply as "the argument from marginal cases." My present interest in this form of argument is threefold. First, I want to go further than others have in clarifying just what it is that proponents of it are arguing; second, I want briefly to investigate the possibility that this form of argument is self-defeating; and third, I endeavor to defend the soundness of this argument while at the same time criticizing various formulations it has received in the hands of others who have used it.

I

Before proceeding, two preliminary points need our attention. The first concerns the conception of rights involved in the argument from marginal cases; the second deals with why I limit my attention to the weaker version of this argument. There are thorny issues lying along the path of my explanation of both points.

First, then, as to the matter of rights, we must ask whether moral rights or legal rights are at issue. As we shall see shortly, different advocates of the argument from marginal cases have used this argument for different purposes, some relying on it as a basis for extending legal rights to animals, others dealing with moral rights only. For the purposes of this essay I restrict my attention exclusively to moral rights, leaving the controversies surrounding legal rights for some possible future occasion. Still, moral rights themselves can be understood in importantly different ways, so it is not enough simply to say that it is moral rights that concern us. How these rights are understood must be explained.

The principal distinction that needs to be made is between basic moral rights and nonbasic moral rights. A basic moral right is itself the ground of a moral obligation; it is not a consequence of our having a moral obligation. For example, if A has a basic moral right to life, then A's having this right is itself the ground of our obligation not to take A's life. More generally, if there are basic rights, we cannot establish, independently of these rights, the full range of our obligations; on the contrary, there is at least a subset of obligations we have to certain beings grounded in their possession of basic moral rights. The existence of basic moral rights thus appears to be inconsistent with any type of consequentialist theory—for example, utilitarianism. For if there are basic moral rights, there will be moral obligations that are grounded in these rights themselves, independently of considerations about how good or bad are the consequences of actions or rules that respect these rights. On what, then, if not the consequences, must the existence of basic moral rights be based? Only, it appears, on some fact about those beings having basic moral rights. Those beings, if any, having basic moral rights must have them, it would appear, just because of the sort of being they are. It is in this sense, and for this reason, that basic moral rights might be termed natural rights.

Nonbasic moral rights differ in conception from those that are basic. If *A*'s right to life is a nonbasic right, then *A*'s having this right is not itself the ground of any obligation we have to *A*; rather *A* will have a right to life only if we have (and then as a consequence of our having) an obligation to *A* not to take *A*'s life. Given that moral rights are nonbasic, in other words, we must first establish to what beings we have moral obligations. In this way, nonbasic moral rights can be correlated with, without themselves being the grounds of, moral obligations. It is therefore consistent for any consequentialist to deny that there are basic moral rights, on the one hand, and, on the other, to maintain that there are nonbasic moral rights; this he can do because nonbasic rights can be grounded in obligations that are themselves based exclusively on the net value of consequences. What no consequentialist can consistently maintain is that some beings have basic moral rights, in the sense explained, just because of the sort of being they are.

Which type of moral right, basic or nonbasic, is meant, when, in the argument from marginal cases, it is argued that animals have rights if marginal humans do? A survey of the literature points decisively to the idea of basic moral rights. Nowhere do we find an advocate of the argument from marginal cases arguing that marginal (or other) humans have certain rights on consequentialist grounds.[3] What we do find, instead, is that these (and other) humans are alleged to have various rights because they are the sort of being they are—for example, because they are sentient beings. When, therefore, in what follows, I examine and defend the ascription of rights to animals, if marginal humans have rights, it is basic moral rights that I shall have in mind and, unless otherwise indicated, it is in this sense that I shall use the word "rights" throughout.

Having said this much, I can now say why I confine my attention throughout to what I have called the weaker form of the argument from marginal cases. This I do because it is far from certain that *anyone* at all has basic moral rights.[4] The issues involved in the dispute over the existence of basic moral rights are among the most heated in moral and political philosophy. To endeavor to resolve them would take me well beyond the limited scope of this essay. What I *believe* about these issues, however, may be worth noting, since this bears on what I take to be the underlying assumption of those who argue from marginal cases.

If I am right, the heart of the controversy over basic moral rights is as follows. Let us agree that there are certain immoral ways of treating (say) marginal human beings; for example, suppose we agree that it is morally wrong to cause them gratuitous pain or arbitrarily to restrict them in their ability to move about as they will. Then, theoretically, the pressing question is: How can we most adequately account for our beliefs (our "intuitions") that such conduct is morally wrong? The history of theoretical ethics is full of diverse answers to this question, none of which can be explored in detail here. What I assume, however, is that those who argue from marginal cases believe that it is *only* by positing the existence of basic moral rights that we can most adequately account for these intuitions. Given any other theory, these thinkers imply, what we find is that it could sanction treating these human beings in ways that clash with these intuitions. Now, perhaps these thinkers are mistaken in believing this; perhaps, for example, a utilitarian, who must deny that there are basic moral rights, could after all adequately account for these intuitions by means of his theory. I do not know (though I do not believe that he could).[5] However this question is to be resolved, my point now is that those who argue from marginal cases, insofar as their argument does commit them to positing basic moral rights, can and should be understood as believing that it is only by means of a theory of such rights that we can satisfactorily account for some of our intuitions about what is morally wrong. This is what I believe these thinkers commit themselves to, and I have occasion to reaffirm this point as we go along. As to whether there *are* basic moral rights, that, once again, is something I myself stop short of affirming. My interest lies only with the weaker argument from marginal cases, the argument that *if* marginal humans have basic moral rights, *then* so do (some) animals. Which rights these humans or animals have, and what animals have them, are questions we have to postpone addressing until much later (Section VI).

II

So much by way of preamble. Now I commence my examination of the argument from marginal cases. And the first thing it is important to realize is that this argument proceeds on two different fronts. For reasons I explain in what follows I call one "the critical phase" and the other "the constructive phase." The initial characterization of both needs to be made more precise. I take up the critical phase first, which initially I summarize as follows:

The Critical Phase₁

1. Given certain criteria of the possession of rights, some marginal humans and not just all animals will be excluded from the class of right holders.
2. Humans, however, including those who are marginal, do have rights and so belong in the class of right holders.
3. Therefore, each and every one of the criteria of which (1) is true must be rejected as setting a requirement for the possession of rights.

I call the form of argument just characterized "the critical phase of the argument from marginal cases" because (*a*) arguments of this form involve an appeal to the assumption that marginal humans have rights, and because (*b*) tokens of this argument form are used to criticize the adequacy of various criteria nominated as requirements for the possession of rights. Tokens of the critical phase do not dispute whether any given criterion is a sufficient condition of right possession. For since no criterion that is merely sufficient can serve as a basis for *excluding* beings from the class of right holders; and since the critical phase quite definitely aims at disputing the adequacy of those criteria that, it is argued, *do* exclude marginal humans; it is evident that advocates of this phase of the argument are not questioning whether the contested criteria set forth sufficient conditions; rather, it is their claim as *necessary* conditions that is being denied. Arguments of the form just outlined, in a word, are advanced, not with the intention of establishing what the necessary and sufficient conditions of right possession *are*; they are advanced with the intention of demonstrating what the necessary conditions of right possession are *not*.

Tokens of the critical phase have been advanced against proposed criteria both of the possession of legal and of basic moral rights, and they have been advanced in enthymematic and in more highly developed forms. Here are two examples, the first from Andrew Linzey's *Animal Rights*,[6] where the adequacy of rationality as a necessary condition of the possession of basic moral rights is contested enthymematically; the second is from an essay by Joel Feinberg,[7] where other criteria of the possible possession of legal rights are contested at greater length.

> If we accord moral rights on the basis of rationality, what of the status of newly born children, "low grade" mental patients, "intellectual cabbages," and so on? Logically, accepting this criterion, they must have no, or diminished, moral rights.

* * *

> No one can deny [that animals are incapable of *claiming* rights or of understanding when their rights are being violated]; but to the claim that [these facts] are the grounds for animal disqualification for rights of animals, philosophers on the other side of this controversy have made convincing rejoinders. It is simply not true, says W. D. Lamont, that the ability to understand what a right is and the ability to set legal machinery in motion by one's own initiative are necessary for the possession of rights. If that were the case, then neither human idiots nor wee babies would have any legal rights at all. Yet it is manifest that both of these classes of intellectual incompetents have legal rights recognized and easily enforced by the courts. . . . If there is no conceptual absurdity in this situation, why should there be in the case of . . . animal[s]?

Despite the possible relevance of the argument from marginal cases to the question of the possession of legal rights, as I remarked earlier, I limit my attention to its relevance to the question of the possession of basic moral rights. For this reason, it is the quote from Linzey which deserves a brief exegesis. If rationality were necessary for right possession, he is claiming, then children and certain mental patients would have "no, or diminished, moral rights." Suppose this follows. Why should it constitute a telling objection against counting rationality as a criterion of the possession of rights? It can only if we make the further *assumption* that these marginal human beings, like those who are not marginal, have certain moral rights—if, in other words, we accept premise (2) of the critical phase. And it is clear, given his final position, about which more later, that Linzey, for one, does accept this. So, although Linzey is less explicit than is Feinberg in asserting that the humans in question do have rights, it is reasonably clear that both thinkers believe that they do and that each makes use of the critical phase of the argument from marginal cases for his particular ends.

And so have others.[8] Armed with it they have done battle with other proposed criteria of the possession of rights—for example, autonomy; the ability to use a language; the capacity to have a conception of one's self. And, like Linzey vis-á-vis rationality, they have argued that since these criteria exclude babies and the severely mentally enfeebled from the class of right holders, or at most grant them "diminished" rights, these criteria must be rejected as defective. Animals, therefore, they have concluded, cannot be excluded from the class of right holders by appealing to any one or any number of the discredited criteria, a position that, assuming it is correct, does not establish that animals do have rights but only that certain attempts fail to show that they do not.

Recently R. G. Frey has disputed[9] the critical phase by contending, in effect, that this part of the argument from marginal cases is self-defeating. Interpreting advocates of the critical phase as holding that (1') "Each and every criterion for the possession of rights that excludes animals from the class of right holders also excludes babies and the severely mentally enfeebled from the class of right holders," Frey urges that "the best defenses" of premise (2) of the critical phase, a premise that, in his words, "is not obvious and requires defense," have the unhappy consequence of specifically *excluding* animals from the class of right holders. Thus, Frey maintains, *either* premise (2) cannot be defended, which it must be if the critical phase is to claim our rational assent, *or* premise (1') is false, a development that would, he thinks, undercut the very basis of this phase of the argument. Whichever alternative is chosen, Frey concludes, "this important argument for animal rights fails."

A more detailed examination of Frey's position is available elsewhere.[10] Here it is sufficient to remark that, as stated, his position rests on a misinterpretation of the critical phase of the argument from marginal cases. Advocates of this phase of the argument do not maintain, nor are they committed to maintaining, the view Frey attributes to them— namely, (1') "*Each and every* criterion for the possession of rights that excludes animals from the class of right holders also excludes babies and the severely mentally enfeebled from the class of right holders." Someone could maintain, after all, that mere membership in the class, human being, is both a logically necessary and sufficient condition for membership in the class of right holders. And this, though rationally a dubious requirement, is enough to show the falsity of Frey's (1'), since here we have a criterion that excludes all animals but no humans. That (1') *is* false, however, provides no grounds for disputing the critical phase, least of all for imputing that this phase of the argument is self-defeating. For since advocates of this phase of the argument neither affirm nor are committed to (1'), its falsity cannot be a possible ground for criticism.

III

Frey's alleged dilemma defused, there is another, possibly fatal, and previously undetected one that seems to lie ahead for users of the argument from marginal cases. It is not to be located, as Frey tries but fails to show, in the critical phase alone; rather, its outlines emerge once this phase is conjoined with the constructive phase. This will become clearer after we have stated and examined this latter phase, whose initial characterization reads as follows:

Constructive Phase₁

4. Humans, including those who are marginal, have rights and therefore belong in the class of right holders.

5. Given the most reasonable criterion of the possession of rights, however, one that enables us to include marginal humans in the class of right holders, this same criterion will require us to include some (but not all) animals in this class.

6. Therefore, if we include these marginal humans in the class of right holders, we must also include some animals in this class.

I refer to this form of argument as "the constructive phase of the argument from marginal cases" because (*a*) like the critical phase, this argument form involves making an appeal to the assumption that marginal humans possess rights, and because (*b*) unlike the critical phase, this form of argument is not used as a basis for criticizing proposed criteria of the possession of rights; rather, its purpose has the constructive point of bringing out an alleged positive implication of the criterion judged to be "the most reasonable" one—namely, that it requires that we ascribe rights to some animals.

Like the critical phase, tokens of the constructive phase also are to be met with in the literature on animal rights. Before examining representative examples, something further should be said about this phase of the argument, both about the methodology employed and about the status of the criterion of right possession referred to in premise (5). As for the matter of methodology, it is important to observe, first, that the constructive phase, like the critical, assumes, and does not itself endeavor to establish, that humans, including those who are marginal, have rights. What is being assumed here, if my earlier speculation is correct, is that there are certain immoral ways of treating these humans which cannot be theoretically accounted for without assuming that they have basic moral rights that this treatment violates. Now, to assume this is to assume a good deal, since, as noted earlier, it is at least controversial to maintain that this is true in the case of paradigmatic humans, let alone that it is true in the case of those who are nonparadigmatic. But to point out that the argument from marginal cases involves an assumption that, in Frey's words, "is not obvious and requires defense," is not to offer a refutation of this form of argument. Rather, it points to its incompleteness as an argument for the thesis that animals *do* have rights. Clearly, to establish that they do, both phases of the argument would need to be supplemented by arguments that support the assumption in question. As I indicated in the above, to pursue these supplementary arguments goes well beyond the modest scope of this essay.[11] My interest is confined to the weaker version of the argument from marginal cases.

A second point about methodology is this. If we assume that humans, including those who are marginal, have rights, we can then go on to ask about the implications this assumption has for the inquiry into the necessary and sufficient conditions of right possession; we can go on to ask, in other words, what are the relevant characteristics that these humans possess in virtue of which we can reach an enlightened position about the criteria of right possession. The methodology here, in a word, is "transcendental": Given that humans, including those who are marginal, have rights, how is this to be accounted for? What is there, in other words, that is true of those beings assumed to have rights which can most reasonably be construed as the grounds of their possessing them? What advocates of the constructive phase aver is that, given the most reasonable answer to this question—given, that is, that answer that more adequately than others illuminates the relevant conditions humans satisfy in virtue of which we can account for their possessing rights, assuming that they do possess them—given this, what we will find is that some nonhuman animals also will qualify as right possessors. Of course, what this condition is, or what these conditions are, is at this stage an open question, one about which advocates of the constructive phase not only may but actually sometimes do disagree. For example, some say the condition is the capacity for sentience; others that it is the capacity to have interests. More on this matter appears below. For the present it is sufficient to note that, though disagreement can and sometimes does exist over how this question should be answered, those who argue from marginal cases appear to be of one mind regarding the methodological point sketched here.

One thing that may not be as apparent is how we should understand the logical status of the criterion of right possession recommended as "the most reasonable" in the constructive phase. Is this criterion supposed to incorporate the most reasonable necessary, sufficient, or necessary *and* sufficient condition of the possession of rights? That it is supposed to incorporate the most reasonable sufficient condition, given the assumption that humans, including those who are marginal, have rights, is clear enough, since the criterion in question is said (in step 6) to require that we *include* some animals in the class of right holders. What perhaps is less clear immediately is whether this same criterion is thought to incorporate a necessary condition. An examination of the relevant literature, however, indicates that this is thought to be so. For those who deploy the constructive phase use the criterion they judge to be "the most reasonable" not only as a basis for including some animals in the class of right holders; they also use this *same* criterion as a basis for *excluding* other animals as well as other sorts of entities (e.g., plants) from this class, a procedure that would be logically askew if the criterion were thought to incorporate only a sufficient condition.

In general, then, the criterion of right possession urged as "the most reasonable" in the constructive phase is to be understood as embodying the most reasonable necessary and sufficient condition(s) of right possession. Thus, what is being argued in this phase of the argument is that, assuming that we must postulate that humans, including those who are marginal, have basic moral rights in order theoretically to account for why it is wrong to treat them in certain ways; and given that, if we make this assumption, we need to give an account of what it is about these beings that underlies their possessing those rights they are assumed to possess; then the account that turns out to be the most reasonable one will yield the conclusion that some animals have basic moral rights also.

Now, tokens of the constructive phase also occur frequently in the literature, though normally in a less explicit form than one that characterizes some instances of the critical phase. The following passage, from Linzey again, in which he commends sentience to our attention as the most reasonable criterion of the possession of rights, may be taken as illustrative.[12]

> We have a choice here. Either we continue to . . . understand moral rights exclusively as the property of human beings, or we widen our perspective to include the rights of non-humans which possess the capacity for . . . sentiency. Either we say that only the species of *homo sapiens* possess moral rights (accepting the difficulties with our criterion with regard to children and mental patients) or we acknowledge a situation where we are bound by difficulties in our criteria to revise our basis of judgment in this matter.

The "difficulties in our criteria" Linzey refers to are the familiar ones. If the criteria of right possession were, say, rationality or the ability to have a concept of one's self, then there will be "difficulties" with respect to children and the severely mentally enfeebled—namely, they will, Linzey thinks, "have no, or diminished, moral rights." Linzey's position is that these "difficulties" are sufficiently severe to prompt us "to revise our basis of judgment"—that is, to revise our criteria. What we must do is accept a criterion that avoids these difficulties, and this criterion, he thinks, is sentience. Not that this criterion will itself be "without difficulties"; it will not. Rather, Linzey's position is that, among the possible candidates for criteria of the possession of rights, this one more than others "more adequately" accounts for the assumption about which humans possess rights. For this reason, then, it is reasonable to interpret Linzey as believing that the capacity for sentience is the most reasonable criterion of the possession of rights, given that humans, including those who are marginal, do possess them. And it is equally reasonable to interpret him as seeing in this most reasonable criterion the means for "widen[ing] our perspective to include the rights of [some] non-humans"—namely, those animals who are sentient—while, at the same time, *not* "widen[ing] our perspective" so much that we include the rights of, say, ice crystals and clouds. Though, in the passage just quoted, Linzey himself does not argue explicitly in the form I have characterized as the constructive phase, there appear to be sufficient grounds for interpreting his argument in this way.

Nor is Linzey alone in this. For if one looks closely at those who have gone beyond deploying the critical phase and have themselves advanced some criterion of the possession of rights, what one finds is that the criterion proposed is one that babies and the severely mentally enfeebled manage to meet. Thus, for example, Peter Singer, like Linzey, submits[13] that it is "the capacity for [sentience] . . . that gives a being a right to equal consideration," while Joel Feinberg locates this in the capacity to have interests, in the sense of having the capacity to have desires, wants, goals, preferences, and the like.[14] But if we ask what it is that recommends these criteria to these thinkers, what we find is that it is because the criteria are, so to speak, "low enough" to permit the marginal humans in question to meet them. It is the assumption that marginal humans have rights, in other words, that underlies the case for the presumed reasonableness of the criteria they recommend, when compared to, say, rationality or autonomy. And it is because many (but not all) animals, not just humans, meet these criteria, that these same thinkers have, in Linzey's words, "widen[ed] our perspective to include the rights of [these] non-humans."

Now, like Linzey, Singer, for example, recognizes that the criterion he recommends (sentience) is not free of "difficulties." But the "difficulties" he and Linzey seem to have in mind stem from the uncertainty that exists concerning how much of nonhuman nature is sentient. Are clams? Oysters? Paramecia? Plants? These are the sorts of "difficulties" both recognize; and there is no denying their importance, given the view that the possession of sentience guarantees certain rights for those beings who have this capacity. Significantly, however, both Linzey and Singer fail explicitly to deal with a "difficulty" that stems from a different quarter, one that, if it cannot be met, renders the entire thrust of their argument rationally impotent. The "difficulty" I have in mind concerns the status, not of certain *non*humans, but of certain *human* beings— namely, the irreversibly comatose.[15] The "difficulty" these humans pose for the argument from marginal cases is that they may seem to render this form of argument self-defeating.

To make this clearer, consider the criterion of sentience. This criterion runs into trouble, given the initial characterization of the critical phase, for the simple reason that there are some marginal humans (namely, those who are irreversibly comatose) who are altogether lacking in this capacity and yet who, given that they are marginal humans and given premise (2) of this characterization, do have rights. Thus, since these humans lack this capacity but, given this characterization, do have rights, it follows, if we accept the soundness of the initial statement of the critical phase, that sentience must be rejected as incorporating a necessary condition of the possession of rights. Now, suppose this is true given *any* criterion proposed as "the most reasonable" in the constructive phase: Given each criterion nominated for this position, suppose it is found that there are some marginal humans (the irreversibly comatose) who fail to meet it and who, therefore, given that the criterion is presumed to set forth not only a sufficient but also a necessary condition of the possession of rights, will be excluded from the class of right holders. Then each criterion will be disqualified, if we assume the soundness of the critical phase, as initially characterized. Now, if this is true, not only of some, but of each and every criterion of right possession proposed as "the most reasonable," then, given the soundness of the initial characterization of the critical phase, *there can be no* "most reasonable criterion" that explains how it is that all marginal human beings possess rights, and the possible success of the argument's constructive phase would seem necessarily to be canceled. If, however, there *is* a "most reasonable criterion" of right possession, but one that, though it allows for some marginal humans to possess rights also *excludes* others from the class of right holders, then it would seem that this "success" of the constructive phase necessarily cancels the unqualified soundness of the critical phase, as initially characterized. In a word, the success of either phase seems to guarantee the failure of the other. It is in this sense, and for these reasons, that a question can and should arise as to whether this argument concerning animal rights is self-defeating.

One possible but foolish reply[16] that comes immediately to mind consists in urging that irreversibly comatose human beings are *not* human beings; thus, in arguing from what is true, or from what is assumed true, of marginal human beings, one is not committed to including these human beings. I say this is a possible but foolish reply because it involves a plain falsehood. Beings can be irreversibly comatose *and* be human beings. If Jones wants to test a drug on a human being and injects it into Smith, who lies abed, irreversibly comatose, Jones *does* inject it into a human being albeit one who is unable to communicate the drug's effects. A colleague with goals similar to Jones might criticize him for administering the drug to an incommunicative subject, but he can hardly criticize him on the grounds that he did not administer it to a human being. The lesson to be learned from this is that any viable reply to the charge that the argument from marginal cases is self-defeating must work with the knowledge that irreversibly comatose human beings *are* human beings.

A second and, to my mind, the correct response to the charge at issue consists in conceding what the first denies—namely, that irreversibly comatose human beings are human beings—and then maintaining that, though they are humans, the irreversibly comatose are not to be included in the class of humans which, in the argument from marginal cases, are assumed to have rights. This reply, in other words, consists in urging that *some, not all* marginal humans are assumed to have rights. In particular, babies and the mentally enfeebled are assumed to have rights, but not the irreversibly comatose. As such, this response continues, it cannot be argued that, since some marginal humans (the irreversibly comatose) fail to meet some favored criterion (say, sentience), it follows, assuming that the argument's critical phase, when properly understood, is sound, that this criterion must be rejected. For since these marginal humans are not assumed to have rights in the critical phase, when properly understood, it can be no objection against a criterion proposed in the constructive phase that it fails to illuminate how it is that they do possess them. In this way, then, the argument from marginal cases can be defended against the charge that it is self-defeating.

Perhaps it will be objected that this defense is question-begging. If some but not all marginal humans are assumed to have rights, it is natural to ask *why* these assumptions are made. Suppose one replies that those who are assumed to have rights are assumed to have them *because* they are, say, sentient, whereas those who are not assumed to have rights are not assumed to have them *because* they are not sentient. Then one *is* assuming that the presence or absence of this particular capacity already has been established to be a decisive consideration concerning right possession, and one does beg the question.

It is not necessary to beg this question, however. True, it happens to be the case that the irreversibly comatose are not sentient. But it does not follow from this that these humans are not assumed to have rights *because* they lack this particular capacity, or some other particular capacity that figures in some tokens of the argument from marginal cases—for example, the capacity to have interests. Rather, these marginal humans are not assumed to have rights because they evidently lack *each and every* capacity that, at this juncture, might plausibly be thought to have a bearing on the question of why human beings have certain rights, if they do. The permanently comatose lack not only the capacities for sentience and for having interests, but also, for example, the capacities to reason, to form a concept of themselves and to make claims or free choices. In making the assumption that, say, the severely mentally enfeebled have rights, those who argue from marginal cases do assume something that is controversial, something, for example, which those who regard the capacity for rationality as a necessary condition of right possession cannot believe. But in not including the irreversibly comatose in the class of humans assumed to have rights, those who argue from marginal cases make an assumption that is common ground between them and those of their philosophical opponents who posit basic moral rights. Nor, again, is there any reason to look with suspicion upon this. Just because the proponents of the argument from marginal cases go further than some others when they assume that *some* marginal humans (e.g., the mentally enfeebled) have rights, it does not follow that they must assume that *all* marginal humans have them.

Moreover, it is pertinent to note that those who argue from marginal cases assume, or can be interpreted as assuming, only that the irreversibly comatose are not to be included in the class of human beings assumed to have rights, an assumption that is logically distinct from assuming that they *do not* have them. Whether they have them or not is an open question, so far as the assumptions that are made in both the critical and constructive phases of the argument are concerned. This is a question that, as in the case of the comparable question about animals possessing rights, can be answered only after we have uncovered the most reasonable criterion of the possession of rights and *then* asked whether the irreversibly comatose can meet it. Below I argue that the most reasonable criterion of right possession leaves this open question open. For the present it is enough to repeat that, by not assuming that irreversibly comatose human beings have rights, those who argue from marginal cases do not beg the question.

The "self-defeating" charge, then, can be met, and this with a gain in understanding. Earlier, when the critical and constructive phases of the argument from marginal cases were characterized, the expression "marginal humans" was used without qualification, a use that allowed that irreversibly comatose human beings might be included in the class of humans assumed to have rights. Now we see that, if the argument is to avoid defeating, or appearing to defeat, itself, these humans cannot be included in this class. And we also see that it is possible to exclude them without making the argument vulnerable to the charge that it begs the question. All this gives rise to more precise characterizations of both phases of the argument, which follow.

The Critical Phase₂

1. Given certain criteria of the possession of rights, some marginal humans who are not irreversibly comatose and not just all[17] animals will be excluded from the class of right holders.

2. Humans, however, including all those who, though marginal, are not irreversibly comatose, do have rights, and so belong in the class of right holders.

3. Therefore, each and every one of the criteria satisfying (1) must be rejected as setting a requirement for the possession of rights.

The Constructive Phase₂

4. Humans, including all those who, though they are marginal, are not irreversibly comatose, have rights and therefore belong in the class of right holders.

5. Given the most reasonable criterion of the possession of rights, however, one that permits us to include all noncomatose marginal humans in the class of right holders, this same criterion will require us to include some, and exclude some other, animals.

6. Therefore, if we include these marginal humans in the class of right holders, we must also include some animals in this class.

IV

Now, all that the argument to this point establishes, if it is sound, is that the argument from marginal cases *itself* does not rule out the possibility of there being a most reasonable criterion of right possession. What it clearly does not establish is what this criterion is, assuming that there is one. Two candidates already mentioned are (*a*) sentience and (*b*) having interests (i.e., having desires, needs, etc.). Now, if it should happen to be the case that either of these criteria proves to be "the most reasonable," the case for extending basic moral rights to animals would be very strong indeed, since in the case of many animals we have very good reason to believe that they are sentient and have interests. But correct as the conclusion that animals have basic moral rights may be, it is not clear that either sentience or interests is the most reasonable criterion of right possession. Partly this is because acceptance of either of these criteria commits us to accepting a still more basic requirement of right possession—namely, that it is only conscious beings, including (perhaps) those that are potentially conscious (e.g., human fetuses), which can have rights (henceforth referred to as "the consciousness criterion"). The consciousness criterion must be accepted by those who favor either sentience or interests because both these latter criteria can only be met by beings that are conscious. *Non*conscious beings (e.g., rocks and trees) fail to qualify as possible possessors of rights, given the sentience or interests criterion, because, *qua* nonconscious beings, they cannot have interests or be sentient. Thus, whether we ought to accept either one or both of these criteria as "most reasonable" involves our asking whether we ought first to accept the consciousness criterion.

Acceptance of the consciousness criterion would, like acceptance of the sentience or interests criterion, have the desired consequences sought by animal rightists: basic moral rights could be extended to many animals, *if* they are attributed to all humans save those who are irreversibly comatose. For we have *very* good reason to regard many animals as conscious. Moreover, that irreversibly comatose humans must be excluded from the class of marginal humans assumed to have rights in the argument from marginal cases, if this argument is to avoid being (or appearing) self-defeating, would seem further to strengthen the case for accepting the consciousness criterion. Nevertheless, I remain unconvinced that consciousness has been shown to be a *necessary* condition of right possession. For reasons I have tried to make clear in other places,[18] the arguments given in support of limiting the class of right holders to the class of conscious beings (even including those that are potentially conscious), *when* arguments are given,[19] seem to me to be defective. I shall discuss this matter very briefly in a moment. The object of primary interest now is not whether my arguments presented elsewhere against the consciousness criterion are sound but whether a more reasonable criterion than either sentience or interests can be articulated, given the assumptions of the argument from marginal cases. I believe one can be.

The criterion of right possession I wish to recommend involves the notion of inherent value. Put most simply the criterion states that a necessary and sufficient condition of having basic moral rights is that one have inherent value (henceforth referred to as "the criterion of inherent value"). Much depends on what is meant by "inherent value." This is an idea that I have addressed on a previous occasion.[20] Here I merely list what I take to be its most noteworthy features. These are (1) that if any given being (x) has inherent value, then x's having value of this kind is logically independent of any other being's happening to take an interest in or otherwise valuing x; (2) that x's having inherent value makes it improper (a sign of disrespect) to treat x as though it had value only as a means (i.e., only if and only so long as it answers another's needs, etc.); and (3) that because x's having inherent value underlies the obligation to treat x with respect, and since something's being good-of-its-kind is not a plausible basis on which to found this obligation, x's being good-of-its-kind is logically distinct from x's having inherent value.[21]

Now, one question that immediately comes to mind, assuming that the concept of inherent value is sufficiently clear, is, What beings have inherent value? A favored answer is that only conscious beings, including (perhaps) those that are potentially conscious (e.g., human fetuses or future generations of human beings), have or can have inherent value. I do not believe that those who favor this answer have succeeded in giving it an adequate defense.[22] It at least appears conceivable that beings lacking even the potential for consciousness (e.g., individual trees or the constituents of inanimate wilderness generally) *might* have inherent value, in the sense explained in the previous paragraph; indeed, it would seem to be the case that it is only if they have value of this kind that we can develop a genuine ethic *of* the environment, as distinct from an ethic *for its use.* In any event, recommending, as I do, that we think of rights as being ultimately grounded in respect for what has inherent value does not by itself commit us to any particular view concerning what beings can and do have rights, and this because it does not commit us to any particular view concerning what beings can and do have inherent value.

Now, some of the beings frequently thought to have inherent value, in the sense explained, are human beings; it is this belief, though it may not be put in just these words, which, for example, underlies the widespread conviction that it is morally wrong to treat human beings in certain ways (e.g., as slaves), since to treat them in such ways is to fail to show respect for their having value in their own right, not merely if or as they are useful as means to certain ends. Thus, in suggesting, as I shall, that thinking of humans as having inherent value contributes to our search for the most reasonable criterion of right possession, I shall not be suggesting something that is totally without philosophical roots.

There are problems, however. For the question remains, Are all human beings inherently valuable, or only some? And, in either case, on what basis ought we to judge their having or failing to have inherent value? A variety of answers is possible. The Kantian answer, for example, appears to be [23] that only some, not all, humans have inherent value, these being those humans who happen to be free and rational. Severely mentally enfeebled human beings, lacking autonomy and rationality, would thus fail to qualify as having inherent value and, if rights are based on having value of this kind, would likewise fail to qualify as even possible possessors of rights. But the Kantian answer, if I am right, must strike us as having morally unacceptable implications. It would have us believe that we do not mistreat, do not show a lack of respect for, the mentally enfeebled if we treat them merely as means to our ends, whatever they may be. Given the Kantian answer, the use of the enfeebled in painful, trivial scientific research, for example, cannot be objected to on the grounds that we are mistreating the enfeebled, or that we are failing to show proper respect for them. At the very most[24] it might be objected that, by engaging in such treatment of the enfeebled, we become more prone to treat those human beings who are inherently valuable, ourselves or others, in analogous ways. But, first, no one has, to my knowledge in any event, succeeded in showing that there is such a strong psychological link between treating the enfeebled and the nonenfeebled in such ways, and, second, even if such a connection were established the question would still remain, Are we not failing to show respect for the enfeebled if we regard them as having value only if or as they happen to be useful to our ends? I do not know how this can be proven conclusively,[25] and I shall not pursue the matter further on this occasion, but I submit that there are certain ways of treating even the severely mentally enfeebled which would fail to show a proper respect for them, and this quite independently of how those who mistreat them are disposed to treat those humans, if any, who are both rational and free.

Suppose I am right: Even the severely mentally enfeebled have inherent value. The question remains, How shall we account for this? This is a question that is not answered merely by rejecting the Kantian position. Neither is it answered just by insisting that even the mentally enfeebled are sentient or have interests (i.e., desires, needs, etc.). For it is unclear how, by itself, the fact that an individual (A) is sentient or has interests illuminates A's inherent value, assuming A has value of this sort. That sentience, for example, is a capacity that gives to its possessor the potential to have certain valuable experiences (namely, pleasant ones) certainly seems true enough; but this shows only that sentience is necessary for having a certain kind of valuable experience, not that sentience itself is inherently valuable or that those beings having this capacity are. And the same is true, for analogous reasons, in the case of having interests. Moreover—and this appears to be decisive—neither of these capacities by itself illuminates why it would be wrong, assuming that it would be wrong, to treat those beings having these capacities merely as a means; yet this is precisely what must be illuminated, if the humans in question have inherent value. So these two leading contenders for the most reasonable criterion of right possession (sentience and interests) fail, it appears, to illuminate why marginal or other humans have inherent value, assuming that they do; and thus they fail also, if I am right, to give us the most reasonable basis on which to found basic moral rights, assuming that the humans in question have them.

Rather than seek an answer to the question at hand by examining the credentials of various particular capacities (e.g., sentience), however, one might ask whether there is anything about the value of the lives of all but the irreversibly comatose which helps illuminate why all but these humans have inherent value, assuming that they do. Now, just such an answer seems possible. For the noteworthy thing about the lives of the humans in question is that certain forms of life are better or worse *for them*; that is, even in the case of the severely mentally enfeebled, there are alternative forms of life concerning which it is intelligible to say that *they* (i.e., the humans in question themselves) are better off or worse off having one form of life rather than another. In a word, *all* of the humans in question, including (even) the severely mentally enfeebled, not only are alive but are *subjects* of a life that itself has value (is better or worse) for the individual whose life it is. Each is, as it were, the center of his/her own universe of value, living through slices of experience that bode well or ill for the subject himself or herself. The suggestion before us, then, is that all but the irreversibly comatose have inherent value because all these humans have a life that is of more or less positive or negative value for them, and this logically independently of whether they (the humans in question) are valued by anyone else. Here, therefore, we have a way of illuminating, what neither being sentient nor having interests are able to do, why it would be wrong to treat these humans merely as a means. This would be wrong because it would fail to acknowledge and respect that they are the subjects of a life whose value is logically independent of any other beings taking an interest in it. Thus, in treating these humans merely as means one treats them as if their value was logically dependent on their answering to the needs, purposes, and the like, of others, when in fact, they, as the subjects of a more or less good life, have value that is logically independent of their being valued as a means by anyone else.

I might summarize the argument of this section, up to now, as follows. The most reasonable criterion of right possession, given the assumptions of the argument from marginal cases, is not that of sentience or having interests, since neither of these by themselves can account for why it is wrong to treat humans who are not irreversibly comatose merely as means; rather, the criterion that most adequately accounts for this is the criterion of inherent value: all those beings (and only those beings) which have inherent value have rights. *Possibly* there are nonconscious beings that qualify as right possessors; that remains an open question. What is more certain is that all those humans who are not irreversibly comatose qualify since, in their case, it is wrong (a sign of disrespect) to treat them merely as a means. Moreover, if we press on and ask what there is about these human beings which illuminates the inherent value they are assumed to have, the capacities of sentience or having interests again leave matters opaque; instead, the needed illumination appears to be provided best by noting that all but the irreversibly comatose are the subjects of lives that are better or worse for the humans themselves, logically independently of any other being's taking an interest in them or finding them useful as a means to this or that end; thus we account best for the inherent value of the humans in question, it appears, by making reference to the value of their life that is logically independent of their being useful as means. In the section that follows I develop the implications of this argument for the question of animal rights. For the present there are two final points that deserve our attention.

The first is that, in maintaining, as I do, that all those humans who are not irreversibly comatose have inherent value, it does not follow that all have equal inherent value. That, too, remains an open question, one that is not answered just by insisting that all have value of this kind. But given the basis recommended here for grounding inherent value in the case of human beings—namely, in their being the subjects *of* a life that is better or worse for them, logically independently of the interests of others—a means is provided for making sense of the idea that not all human beings are equal in inherent value. This might be made clearer by drawing a distinction between (*i*) those beings that can *lead* a life that is better or worse for them and (*ii*) those beings that can *have but not lead* such a life. To speak of a being (*A*) as "leading" such a life is to convey at least that *A* exercises some control over the conduct of his life, that *A* directs it by, say, setting certain goals and then selecting between alternative means of achieving them. Normal, adult human beings are paradigms of such beings. These are the humans who, if any do, embody the capacities of autonomy and rationality, the importance and value of which are justly so celebrated by Kant. For these are the human beings who, if any can be, are capable of moral agency and thus can lead a life that is better or worse for them relative to the comparative presence or absence of the moral virtues. And these are the human beings, too, who, if any can, can lead a life that is better or worse for them in terms of the comparative presence or absence of the intellectual virtues.

Not all human beings *can* lead such a life. Certainly the severely mentally enfeebled cannot, and this because they lack the intellectual prerequisites that would enable them to exercise willful control over the course of their lives. For them there is no possibility of moral agency or intellectual and artistic development; for them, therefore, there is no possible life whose value is enhanced by the presence of the moral and intellectual virtues. These are humans who cannot so much lead a life as have one. It is not implausible to suppose that normal, adult humans, because they can lead a life that can have a range of values (e.g., moral virtues) not obtainable by the severely mentally enfeebled, can be regarded as themselves having greater inherent value than the enfeebled. Thus, if, in bizarre life-and-death circumstances (e.g., familiar philosophical examples about survivors on a lifeboat), it came down to choosing between saving the life of a normal adult or that of a severely mentally enfeebled child, it perhaps would not be unreasonable, other things being equal, to choose to save the former on the grounds that he/she was of greater inherent value than the unfortunate child. How such cases ought to be resolved, however, is not something that needs to be resolved here, though it bears remarking that the view that not all humans are equal in inherent value does not entail that those with greater inherent value can treat those with less in any way they please (e.g., as slaves). This does not follow because, so long as a human being has some inherent value, in the view proposed here, it would be wrong (a sign of disrespect) to treat the human in question as if he/she had value only as a means (e.g., only as a means to the ends of those humans of greater inherent value). In a word, some humans having greater inherent value than others does not sanction the exploitation of the lesser by the greater. These difficult matters set to one side, the particular point that needs emphasis here is that mentally enfeebled human beings, though they lack the intellectual wherewithal to lead a certain kind of valuable life, nonetheless can, relative to the satisfaction of their desires, needs, and the amount of suffering they experience, *have* a life that is better or worse for them, logically independently of whether anyone else takes an interest in them. True, it will fall to others to ensure as best they can that the needs of the enfeebled will be met; and, true, their having a better rather than a worse life is *causally* dependent on the interested care extended to them by others; nevertheless, so long as we have grounds for believing that they have needs *and* that it is not a matter of complete indifference to them whether they are filled or not, we have sufficient grounds for thinking that some forms of life are better or worse for them, in the sense explained.

Lamentably, the same is not true in the case of those humans who are irreversibly comatose. In their case there is no better or worse life *for them*; there is only the being alive. Thus, in their case we cannot argue that they have basic moral rights because they can have or lead a life that is valuable for them, logically independently of the interests of others. Whether it follows from this that they cannot have rights, period, is a question I explore briefly in the following section.

The final point of this section concerns the greater explanatory power of the criterion of inherent value when compared to the sentience and interests criteria, given the assumptions of the argument from marginal cases. The criterion of inherent value, if I am right, has greater explanatory power because it enables us to illuminate the prima facie relevance of these other criteria to the question of right possession in a way that neither criterion by itself is able to do. Take the criterion of sentience first. In the preceding it has been argued that this criterion fails to illuminate why beings who are sentient have rights, even assuming that sentient beings have them. If, however, sentience is viewed against the backdrop of the criterion of inherent value, its place in grounding rights can be seen more clearly. If beings having inherent value have rights; and if beings have inherent value if they can have or lead a life that is better or worse for them, logically independently of whether they are valued by any other being (and here again I leave it an open question whether it is *only* such [conscious] beings that can be inherently valuable); then sentience is relevant because sentience is a logically necessary condition of some being's having or leading *one* form of life that is better or worse for them—namely, the form of life where pleasure outweighs pain or pain outweighs pleasure. And a similar account can be given of the relevance of interests: That a being has interests is a necessary condition of its having or leading a certain form of life that is better or worse for it—namely, one where its desires, and the like, are more or less fulfilled. Thus, sentience and interests *are* relevant to the question of right-possession. But their relevance is not transparent and stands in need of elucidation. The criterion of inherent value, if the argument of this essay is sound, provides this needed elucidation, which further enhances its claim to being the most reasonable criterion of right possession, given the assumptions of the argument from marginal cases.

V

The implications of accepting the criterion of inherent value for the question of animal rights are obvious and direct. For if it is true, as I have argued, that this criterion better explicates why those humans who are said to have rights in the argument from marginal cases do have them, if they do, then consistency requires that any other beings meeting this criterion must also be assumed to have rights. Thus, whether consistency requires that we think of any nonhuman animals as right possessors, if we think of marginal humans in this way, comes down to this: Is it true that any nonhuman animals have inherent value? And this question, given the preceding, comes down to this: Is it true that any nonhuman animals can and do have forms of life that are better or worse *for them*, logically independently of their being the object of another's interests or useful as a means to another's ends? I do not know how this might be *proven* true, either in the case of many animals or in the case of humans generally, but it is difficult at best to understand how anyone could reasonably deny that there are many, many species of animals whose members satisfy this requirement. Certainly there is ample reason to believe that there are many animals that can *have* a life that is better or worse for them in terms of the comparative amounts of pleasure and pain they experience, or in terms of the satisfaction or frustration of their interests generally, logically independently of whether anyone else finds them useful, and so on. So, as in the case of those humans who are severely mentally enfeebled, we here have very good reason to believe that these animals can and do *have* a form of life that is better or worse *for them*; thus, in their case it must be just as reasonable as it is in the case of the mentally enfeebled to think that *they* have a type of value that is logically independent of any other being's happening to find them useful; thus, in *their* case, given the case of severely mentally enfeebled, consistency must drive us to the conclusion that it is morally wrong to treat these animals as if they were valuable only if or so long as they happened to fulfill our needs, or satisfy our desires; thus, consistency must drive us to maintain that these *animals*, like the humans in question, have basic moral rights *and* that these rights are violated whenever we treat them as if they had only instrumental value.

Now, whether, in addition to having a kind of life that is better or worse for them, there are animals that can lead a life, in the (rough) sense of "lead a life" explained earlier, is, so far as the present argument is concerned, an open question. Certain primates would seem to suggest by their behavior the presence of the abilities to choose between alternative goals and between alternative means of achieving them. Moreover, the more reason we have to believe that these animals are capable of intellectual feats once thought the private domain of humans, and that they have a highly structured social organization that assigns each individual a certain "station" and requires certain loyalties, the more reason we may have to wonder whether there might be nonhuman animals whose lives can be marked even by intellectual and moral pleasures. Possibly this is to push things too far. I do not know. The issues are complex. Certainly I do not feel competent to make an authoritative judgment. Quite apart from these matters, however, the fact remains that there are many, many species of animals whose members can have a life that is better or worse for them, logically independently of whether anyone else takes an interest in them. And this is sufficient, in view of what has been argued (assuming it is sound), as a basis for attributing basic moral rights to these animals, if marginal humans are assumed to have them.

From the moral point of view, it is worth noting that some of the animals in question *are* frequently treated as if they had value only relative to their usefulness as means to human ends. For example, the way animals are treated as a result of "modern" intensive rearing methods[26] and as subjects in gratuitous "scientific research"[27] testifies to the widespread tendency of man to regard himself as "the measure of all things," including all that is valuable, in the sense that nothing has value unless it is of value to us. It is just this view of the world that this essay aims to challenge. What the argument from marginal cases forces us to concede, if it is sound, and if the criterion of inherent value is accepted as most reasonable, is that there are nonhuman animals that have value, logically independently of our valuing them, if this is true in the case of marginal humans. Thus, if, in the case of these humans, we would object to their being treated as if they had value only as a means to someone else's ends, and if we would object to this manner of treatment on the grounds that it violated their basic moral rights, then we must also hold the same positions in case (certain) animals are treated similarly.

As for those humans not assumed to have rights in the argument from marginal cases—namely, irreversibly comatose humans—the criterion of inherent value leaves it an open question whether they can or do possess rights. Permanently lacking as these humans are in consciousness, there is no basis for believing that they can have let alone lead a life that is better or worse for them; so rights cannot be attributed to these humans on this basis. Moreover, within the class of irreversibly comatose humans, it appears to be true but irrelevant that there may be some who are better of their kind than others. Something's being good of its kind is not equivalent to its being inherently valuable; thus, in conceding that some irreversibly comatose humans may be good of their kind we are not conceding that they are inherently valuable, nor that they have rights because some can be better or worse of their kind. Nevertheless, to the extent that we leave it an open question whether *non*conscious beings can have inherent value, to that extent we cannot exclude irreversibly comatose humans from the class of right holders simply on the grounds that *they* are nonconscious. That *would* be inconsistent. This is why the criterion of inherent value leaves it an open question, whether these humans can or cannot, do or do not have basic moral rights. Of course, certain more elaborate arguments might be coupled with this criterion to reach the conclusion that these humans cannot or do not have such rights. For example, one might argue as follows:

1. Beings that belong to a species whose normal members are conscious can have rights only if they are (or are potentially) conscious.
2. Irreversibly comatose humans belong to such a species and are not conscious, not even potentially so.

3. Therefore, irreversibly comatose human beings cannot have rights.

I am not certain what to say of this argument. Step (1) is not self-evident and thus itself stands in need of supporting argument (as well as conceptual elucidation: for example, what is meant by "normal members?"). For the purposes of this essay, however, it is not essential to defend or criticize this argument in particular, or to reach a settled conclusion regarding the more general question, Can irreversibly comatose humans have basic moral rights? This is not essential because neither the soundness of the argument from marginal cases nor the correctness of the criterion of right possession I have recommended (namely, inherent value) depend on how these issues are resolved. Thus, in saying that the status of the irreversibly comatose is left an open question, given the argument of this essay, it should not be inferred that it is therefore a potentially damaging one.

VI

There is one other important question that remains open, given the preceding characterization and defense of the argument from marginal cases. This is the question, What *particular* basic moral rights do marginal humans and animals have, assuming that they have any? This remains open in the case of marginal humans because, given the argument from marginal cases, marginal humans are not assumed to have any *particular* right(s), only a particular *kind* of right (namely, basic moral rights); thus, this remains an open question in the case of animals too, since one cannot infer that they must have this or that particular right if marginal humans are not assumed to have particular rights and if one argues for animal rights from marginal cases. But while this vital question remains an open question, for the reasons given, and while a theoretically complete answer cannot be attempted on this occasion, some concluding remarks on this matter may not be out of order.

The short answer to the question of what *particular* rights marginal humans have (assuming that they have basic moral rights) is: This varies; that is, different marginal humans might have different basic moral rights. The long answer attempts to elucidate the short answer. Essential to this elucidation is the recognition that one can have a particular right to have (or to do) something only if one *can* have or do what having the right would give one the right to have (or to do). For example, in the case of having a right to freedom of movement, this is a right that a being can have only if it has the capacity to carry out intentional bodily movements; lacking this capacity, this right cannot be possessed. Whether those beings that have this capacity and thus *can* have this right, *do* have it, is of course, quite another matter. The point to notice now is that there are some marginal humans who have, and some who lack, the capacity to carry out intentional bodily movements. Thus, if the possession of a right to freedom of movement depends on the capacity to carry out intentional bodily movements, there will be some marginal humans who could have this right while others could not. And the same variation is likely to obtain in other cases—for example, with regard to the right to pursue one's happiness, it might well be the case that there are some marginal human beings who are so intellectually deficient that they cannot be said literally to have the capacity to pursue anything (i.e., to set goals or objectives, select between alternative means of achieving them, etc.). Thus, the intellectually deficient could not possibly possess the right in question, whereas the less mentally incompetent marginal humans could.

I do not say that the preceding is a complete telling of the "long answer" to the question of what particular rights marginal humans have, assuming that marginal humans have basic moral rights, but only that this answer would have along the lines indicated and could give an intelligible explanation of how it is that, though all those marginal humans who figure in the argument from marginal cases do have (some) basic moral rights, not all of them would necessarily have the same ones. That is a matter that would have to be settled by considering subclasses of the general class, marginal humans, paying particular attention to the relevant capacities of the members of the respective subclasses.

This being so, it should be no surprise that a similar finding ought to be reached regarding the question (assuming the soundness of the argument from marginal cases), What particular rights do *animals* have? In their case, too, what rights are possessed, assuming that some are, may well vary from case to case, depending on the presence or absence of relevant capacities. Thus, one cannot argue that all animals have certain particular rights because (or if) all (or some) marginal humans do. One must proceed more cautiously, recognizing the possibility that some animals might possess rights not possessed by others, that some animals might not possess any rights whatever, that some animals might possess some rights not possessed by some humans, and so forth. Now, it does not follow from this possibility of variation that the attempt to answer the question, What particular rights do animals possess?, is devoid of rational boundaries. On the contrary, what can be argued in the case of animals, assuming that a sound defense of the agument from marginal cases is possible, is that those animals, which are like the members of a certain subclass of marginal humans in the relevant respects, have those particular basic moral rights possessed by the marginal humans in question, assuming that these humans have these particular rights. What the "relevant respects" are will be a function of the relevant capacities of the humans in question (e.g., whether they can move willfully, form intentions, make plans, experience pleasure or pain). Thus, if, for example, we are led to ascribe the right not to be made to suffer gratuitously[28] to a subset of marginal humans, then, assuming that the argument from marginal cases is sound, we shall have just as much reason to ascribe this same right to those animals like the humans in the relevant respect (i.e., like them in having the capacity to suffer). In this essay no attempt has been made to show that marginal (or paradigmatic!) humans *do* have basic moral rights, or, assuming that they do, what particular rights are possessed by what humans. To show this would require arguing for what at the outset was referred to as "the stronger" version of the argument from marginal cases. And to argue in support of that version of the argument would involve clarifying and defending (at the very least) the controversial positions characterized in an earlier section (Section I). The object throughout has been to defend the weaker version, the argument (roughly speaking) that if marginal humans have basic moral rights, so do many animals. As to what particular rights the humans and animals have, assuming that each has some, this is a matter only briefly touched upon in this concluding section. The weaker argument from marginal cases does not itself answer that question. But it does help prepare the way for its serious consideration, which is why an examination and defense of it are important.[29]

NOTES

1. R. G. Frey, "Animal Rights," *Analysis* 37 (1977).
2. Jan Narveson's critical notice in the *Canadian Journal of Philosophy* 2 (1977): 161–178, are of Tom Regan and Peter Singer, eds., *Animal Rights and*

Human Obligations (Englewood Cliffs, N.J.: Prentice-Hall, 1976) and Peter Singer, *Animal Liberation* (New York: A New York Review Book, distributed by Random House, 1975; New York: Avon Books, 1977). For a critical discussion of Narveson's objections to the argument from marginal cases, see Tom Regan, "Narveson on Egoism and the Rights of Animals" in this same issue of the *Canadian Journal of Philosophy* 7, 2 (1977):179–186. In this essay I concentrate on mentally enfeebled humans; human infants present difficulties about potentiality which I do not consider here.

3. Though what Singer writes in *Animal Liberation* (see esp. pp. 8–9) suggests that he accepts both (*a*) the view that animals have certain moral rights and (*b*) that these rights are basic, in the sense explained, he has more recently dissociated himself from this position. See his "The Fable of the Fox and the Unliberated Animal," *Ethics* 88, 2 (1978), esp. p. 122. (See also essay 2, above.)

4. I have developed this argument at greater length in my essay on Narveson, "Narveson on Egoism," and in an essay critical of Singer's views, "Utilitarianism, Vegetarianism and Animal Rights," *Philosophy and Public Affairs* 9, 4 (1980), essay 2, above.

5. On this point, see essay 2, above.

6. Andrew Linzey, *Animal Rights* (London: SCM Press, 1976), p. 24.

7. Joel Feinberg, "The Rights of Animals and Unborn Generations," in W. Blackstone, ed., *Philosophy and Environmental Crisis* (Athens: University of Georgia Press, 1974), pp. 46–47.

8. See, e.g., Singer, *Animal Liberation*, and Tom Regan, "The Moral Basis of Vegetarianism," *Canadian Journal of Philosophy* 5 (1975), (essay 1, above).

9. Frey, "Animal Rights."

10. Dale Jamieson and Tom Regan, "Animal Rights: A Reply to Frey," *Analysis* 38, 1 (1978):32–36.

11. On this, see again my essays critical of Narveson, "Narveson on Egoism," and of Singer, "Utilitarianism," n. 4, above.

12. Linzey, *Animal Rights*, pp. 27–28.

13. Singer, *Animal Liberation*, p. 8.

14. Feinberg, "The Rights of Animals and Unborn Generations."

15. Given the literature presently available, Joel Feinberg is a noteworthy exception. See his "The Rights of Animals and Unborn Generations." At one point in one of his essays Singer reminds us of "the existence of some humans who quite clearly are below the level of awareness, self-consciousness, intelligence, and sentience, of many non-humans." "I am," he says, "thinking of humans with severe and irreparable brain damage," "All Animals are Equal," *Philosophic Exchange* 1, 5 (1974), reprinted in Regan and Singer, eds., *Animal Rights and Human Obligations*, p. 160. In this essay, however, Singer does not examine the importance of these humans in the argument from marginal cases. For a more complete examination see his essay "Animals and the Value of Life" in Tom Regan, ed., *Matters of Life and Death* (New York: Random House, 1980).

16. So far as I know, I am the only one who has advanced this bit of foolishness. See my "The Moral Basis of Vegetarianism."

17. Even this is not quite precise, since some of the criteria that exclude, say, the severely mentally enfeebled arguably do not exclude *all* nonhuman animals. If the capacity to reason is thought to be a necessary and sufficient condition of right possession, then all severely mentally enfeebled, but not all non-human animals, would seem to be excluded from the class of right holders. It is not necessary for my present purposes to attempt to remove this area of imprecision from the characterization of the critical phase.

18. See my "The Nature and Possibility of an Environmental Ethic," *Environmental Ethics* 3, 1 (1981), (essay 9 below).

19. Singer appeals to what is "meaningless" in this connection, and Feinberg invokes an appeal to what is "inconceivable." See Singer, "All Animals are Equal," and Feinberg, "The Rights of Animals and Unborn Generations." It is not clear that such appeals constitute arguments.

20. See my "The Nature and Possibility of an Environmental Ethic," essay 9, below, and my "Feinberg on What Sorts of Beings Can Have Rights," *Southern Journal of Philosophy*, Winter 1976, (essay 8, below).

21. I am myself confused about this point in my essay on Feinberg, ibid. Despite the largely critical tone of this essay, I have been strongly influenced by Professor Feinberg's work on rights.

22. See, again, my "The Nature and Possibility of an Environmental Ethic."

23. See I. Kant, *"The Ground Work of the Metaphysic of Morals*, H. J. Paton, trans. (New York: Harper and Row, 1964).

24. The grounds for this conjecture are to be found in Kant's remarks about our duties to animals. See his "Duties to Animals and Spirits," in *Lectures on Ethics*, Louis Infield, trans. (New York: Harper and Row, 1963). Relevant portions are reproduced in *Animal Rights and Human Obligations*, pp. 122–123.

25. I examine Kant's position vis-à-vis the treatment of marginal humans at slightly greater length in my "Utilitarianism, Vegetarianism, and Animal Rights." For an examination of his views regarding our duties to animals, see my "Exploring the Idea of Animal Rights" in David Paterson and Richard Ryder, eds., *Animals' Rights: A Symposium* (London: Centaur Press, 1979). The arguments for animal rights presented there are not quite on target, if the argument advanced in this essay is sound. I defend Kant against the criticism given his views on our duties by others in my "Broadie and Pybus on Kant," *Philosophy* 51 (1976):471–472. See Elizabeth Pybus and Alexander Broadie, "Kant's Treatment of Animals," *Philosophy* 49 (1974): 375–383.

26. See esp. Singer, *Animal Liberation*, chap. 1, and Ruth Harrison's *Animal Machines* (London: Stuart, 1964).

27. See esp. Singer, *Animal Liberation*, chap. 1, and Richard Ryder, *Victims of Science* (London: Davis-Poynter, 1975).

28. For some comments on this right, see my "On the Right to be Spared Gratuitous Suffering," *Canadian Journal of Philosophy* 10, 3 (1980). The occasion for this note is Donald VanDeVeer's "Animal Suffering," ibid.

29. Many people have given me the benefit of their criticism of earlier drafts of this essay. It is a pleasure to thank them for their interest. The following, in particular, have made valuable suggestions: Dale Jamieson, W. R. Carter, A. Donald VanDeVeer, R. G. Frey, Bonnie Steinbock, Sidney Gendin, L. W. Sumner; the members of the philosophy department, University of Calgary, especially John Heintz and Kai Nielsen; the members of the philosophy department, University of Kansas, especially Richard De George and Rex Martin; the members of the philosophy department, Northern Illinois University, especially Harold Brown, Donald Cress, and William Tolhurst. With the assistance of so many one might hope that errors would be few. Understandably I do not know if the hope is borne out in this case. I do know that the kind attention of the persons mentioned has appreciably helped my thinking.

7
Animals and the Law: The Need for Reform

This essay on the legal status of animals was presented at a World Congress on Philosophy of Law and Social Philosophy held at Basel University, Basel, Switzerland, in August 1979. It was the first large-scale international conference I had attended, and I was somewhat awestruck by its size and scope. Another participant attempted to salve my apprehension. He had been to such conferences before. There were entirely too many papers, he said, and the criteria used for accepting submissions were always suspect. "Why, there's even a paper on *animals* and the law!" he told me, his voice a polished combination of disdain and disbelief. I did not have it in me to admit that I had known of that paper prior to his revelation, but what he said helped prepare me for the incredulity with which the paper was viewed and encouraged me to believe that I had come to the right place to give it.

This participant's reaction to a paper on animals and the law speaks volumes about human prejudice. We who are humans, it is widely supposed, do have *bona fide* legal status and legitimate legal rights —or, if we do not have them, we should. The "laws of the land" ought to protect the legitimate interests of individual citizens; that is the primary, if not the sole, function of the law. When it comes to non-human animals, however, the legal situation is and should be different. They neither have, nor should they have, genuine legal status or, in any full sense, legal rights. Seriously to challenge these widespread convictions is almost certain to be viewed as a symptom of a mind gone wrong. This essay makes this challenge, seriously, arguing that the refusal to accord animals full legal status or to protect their vital interests against human intervention by according them legal rights is a product of unexamined, indefensible prejudice.

There is another side to this issue or, to put the point differently, another audience to whom this essay is addressed. Among those who labor for the better treatment of animals, some think that animals *already have* legal rights—that they *already are* recognized as "legal persons." How far this is from true is another point this essay seeks to establish. We are not likely to challenge the prejudicial basis for denying animals their proper place in the law if we operate on the assumption that they already occupy it.

One final point. One of those who gave my paper a polite hearing was visibly incredulous. "Would you have dogs judged by a jury of their peers—other dogs?" he wanted to know. The point of the question, it seemed, was that since animals cannot *judge* legal guilt or innocence, they cannot *have* legal rights that others might abridge. To champion their "legal rights" thus makes about as much (that is, as little) sense as calling for the "educational rights" of, say, hogs to have courses in advanced physics. The question, and the preconceptions that lie behind it, are a special instance of the widespread acceptance of double standards, one standard for humans, another for animals. For there are, after all, some *humans* who cannot judge legal guilt or innocence (e.g., children, the retarded) and yet who are recognized as "legal persons" and are accorded legal standing. That being so, what arguments are there, and how good are they, for persisting in judging and treating the case of all nonhuman animals differently? That is the central question explored here.

Comparatively little has been written on the legal status of animals. Of those who have recently written on the topic, Joel Feinberg's work is the most supportive of the cause for reforming our understanding of animals' legal rights. See his "The Rights of Animals and Unborn Generations" in W. Blackstone, ed., *Philosophy and Environmental Crisis* (Athens: University of Georgia Press, 1974), pp. 43–68, and "Human Duties and Animal Rights" in R. K. Morris and M. W. Fox, eds., *On The Fifth Day* (Washington, D.C.: Acropolis Books, 1978), pp. 45–69. A helpful historical review of positions on both the moral and legal status of animals, which contains specific legislative proposals, is

Stephen I. Burr, "Toward Legal Rights for Animals," *Environmental Affairs* (Boston Law School) 4, 2 (1975): 205–254. An enormously helpful resource is the "Animal Rights Reporter," edited by Henry Mark Holzer, published and distributed by Society for Animal Rights, Inc., 421 South State Street, Clarks Summit, Pa. 18411.

"Animals and the Law: The Need for Reform" is forthcoming in the Proceedings of *Internationalen Vereinigung für Rechts—und Sozialphilosophie (IVR)*, World Congress, 1979, Volume II.

Historically, animals have occupied an interesting, if ofttimes unenviable, position within and before the law. From the ancient Greeks, through the Middle Ages, even into the twentieth century; from the East and the West; in a word, across both cultural and temporal boundaries, the legal landscape is dotted with records of the criminal prosecution of animals. Those animals brought to trial, before ecclesiastical and civil authorities, include but are not limited to beetles, bulls, cows, dogs, dolphins, field mice, horses, moles, rats, sheep, slugs, swine, termites, wolves, and worms. The charges brought against these animals varied from unlawful occupancy to murder, and the modes of punishment varied as well; the Russian courts, for example, displaying a not untypical inclination to banish animals (for example, toward the end of the seventeenth century a he-goat was exiled to Siberia) while some courts, especially those in Europe in the Middle Ages, went so far as to execute animals. Indeed, one of the most famous of these latter cases took place here in Basel. The year was 1474. The accused was a certain rooster. The offense: Having laid an egg. Walter Woodburne Hyde describes the proceedings as follows:[1]

> During the proceedings it was shown that cock's eggs were of use in mixing certain magical preparations and that sorcerers were therefore eager to get them. The defendant's lawyer frankly admitted this, but contended that the laying of the egg in this particular case had been entirely unpremeditated and involuntary, and that consequently the occurrence was not punishable by law, and further, that his client was innocent since no records could be adduced to show that Satan had ever made a compact

with any of the brute creation. The prosecution replied that it was not a case of the devil making a compact with brutes, but that Satan actually entered into them on occasion . . . . On this argument the cock was condemned and was actually burned at the stake before a great crowd of onlookers.

Three further cases will have to suffice as illustrative of the variety of charges that brought animals before the bar. (1) In Saigny-sur-Etang, in Bourgogne, France, in January 1457, a sow and her six piglets were tried for murdering and partly devouring an infant. The piglets, because of their youth, innocence, and the corrupting influence of their mother, were pardoned; the sow was found guilty and hanged. (2) In New Haven, Connecticut, in June 1662, a man named Potter, described as being "devout in worship, gifted in prayer, forward in edifying discourse among the religious, and zealous in reforming the sins of other people," was found guilty of the crime of bestiality. Like the French sow, Potter, together with a cow, two heifers, three sheep, and two sows, was also sentenced to death by hanging. (3) Lastly, we have a less disquieting but a still instructive case, this time from an ecclesiastical court, but from France again, the year 1552, the court of Austin. The accused: Some rats. The charge: Having eaten and wantonly destroyed some of the district's barley crops. Their defense counsel: Bartholomew Chassenee. Hyde describes the proceedings as follows:[2]

> The culprits were cited to appear on a certain day. As the rats failed to appear, their advocate Chassenee, trying by every means to find a loophole in the law for his clients, pleaded that the summons had been too local and of too individual a character, and that not some but all of the rats of the diocese should be summoned. In consequence the curates of all the parishes under the bishop summoned every rat to appear on a certain day; but still no rats put in an appearance. Then Chassenee argued that, inasmuch as the rats were dispersed in many villages, great preparations for a migration had to be made and that this required time. So a delay in the proceedings was granted; but still no rats. Their absence this time was excused by their advocate on the ground that a summons implied full protection to the parties summoned while coming and going; but that his clients, though anxious to appear, were afraid of their natural enemies the cats, which belonged to the plaintiffs. He therefore demanded that the plaintiffs be bonded under penalty to keep their cats from frightening the rats. This plea seemed to the court to be valid, but the plaintiffs demurred, and in consequence the period for the appearance of the rats was ajourned *sine die* and judgment was given by default.

Would that some humans were as lucky as the rats of the diocese of Austin to have so clever and persistent a defense counsel!

These examples illustrate well the progress we have made in our ascent toward a more enlightened view of the world. That rats should be charged with a crime must today strike us as bizarre; that a human being and sundry animals should be put to the death because of their sexual adventures, tragic. So, yes, discernible progress has been made (though it is good to remind ourselves that the practice of prosecuting animals and subjecting them even to capital punishment survived into the twentieth century). But despite this progress, and in spite of the increasing protection animals are provided by both humane and environmental legislation, the law has yet to grant to animals themselves either legal rights or legal standing. The time to do so has come, I believe; indeed, the time to do so is now overdue. In the remainder of this essay this is the case I myself endeavor to prosecute. My argument begins with a critical examination of specimen arguments that deny the intelligibility of the very idea of animals having legal rights;[3] next I advance my principal argument for granting legal rights to animals; lastly, I defend my argument against forseeable objections and endeavor to indicate why, though so much is uncertain, the movement for animal rights ought to go forward, not in opposition to the power of "the law" but with its assistance.

I. Arguments Against the Intelligibility of Animals Having Legal Rights

Not all possible arguments against the intelligibility of animals having legal rights can be considered here. Those that are examined seem to be the best of a bad lot. For convenience's sake, I give names to the arguments. The first I call the Person Argument and formulate it thus:

The Person Argument

Premise 1. All and only persons can have legal rights.

Premise 2. Animals are not persons.

Conclusion. Therefore, animals cannot have legal rights.

The major weakness in this argument concerns premise 2. If by "persons" is meant "human beings," then that premise is true: Animals decidedly are not human beings. But this cannot be what is meant by "persons" within the present context. For there are "persons" within the law ("legal personalities") who, whatever else they may be, certainly are not human beings. For example, corporations are persons within the law, as are ships. Thus, premise 2 must mean something other than that animals are not human beings. But what else might it mean? Only, it appears, that animals are not legal persons—that is, animals *do not* have legal rights. Thus repaired, the Person Argument remains glaringly deficient. For now the conclusion does not follow from the premises. That is, it does not follow that something cannot be the case simply because it is not the case. Indeed, we need go no further than the history of the law itself to make this plain. For example, corporations have not always had the status of legal persons. The same could, then, hold true in the case of animals. Granted, they do not *now* have legal rights; granted, they are not *now* recognized as legal persons; nevertheless, it does not follow that they cannot in the future bear these rights or enjoy this status.

A second argument is the Injury Argument.

The Injury Argument

Premise 1. All and only individuals who can be injured can have legal rights.

Premise 2. Animals cannot be injured.

Conclusion. Therefore, animals cannot have legal rights.

The mere statement of this argument is its undoing. Except for some few latter day Cartesians, no one will find premise 2 credible. If a dog is beaten to a whimpering heap by his master, the dog is injured, and injured in a literal, not a metaphorical sense of the word. Someone will say, "Still, the dog cannot be injured the way persons can. For example, he cannot be injured by having malicious rumors spread about his integrity or honesty in business affairs." Indeed. Neither can human infants, nor the senile; neither can ships (in any literal sense). Yet the law grants rights to these individuals. And if these individuals are not excluded as subjects having legal rights, though they cannot be injured in all the ways paradigmatic human beings can, then neither can we rationally deny that animals can have legal rights for this reason. Nor can we rationally exclude animals by appeal to the Benefit Argument.

The Benefit Argument

Premise 1.   All and only individuals who can be directly benefited can have legal rights.

Premise 2.   Animals cannot be directly benefited.

Conclusion.   Therefore, animals cannot have legal rights.

This argument is as weak as the Injury Argument and for similar reasons. Animals not only can be, they frequently are the direct beneficiaries of what befalls them. Imagine your cat has worms, and you take her to the veterinarian for treatment. The diagnosis is correct, the prescribed medication effective, and the cat recovers her normal good health. You, as the owner, are relieved, elated perhaps; you, as one who has an interest in the animal, are a clear benefactor of the veterinarian's services. But so is your cat! And directly. *She* does not have to wait to see if *you* are a benefactor! Suppose that, before she recovers, you die. Would it follow from your being dead that she could not benefit from her medical attention? It is preposterous to think it would. It is a symptom of human arrogance to suppose that things can happen to nonhuman individuals that benefit or injure them only if or as we humans are in turn benefited or injured. Such is also a mark of of an infantile view of the world. Like our fellow humans, our fellow animals can be direct beneficiaries of what is done to them. This being so, let us go on to consider the Interests Argument.

The Interests Argument

Premise 1.   All and only individuals having interests can have legal rights.

Premise 2.   Animals do not have interests.

Conclusion.   Therefore, animals cannot have legal rights.

In reply to this argument it is relevant to distinguish between two senses of "interests."[4] In the first (which I shall call " the desiring sense"), to say that an individual (*A*) "has an interest in" something (*x*) means that *A* wants, desires, craves, lusts after, aspires to have *x*; in the second ("the welfare sense"), to say "*A* has an interest in *x*" means "*x* is in *A*'s welfare—that is, having *x* would promote *A*'s welfare (or keep it stable)." The two senses certainly are different—for example, individuals do not always desire what is actually in their welfare. So, the Interest Argument might be interpreted in two quite different ways, depending on which sense of "interest" is intended. Whichever sense is intended, however, the argument is equally deficient. This is because there are many species of animals whose members have interests in both the desiring and the welfare sense. For example, veal calves not only want to suckle; their being permitted to do so is beneficial to them: Other things being equal, *they* are better off in terms of their physical and psychological well-being if they are given the opportunity to suckle than if they are denied this opportunity. Thus, the Interest Argument will not do the job of excluding all animals from the class of possible possessors of legal rights.

Finally there is the Claims Argument.

The Claims Argument

Premise 1.   All and only those individuals who can themselves press claims can have legal rights.

Premise 2.   Animals cannot themselves press claims.

Conclusion.   Therefore, animals cannot have legal rights.

This argument at least has the distinction of containing a second premise that is true. Its problem is that its first premise is manifestly false. Human infants cannot press their own claims; nor can the senile; nor the mentally incompetent. Yet the law does not *now* (though it once did) withhold legal rights and standing in their case. For the law allows that the interests of these individuals can be represented by another competent or concerned individual who, acting on their behalf, can make and press those claims that, say, infants and the senile themselves can neither make nor understand. Logically, the case of animals is no different. *They* cannot speak. *They* cannot understand, make, or press any claim they might have upon others to cease and desist from doing what is injurious to them or to institute policies that would redound to their benefit. But it is intelligible to imagine other, interested, competent individuals doing so on their behalf. If being condemned by nature to ignorance and muteness is no bar against granting legal rights to dumb mute humans, a similar natural limitation should be no logical bar to granting legal rights to animals.

I conclude this section of my essay, therefore, as follows: First, those arguments fail which attempt to show that animals are not even intelligible or possible bearers of legal rights; and second, to the extent that intelligible bearers of rights are individuals who can be injured, or benefited, or have interests, or can have claims made by themselves or on their behalf, to that extent we have ample reason to believe that the idea of animals having legal rights—the idea of their being legal persons—is at least intelligible.

II. An Argument for Granting Animals Legal Rights

I turn now to my second task, that of presenting an argument for actually granting legal rights to animals. To some this will seem a case of wasted labor since, they will affirm, animals *already* have legal rights. Now, it is true that animals already are the beneficiaries of various national and international laws—for example, the Endangered Species Act in the United States, a wealth of anticruelty legislation throughout the world, and the Council of Europe's "Convention for the Protection of Animals during International Transport." And it is not uncommon for people to infer that animals have legal rights because they are protected by such legislation. Thus, for example, in the recent, extremely helpful book, *Animals and Their Legal Rights*, Emily Stewart Leavitt and Diane Halverson, after quoting the first anticruelty law enacted in the United States, passed by the New York State Legislature in 1828, write that "although this law limits the protected animals to owned horses, cattle, sheep, it does give these animals the right to be protected from their owner's cruel treatment . . . (and gives) them the legal right to be well treated."[5] But this interpretation of the New York law and other, comparable legislation overlooks the legal distinction between (*a*) being protected by a law and (*b*) having a legal right that is created or acknowledged by a law. For not everything protected by a law itself has a legal right. To illustrate this, consider the legal status of great works of art or architecture—say, the Pieta. Anyone who defaces or in other ways damages the Pieta is liable to be charged with a criminal offense and, if found guilty, judicially punished. Thus, the Pieta is protected by the law. But it does not follow that the Pieta itself has legal rights. For the law protects the Pieta, not for its own sake, but for the sake of others—in particular, for the sake of the interests of present and future generations of human beings, who have an interest in preserving great works of art and architecture. So, though these works of art are protected by the law, though they are its "beneficiaries," they have no legal rights. Similarly in the case of existing animal legislation: Such legislation does (or at least is intended to) protect animals. But this protection by itself does not establish that these animals thereby have either legal rights or legal standing.

The issue before us is not, however, "Does the law now grant animals legal rights and standing?," to which the answer evidently is, no. The question is, "Ought the law to do so?," to which I answer, yes. The grounds on which I argue this are mostly moral in nature. Indeed, my short answer to the question, "Why ought the law to grant legal rights to animals?" is, "because morality will not be satisfied with anything less." My longer answer, as I now explain, albeit sketchily, involves considerations about the moral status of animals, the history of human prejudice, and the interplay between enlightened morality and progressive legislation.

I begin with some remarks about prejudice. Prejudice characteristically involves a disposition to deny, ignore, or undervalue the interests and importance of those against whom one is prejudiced. In two of its most glaring forms, prejudicial discrimination is meted out along racial or sexual lines: The color of one's skin or the gender of one's sex are themselves taken to be grounds for denying, ignoring, or undervaluing the interests or importance of others.[6] Morally, we are agreed that such prejudices are indefensible. Legally, in the United States and elsewhere, steps have been and are being taken to give full and equal legal status to those against whom prejudice has historically prevailed. Egalitarian considerations are winning the day. But the vision and impetus to vouchsafe the growing defeat of prejudice came not from the positive law alone. It came from a morality that would not be satisfied with a system of law that provided legal protection for, as it itself helped to institute, the very prejudices in question.

Two important lessons may be learned from this, I think. These are, first, that the body of positive law up to any given point in time might itself encapsulate and, from a legal point of view, legitimize prejudice and, second, that, if the law is not simply to be a handmaiden of the special interests prejudice serves, it must be open to moral criticism and direction. The history of our legal systems shows that they *can* be made to be responsive to egalitarian moral considerations. The present movement to grant animals legal rights is another chapter in this ongoing history.

Now, to many, the idea of "animal rights" will be laughable, analogous in terms of seriousness to the suggestion made some years back by an anonymous person that animals be required to wear clothes in public since otherwise they are in violation of well-established antinudity legislation. The task of changing the laughers will not be easy, if possible at all. The point to realize, however, is that what we find laughable sometimes tells us more about ourselves and our time than we might suppose.[7] We would be fooling ourselves if we thought that racists or sexists did not find the idea of the rights of blacks or women laughable. We must beware of our laughter, lest we count it as evidence of the truth or reasonableness of the prejudice it sometimes expresses. So, though some may laugh, that is no substitute for argument. And argument is what is wanted.

The moral underpinning of the case against racism and sexism, I think, comes to this: We come to see that blacks and females *themselves* have interests; *themselves* can be injured or benefited; *themselves* have valid claims against others; *themselves* not only are alive, but have a life that is better or worse for them as individuals, logically independently of whether they are valued by, or of value to, anyone else; *and*, once having seen this, we are brought to see that we can no longer tolerate laws and institutions that deny or subvert these truths—for example, we can no longer tolerate viewing another human being as the legal property of another human being, so that, if questions of injury or benefit were to arise, these must be answered from the point of view of the owner, not the slave. To view other humans merely as property is to deny them both moral and legal personality—is to deny them both moral and legal rights. To go on quietly condoning or supporting a body of law that tolerates or protects such a view of other humans, based on racial or sexual grounds—or, say, religious ones—is implicitly to serve the ends of prejudice. The hands of docile "law-abiding citizens" are not clean.

Not surprisingly, those who, like myself, call for granting legal rights to animals also call for a concomitant change in our vision and understanding of them. We are not to see them, as Descartes did, as nature's machines; nor, as Plato did, as lawless beasts; nor, as the marketing mentality does, as commodities or renewable resources. We are not to see them thus because each view is symptomatic of the same, deep, slumbering falsehood—namely, that humans are different *in kind* from animals. After all, *we* are not lawless beasts; *we* are not commodities or renewable resources. But all such attempts to mark a qualitative chasm that separates man from the beasts must fail, not just because we are *like* animals, but because, as Mary Midgley notes, we *are* animals.[8] This does not mean that there are no significant differences between the human and other animal species. It means, rather, that the difference can no longer be supposed to be as great as was once widely believed—and perhaps, too, as Midgley argues, that the difference must be looked for in a different place. The general point we must recognize, however, comes to this: That humans and animals are *cohabitants* of the earth, neither of us the other's natural owner or slave; that, like us, they, too, can be injured and benefited; that, like us, they, too, have interests; that, like us, they, too, can be viewed as having valid claims against others; and that, like us, they, too—or members of many species of them—not only are alive, they have a life that is better or worse for them as individuals, logically independently of whether they are valued by, or are of value to, anyone else—in particular, any human being. To regard the value status of animals otherwise—to go on believing and acting as if nonhuman animals had value only if or as they served human interests—is to give regrettable testimony to the very prejudice here being challenged.[9]

In an earlier time, what I have just said about animals might well have been dismissed as "sentimental anthropomorphism," hardly supported by science—at odds with science, in fact. But such apologies are not in order today. For today (actually, at least from Darwin's day forward) the evidence for the view that animals have interests, that they can be injured or benefited, comes, not from the armchair speculations of so-called "animal lovers" (compare the rhetorical use of this expression with that of "nigger lover") but from scientists themselves, especially ethologists.[10] *I* have not made these things up. *They* are finding them out.

So we have, I submit, a glaring discrepancy. On the one hand, human beings,[11] of whatever color, gender, or religious persuasion, are recognized as having interests; are understood to be subjects who can themselves be benefited or injured; are viewed as individuals who can themselves press their claims or have them pressed by others acting on their behalf; are acknowledged to be possessors of a life that is better or worse for them considered as individuals, logically independently of their value to others; *and* are not relegated to the legal status of property but themselves have legal rights. On the other hand we have nonhuman animals, members of many species which are now known to be like humans in the relevant respects—for example, they have interests and can be benefited or injured—but who are relegated to the legal status of property and who are denied legal rights. And my question is: Is there any satisfactory way to explain this discrepancy that does not itself bespeak the very prejudice at issue? Not surprisingly, I think not. But there are two arguments worth considering in this regard.

The first is an argument involving the idea of benefits again. Roughly, the argument is that, since animals already benefit from protective legislation, without our having to grant them legal rights, it is therefore unnecessary to grant them these rights. Indeed, by appealing to a legal version of Occam's razor ("Never multiply legal rights beyond necessity") we are able to arrive at the stronger conclusion that we ought not to grant rights in their case.

This argument cannot find a thoughtful audience. We do not say that, because human beings already benefit from various laws, therefore legal rights are unnecessary in their case—or, stronger, that the law ought not to grant or acknowledge them. Thus, uncritically to persist in treating the two cases differently, maintaining that humans (rightly) have legal rights while animals (rightly) do not, merely on the grounds that animals already are protected by (are the beneficiaries of) various laws, is not to engage in the debate at hand. It is unwittingly to testify on behalf of the prejudice at issue, rather than to examine it.

Despite its shortcomings, this argument does call attention to one aspect of the fundamental issues under debate. For the question we must ask is not, "Are animals protected by legislation?" but, "What is the *basis* of such protective legislation?" In the nature of the case, two possible bases are possible. The first is human centered: We are to protect various animals because it is in our interest to do so. Thus, for example, we may protect endangered species for the sake of future generations of human beings, so that they may see and appreciate these rare creatures; or we may make cruelty to animals illegal because it offends humans (or some of them). On this way of viewing matters, it matters not that the animals themselves are injured, except insofar as this affects human interests. The second possible basis is animal centered: We are to protect various animals, not if or as this coincides with human interest; we are to protect them because they themselves have a legitimate interest in being protected. Thus, even granting that animals are in fact protected by various laws; more, even supposing that they are protected as much by such laws without granting them legal rights as they would be if they had such rights; the question would still remain, "What is the basis of such legislation: human interests or animal interests?"

In view of what I have said up to now, it should come as no surprise that the basis I would defend is animal centered, and this because, first, this basis, and not the human-centered one, is the one that recognizes the independent value of animal life (the human-centered basis would have us suppose that animal life and interests ought to be protected *only if or as* these are in harmony with human life and interests); second, because the human-centered basis would perpetuate the very prejudices I wish to expose and move beyond; and, third, because legislation grounded in a human basis as a matter of fact can be shown to run counter to the interests of animals. For consider: Are we seriously to suppose that cocks have an interest in cockfighting? That it causes them no injury? That they are the beneficiaries of this "sport"? It is grotesque to offer an affirmative answer on their behalf. But the law, by allowing human interest to be its guide, can and has seen things otherwise, as witness this 1953 decision of the New Mexico Supreme Court:

> While it is true that in the minds of some men, there is nothing more violent, wanton, and cruel, necessarily producing pain and suffering to an animal, than placing a cock in a ring with another cock, both equipped with artificial spurs, to fight to the death, solely for man's amusement and sport, others consider it an honorable sport mellowed in the crucible of time so as to become an established tradition not unlike calf-roping, steer riding, bulldogging, and bronco busting.

Thus does the court say that cockfighting is on solid legal ground! And small wonder. For the court views the issue from the vantage point of "the minds of men" and of human interests generally. The court says, in effect, that just because some men find cockfighting ghastly, it ought not to be stopped; for other men find it "an honorable sport mellowed in the crucible of time." In this case, then, the human interest in preserving "an honorable sport" outweighs the interest other humans have in having an end to armed cocks fighting one another. But the whole procedure is ill arranged, the entire perspective ill focused. Human interests are not the measure of animal interests. Were we to have laws founded on the recognition of the interests of animals themselves—if, that is to say, animals themselves had legal rights—the court would be obliged to proceed differently: Not human interest, but the interests of animals themselves would be decisive. The court, then, would be obliged to rule differently, not only in the case of cockfighting, but in many other cases besides, some of which the New Mexico Supreme Court lists (calf-roping, etc.), but some of which it does not. For example, bullfighting, which could not last a legal day if the bull's, not man's (or some men's) interests were the measure of its legality (will anyone suggest that the bulls are not injured?). "Mellowed in the crucible of time" indeed. One can imagine a similar line of legal defense for casting Christians to lions, had a complacent morality and indolent legislation permitted that "entertainment" to endure.

A second attempt to defend the discrepancy outlined earlier— humans have legal rights, but animals do not, despite their relevant similarities—is what I call the Pandora's Box argument, or the argument that, once the lid to the legal rights of animals is opened, there will be no end to the number of animals having such rights or the variety of the rights they have, with the net result that the law, both at its theoretical and practical level, both of which are already on the messy side, will plunge into anarchical chaos. Thus, legal rights ought not to be accorded nonhuman animals.

This criticism is unkind to animal rights' arguments. There *are* relevant differences between humans and other animals—or, to speak more precisely, between some humans and some animals. As such, one is not committed to maintaining that every animal must have each and every right that any human being has—for example, that pigs must have a right to an education or giraffes a right to vote. Moreover, one is not even committed to the view that all animals must have some legal rights. The operative question must be whether a given animal can itself literally be benefited, or injured; can itself literally be said to have interests; can literally have claims pressed on its behalf; or can literally be viewed as having a life that can be better or worse for it, considered as an individual. Only in those cases where the answer to these questions is affirmative do we have reason to raise the lid to animal rights; but even before we open it, we have ample reason to believe that not every creature we call an animal will be found inside—for example, neither clams nor oysters, amoebae nor paramecia are likely to be found there. So, no, the road to the legal rights of animals is not destined to lead to chaos.

But lest my remarks in the foregoing seem lacking in proper humility, let me hasten to add in closing that *of course* there is much that is uncertain, at both the level of theory and of practice. Certainly I am unsure where, or how, this chapter in legal history will end, if it is begun. Whether, for example, animals ought to be accorded a legal right to life and, if so, what impact this would have on the human institutions of hunting, scientific research involving animals, and raising animals as a food source—these questions certainly remain open to informed debate. But our uncertainty here should not prevent us from pushing on. The point we must recognize, the truth we must emphasize, is that just as blacks do not exist for whites, or women for men, so animals do not exist for us. They are not part of the generous accomodations supplied by a benevolent deity or an ever-so-thoughtful Nature. *They* have a life, and a value, of their own. A morality that fails to incorporate this truth is empty. A legal system that excludes it is blind.[12]

NOTES

1. Walter Woodburn Hyde, "The Prosecution and Punishment of Animals and Lifeless Things in the Middle Ages and Modern Times," *University of Pennsylvania Law Review* 64 (1916): 708. The three further cases given in the main body of my essay also are to be found in Hyde's essay. For further treatment of the topic of animal prosecution, see Edward Evans, *The Criminal Prosecution and Capital Punishment of Animals* (London: Heinemann, 1906) and, more recently, Gerald Carson, *Men, Beasts, and Gods* (New York: Charles Scribner's Sons, 1972), chap. 3, "Bugs and Beasts Before the Law."
2. Ibid., pp. 706–707.
3. For an important discussion of this topic, and one to which I am much indebted, see Joel Feinberg, "The Rights of Animals and Unborn Generations" in W. Blackstone, ed., *Philosophy and Environmental Crisis* (Athens: University of Georgia Press, 1974).
4. I have discussed this difference elsewhere. See my "McCloskey on Why Animals Cannot Have Rights," *Philosophical Quarterly* 26, 104 (July 1976): 251–257.
5. Emily Stewart Leavitt, *Animals and Their Legal Rights: A Survey of American Laws from 1641 to 1978* (Washington: Animal Welfare Institute, 1978), p. 12.
6. The Australian philosopher, Peter Singer, has written powerfully about the similarities between racism, sexism, and what has come to be called "speciesism"—that is, those prejudices against animals based on species membership. See, in particular, his *Animal Liberation* (New York: A New York Review Book, distributed by Random House, 1975; New York: Avon Books, 1977).

7. Christopher Stone makes a similar observation in his *Should Trees Have Legal Standing? Toward Legal Rights for Natural Objects* (Los Altos: William Kaufman, 1974), p. 8, n. 23*a*. Shortly thereafter Stone writes that he "essentially limit(s) (himself) to non-animal but natural objects" and, further, that some animals "already have rights in some senses," p. 9, n. 26. He gives no explanation, however, of what these "senses" are; thus, it is not possible to dispute, or concur with, what he says. Nothing that I say entails that nonanimals stand on all fours with animals, when it comes to the question of legal rights.

8. Mary Midgley, *Beast and Man* (Ithaca: Cornell University Press, 1978).

9. I have explored these themes elsewhere. See, especially, "An Examination and Defense of One Argument Concerning Animal Rights," *Inquiry* 22 (Summer 1979):189−219 (essay 6, above) and "Animal Rights, Human Wrongs," *Environmental Ethics* 2, 2 (1980):99−120 (essay 4, above).

10. See, for example, Irenaus Eibl-Eibesfeldt, *Love and Hate*, trans. Geoffrey Strachan (London: Methuen, 1971); Heinz Friedrich, ed., *Man and Animal* (London: Paladin, 1972); Jane Goodall, *In the Shadow of Man* (Boston: Houghton Mifflin, 1971); Konrad Lorenz, *King Solomon's Ring*, trans. M. K. Wilson (Boston: Houghton Mifflin, 1955); and Niko Tinbergen, *Social Behavior in Animals* (London: Methuen, 1953). A more extensive bibliography is provided at the end of the Midgely volume, *Beast and Man*.

11. There are problems here, especially involving the moral and legal status of irreversibly comatose human beings. On this, see "An Examination and Defense of One Argument Concerning Animal Rights" (essay 6, above).

12. I have been stimulated and helped by discussions with Theodore S. Meth on the topics covered in this essay. I would be the first to insist, and he the second, that the conclusions I come to are mine, not his.

8
What Sorts of Beings Can Have Rights?

"What Sorts of Beings Can Have Rights?" marks my first published attempt to address a question that forms part of the normally unarticulated conceptual background of arguments for animal *or* human rights. The question, quite simply, is whether rights *must* be limited only to conscious individuals. This is not a question about which beings *do* have rights. Even if no one has rights we could still ask what sorts of beings could, just as, analogously, we might ask what beings could be immortal, even if none is immortal in fact. Like this analogous question, the question about which beings can possess rights obviously presupposes that we know what we are looking for and thus know how to assess alternative answers. In the case of the question about rights, what is assumed is that we have reasonable criteria for deciding possible possession of rights. If we have such criteria, then any individual who satisfies them will qualify as a possible possessor of rights, while any individual who fails to satisfy them will be reasonably disqualified as a possible possessor of rights. The central question this essay explores is whether a particular, highly plausible account of the criteria of possible right possession shows that inanimate, nonconscious objects (e.g., trees) *cannot* possess rights. With this essay, then, the attempt is made to strike out in a new direction, one that was hinted at but not explored systematically in "An Examination and Defense of One Argument Concerning Animal Rights" (essay 6, n. 18). The question is not merely, or not primarily, whether *animals* can have rights; it is whether *inanimate* things can.

The influential ideas of Joel Feinberg are critically examined with a view to exploring this question. Feinberg, perhaps unwittingly, arguably sets forth different criteria for possible possession of rights (the interest principle and the goodness principle). Inanimate objects arguably meet the latter principle, though not the former, given one interpretation of "having an interest." Thus, if the goodness principle is a satisfactory basis for determining which beings *can* possess rights, nonconscious, inanimate things (trees, sagebrush, rivers) *could* have rights, in which case we could not dispense with the need to investigate whether they have them by denying that they do on the grounds that they cannot. The primary objective of the essay thus is to block this move and to force us to come to honest terms with the complexities of the issues.

As in other essays, the notion of inherent value (of having a good of one's own) plays a prominent role. Feinberg's goodness principle is interpreted in these terms: For any *x*, *x* can have rights if *x* is inherently good (i.e., if *x* has a kind of value that is distinct from its utility for others and is independent of *x*'s being the object of another's interests). Aside from the arguments interpretive of Feinberg, those that seek to defend the *intelligibility* of viewing inanimate objects as having a good of their own, in the sense explained, are the arguments that matter most. They briefly resurface in essay 9.

The ambiguity of "having an interest," remarked upon in the interpretation of Feinberg, was originally noted in my "McCloskey on Why Animals Cannot Have Rights," *Philosophical Quarterly* 26, 104 (July 1976): 251–257. The distinction is noted and used in a somewhat confusing way by R. G. Frey in "Rights, Interests, Desires, and Beliefs," *American Philosophical Quarterly* 16, 3 (July 1979): 233–239, and in *Interests and Rights: The Case Against Animals* (Oxford: Clarendon Press, 1980), pp. 18–27. Robert Elliott challenges my principal arguments and conclusions in "Regan on What Sorts of Beings Can Have Rights," *Southern Journal of Philosophy* 16 (Spring 1978): 701–705. The references cited in the introductions and the footnotes to essays 7 and 9 are relevant to the issues explored in the essay that follows.

"What Sorts of Beings Can Have Rights?," originally titled "Feinberg on What Sorts of Beings Can Have Rights," first appeared in the *Southern Journal of Philosophy* 14, 4 (Winter 1976): 485–498, and is reprinted here with permission of that journal.

What sorts of beings can have rights?[1] In particular, can *inanimate* beings—flowers or trees—have rights? Or is the concept of a right necessarily limited to animate beings, so that, even if it should turn out that *not all* animate beings, not all animals, have rights, it would at least be true that *only* animals can have them? The possibility of inanimate beings having rights is the central question examined in this essay. How this question is answered has immediate and important implications for the kind of environmental ethic we can consistently develop. By an "environmental ethic" I mean (roughly) a set of principles that sets forth how we morally ought to behave, if and when the effects of our actions affect the life or being of nonhumans, including fauna *and* flora. *If* it could be reasonably argued that flora (living but inanimate beings) have rights, then the principles that comprise our environmental ethic would have to take this into account. These principles could not be through and through anthropocentric, laying down that we have obligations to act thus and so, or to refrain from acting thus and so, if and only if the lives of human beings are affected for good or ill, nor could they draw moral boundaries exclusively in terms of the interests of animals, human or otherwise. If flora have rights, constraints would have to be placed on how we behave with respect to their rights—the rights of trees, flowers, and the like. Such an ethic of the environment would thus commit us to a far larger view of what individuals, and possibly what groups of individuals (e.g., ecosystems), are of direct moral significance. And this is bound to make a difference in how we perceive both their and our own status in the world. So it is no idle, no unimportant question, to ask what sorts of beings can have rights and, in particular, whether inanimate beings can have them.

To offer a reasoned answer to this question obviously presupposes that we have worked out and defended a basis for deciding who or what can have rights—some criterion of right possession. This is no easy task, certainly, nor is it one to be accomplished of an essay's writing. My more modest objective is to approach this question by reflecting on the position of a leading thinker—quite possibly *the* leading thinker—on the nature of rights and to indicate what I take to be the implications of his position regarding the question, What sorts of beings can have rights?, especially as these implications bear on the nature and possibility of developing an environmental ethic that includes a principle that bids us to respect the rights of inanimate natural objects. The thinker I have in mind is Joel Feinberg, and the particular work of Feinberg's I propose to examine is his influential essay, "On the Rights of Animals and Unborn Generations."[2]

In this essay Feinberg makes use of several general claims involving the idea of "interests" in his effort to illuminate some of the dark corners of our thinking about rights—for example, "Can animals have rights?" "Can plants?" "Can unborn generations?" Here are two of the things Feinberg says:

> (1) The sorts of beings who *can* have rights are precisely those who have (or can have) interests (p. 51).
>
> (2) What is incapable of having interests is incapable of having rights (p. 57).

Feinberg refers to the principle expressed in (1) and implied by (2) as "the interest principle."[3] His view is that a logically necessary and sufficient condition for a being's possibly possessing rights is that it meet this principle. I have more to say about the interest principle in what follows. First, though, we need to realize that there is another principle concerning the sorts of beings that can possess rights which is implied by other things Feinberg says but to which he gives no name. This can be made clear by considering these additional claims:

> (3) A right holder must be capable of being a beneficiary in his own person and a person without interests is a being that is incapable of being harmed or benefited, having no good or "sake" of its own (p. 51).
>
> (4) Without interests, he (the catatonic schizophrenic or the human "vegetable") cannot be benefited; without the capacity to be a beneficiary, he can have no rights (p. 61).
>
> (5) Without interests a creature can have no "good" of its own, the achievement of which can be its due (p. 50).

These latter claims of Feinberg's differ from the earlier ones in that they involve not only the ideas of "rights" and "interests" but also the ideas of "benefit" and "a good of his/its own." It seems reasonable to assume, therefore, that Feinberg thinks there are important connections between the members of this family of ideas. Here I trace two of the implied connections.

First there is an implied connection between (*a*) a being's capacity to be a beneficiary in his own person and (*b*) that being's possibly having a good of his own. This becomes clear if we look carefully at what (3) says. What it says is that a being without interests cannot be a beneficiary in his own person. But if we ask *why* this is so, the implied answer is that, lacking interests, he can have no good of his own. The most natural reading of (3), in other words, is that a being without interests cannot himself be benefited or harmed—cannot be the sort of being *whose good* can be positively or negatively affected—because such a being can have no good of his own to begin with. Thus, (3) yields the view that a being who can have no good of his own cannot himself be a beneficiary, which implies that the only sorts of beings who can be beneficiaries in their own person are those who can have a good of their own.

A second thing that is implied concerns (*c*) those beings who can have a good of their own and (*d*) those beings who can possess rights. Claim (3) tells us that a right holder must be capable of being a beneficiary in his own person. We have just seen, however, that the only sorts of beings who can be beneficiaries in their own persons are those beings who can have a good of their own. It follows, therefore, that the only sorts of beings who can have rights are those beings who can have a good of their own. Hereafter I shall refer to this latter proposition about the sorts of beings who can possess rights as "the goodness principle."

In what follows I examine both of Feinberg's principles. First I explain why both depend on an understanding of interests that Feinberg has failed to illuminate to a satisfactory extent. As such, I argue that it would be premature for anyone to accept either the interest principle or the goodness principle, as Feinberg understands them, even if they were otherwise free of difficulties. But, second, I argue that they are not free of other difficulties and that, in particular, they lead to inconsistent results concerning what beings can and what beings cannot possess rights. This I show by arguing, contrary to Feinberg's judgments, that mere things and plants can meet his goodness principle though they cannot meet the interest principle.

Fundamental to both of Feinberg's principles is the idea of interests. Even in the case of the goodness principle, as (5) (above) makes plain, the basis Feinberg uses for determining which beings can and which cannot have a good of their own is the presence or absence of interests. A natural place to begin our assessment of Feinberg's position, therefore, is by asking how he understands this idea. Here we encounter an important ambiguity, one that we shall have occasion to remark upon again. For when we speak of a being (*A*) as "having an interest" in something (*x*), we may mean either (*a*) that *x* is in *A*'s interests, that *x* is conducive to *A*'s good, or (*b*) that *A* is interested in *x*, that, for example, *A* likes or desires or is aiming at *x*. Suppose we refer to these two senses of "*A* has an interest in *x*" as interest₁ and interest₂ respectively. And let us note that the two senses really are logically distinct: A being can be interested in something that is not in his interests, and something may be in a being's interest though he is not interested in it. Then we can ask, which sense of "having an interest" Feinberg has in mind, when, as in the quotes given above, he speaks of beings as "having" or of "being without interests." The answer here is that it is interest₂ that Feinberg has in mind. That this is correct is shown when he turns to the task of saying what is involved in the idea of "an interest." It is "an interest" in the sense of interest₂ that he discusses. What he says is this (p. 52):

> An interest, however the concept is finally to be analyzed, presupposes at least rudimentary cognitive equipment. Interests are compounded out of *desires* and *aims*, both of which presuppose something like belief, or cognitive awareness. A desiring creature may want *x* because he seeks anything that is ϕ , and *x* appears to be ϕ to him; or he may be seeking *Y*, and he believes, or expects, or hopes that *x* will be a means to *Y*. If he desires *x* in order to get *Y*, this implies that he believes that *x* will bring *Y* about, or at least that he has some sort of brute expectation that is a primitive correlate of belief.

This is a difficult passage to interpret. In particular, it is unclear how the idea of belief is to be understood. It is not clear whether Feinberg thinks (*a*) that a being merely has to have the capacity to form a belief of one kind or another (and, thus, of no particular kind) if he is to have aims and desires, and, with these, interests, or (*b*) that a being must be able to form beliefs of a particular kind if he is to have interests. Feinberg's examples suggest the latter. For notice, first, that the beliefs of the desiring creature he mentions are not just beliefs about this or that; they are beliefs about what the desiring creature aims at or desires. And notice, second, that these beliefs are not just beliefs about these things; they are beliefs that bear on what the creature will or ought to do if he is to satisfy his desires or to achieve his aims. So, if Feinberg's examples are to be taken as a guide, it would seem to be the case that, on his view, it is not the mere capacity to have beliefs that is necessary if a being is to have desires and aims, and, with these, interests; it is the capacity to have beliefs of a requisite kind (that is, beliefs that have the aforementioned properties) that is necessary; either this, or their "primitive correlates."

But assuming, as I shall, that Feinberg does not believe what is obviously false, it follows that we should not interpret his remarks about the connection between having beliefs and having interests in this way. For we can easily conceive of beings who lack the capacity to form beliefs of the kind just characterized but who can have beliefs, desires, aims, interests, and a good of their own—for example, severely disoriented, retarded but sentient offspring of human parents, beings concerning whom it would be grotesque to say that "they cannot be benefited" or that, for example, "they do not desire anything to ease the pain of an abcessing tooth," a desire that, it bears emphasizing, they can have without being able to form beliefs of the type, "If I want x, then I must do Y" or "Since I want x, and Y appears to be x, I must (ought to) get Y." So, it is doubtful that Feinberg should be interpreted as being committed to a view that would imply that such beings cannot have desires, and the like. Even so, however, this only helps us see what it is likely that Feinberg does not believe about the connection between having beliefs and having interests; it does not contribute to our understanding of what he does believe on this important matter. Certainly it would seem to be the case that he must believe that it is more than the mere capacity to form beliefs that must be present if a being is to have desires or aims and, with these, interests. It would seem that the beliefs must be *connected* with (to) the desires, in some way, that, to take an extreme case, A's capacity to form the belief "Grannie knits afghans" is not a sufficient basis for supposing that A can have the desire to swim the English Channel. But the problem remains how to explain what this connection is, and to explain it in such a way that we do not exclude some beings who plainly can desire things— for example, the offspring of humans referred to above—from having the desires they have. All this and more, in short, remains to be done by one who, like Feinberg, would maintain, what may well be true, that beliefs are necessary for desires, aims, interests, and so on. And this is to say that, since Feinberg has not done this on this occasion—and Feinberg himself is aware that his analysis is incomplete; my remarks are intended to show that it is—he has failed to make it clear what acceptance of the interest and the goodness principles would commit us to. As such, it would be rash to accept either, as he understands them.

But suppose we grant Feinberg his view that the having of beliefs is necessary for the having of interests, in the interest$_2$ sense of interests; the sense in which to say "*A* has an interest in *x*" means "*A* is interested in *x*." Then we can turn our attention to his arguments against the possibility that plants and mere things can have rights, arguments that we may reconstruct in the following way, making use of the interest principle (IP) first and then the goodness principle (GP) (pp. 51–55).

The Interest Principle (IP) Argument

1. The only beings who can have rights are those who are (or can be) interested in things.
2. The only beings who are (or can be) interested in things are those who can have beliefs.
3. The only beings who can have beliefs are those who have some form of cognitive awareness.
4. Plants and mere things do not have any form of cognitive awareness.
5. Therefore, plants and mere things cannot have beliefs.
6. Therefore, plants and mere things are not (and cannot be) interested in things.
7. Therefore, plants and mere things cannot have rights.

The Goodness Principle (GP) Argument

1. The only beings who can have rights are those who can have a good of their own.
2. The only beings who can have a good of their own are those who are or can be interested in things.
3. The only beings who are or can be interested in things are those who can have beliefs.
4. The only beings who can have beliefs are those who have some form of cognitive awareness.
5. Plants and mere things do not have any form of cognitive awareness.
6. Therefore, plants and mere things cannot have beliefs.
7. Therefore, plants and mere things cannot be interested in things.

8. Therefore, plants and mere things cannot have a good of their own.

9. Therefore, plants and mere things cannot have rights.

Both these arguments appear to be formally valid, so to challenge Feinberg, if we ignore the problems he has yet to address concerning the matter of belief, we must come at him from outside the scope of formal logic. I begin here by addressing myself to the GP argument and, in particular, to the second step in this argument.

The first point to notice is that the "can" in "the only beings who *can* have a good of their own" should be understood as the "can" of logical possibility, that, in other words, step 2 in the GP argument implies that it is logically impossible for a being to have a good of its own if it lacks the capacity "to be" interested in things. This is the interpretation that is required since, throughout his essay, Feinberg is interested in what sorts of beings can have rights in this same sense of "can." When he says that plants and mere things cannot possess rights, he means that it is logically impossible for them to do so, that rights cannot be meaningfully predicated of them. Thus, if Feinberg's beliefs about what sorts of beings can have a good of their own are to support his conclusions about what sorts of beings can have rights, the former, like the latter, must be understood in terms of logical possibility and impossibility.

Second, the question must arise, "How are we to understand Feinberg's idea of 'a good of his/its own?' " Unfortunately, this is an idea about which Feinberg has little to say on this occasion but the contrast he implies in this essay[4] is that between those beings, on the one hand, who can have a good independently of the interests other beings happen to take in them, and those beings, on the other hand, whose goodness depends, as he puts it (p. 50), "entirely on their being the objects of other beings' interests." Beings who can have a good of the former kind, what I call an "inherent good," can have a good of their own; those beings who can have a good only if and so long as other beings take an interest in them cannot have an inherent good of their own. Humans and (some) animals are given as examples of beings who can have an inherent good; "mere things," such as buildings and plants are said by Feinberg not to have a good of their own; these latter are not, in Feinberg's words, "the loci of value in their own right" (ibid.). Thus, given that the "can" in step 2 of the GP argument is the "can" of logical possibility; and given Feinberg's conception of what sorts of beings can have a good of their own; his position, as set forth in the step in question, is that the only sorts of beings of whom it is logically possible that they can have a good of their own are those who have interests, in the sense that they are or can be interested in things.

Against this view it might be objected that we do speak of certain things as being "good" or "bad" for, and as being "beneficial" or "harmful" to, beings that are admittedly incapable of being interested in things—for example, plants. Moreover, this way of speaking, as Feinberg acknowledges (p. 52), does suggest, contrary to his view, that such beings might have a good of their own. It will be instructive to consider how Feinberg responds to this.

Here, he thinks, we should not take "what we say" seriously. "We also say that certain kinds of paint are good or bad for the internal walls of a house, and this does not commit us to a conception of walls as beings possessed of a good or welfare of their own" (pp. 51–52). Besides,

> all are agreed that plants are not the kinds of beings that can have rights. Plants are never plausibly understood to be the direct intended beneficiaries of rules designed to "protect" them. We wish to keep redwood groves in existence for the sake of human beings who can enjoy their serene beauty, and for the sake of human beings yet unborn. Trees are not the sorts of things who have their "own sakes," despite the fact that they have biological propensities. Having no conscious wants or goals of their own, trees cannot know satisfaction or frustration, pleasure or pain. Hence there is no possibility of kind or cruel treatment of trees. In these morally crucial respects, trees differ from the higher species of animals (p. 53).

Here Feinberg is assuming the greater part of what he has to show. All that his observations about plants could show is that they could not have a certain kind of good of their own—namely, the kind of good that we tend to equate with the integrated satisfaction of our desires—that is, "happiness." What this cannot show is that plants cannot have a good of their own of some other kind. Similarly, Feinberg's remarks about "kind or cruel treatment" could at most show that plants cannot be benefited or harmed in these ways; what they could not show is that they cannot be benefited or harmed in some other way. For to benefit something, in the relevant sense of "benefit" in question, is to contribute to its good, while to harm it is to do something that is the opposite. And though being kind or cruel to some beings may be to benefit and harm them, respectively,

Feinberg has given us no reason to believe that this is the only way to benefit or harm beings, or that the only beings concerning whom it is logically possible that they be harmed or benefited are those who can be treated kindly or cruelly.

This same point can be made in a different way. Recall the two senses in which we speak of beings as "having interests." In the interest$_1$ sense to say "A has an interest in x" means "x will contribute to A's good." In the interest$_2$ sense, "A has an interest in x" means "A is interested in (desires, etc.) x." Suppose we grant, what I think is an evident (tautological) truth, that only those beings who can have a good of their own can have things that are in their interests (i.e., things that can promote *their* good). Granting this, it does not follow that the only beings who can have a good of their own are those beings who can be interested in things. That remains an open question, even if we grant that beings who are or can be interested in things can have a good of their own. For there is nothing in this line of reasoning that can show that the kind of good these beings can have is the only sort of good that is an inherent one, or that there is something logically untoward involved in the suggestion that things can be in the interests of beings who are not themselves capable of being interested in things. Feinberg, it appears, has overlooked this point, possibly because he was misled by the ambiguous character of speaking of beings as "having interests." But this is conjectural. What is not is that he has gone no way toward showing that "happiness" is the only intelligible sort of inherent good, or that it is only beings who can have an inherent good of this kind who can themselves be the beneficiaries of what is done to or for them.[5]

What remains to be shown is that we can make sense of the idea that beings who cannot be interested in things nevertheless can have a good of their own, and that we can, therefore, literally speak of what will benefit or harm them and of what is and what is not in their interests. I propose to show this by taking examples of beings who cannot literally be supposed to be capable of happiness, beings who Feinberg thinks cannot have a good of their own. The sorts of beings I have in mind are (1) "mere things" and (2) plants. My strategy is to consider arguments that might be advanced against the possibility that these sorts of beings can have a good of their own and to indicate why I think these arguments fail to show this. A strategy of this kind must suffer from a degree of incompleteness. Not all possible arguments against this possibility can be considered here. Those I do consider appear to me to be the most important.

Let us begin with the most difficult case, that of mere things—for example, cars, an example Feinberg himself uses. I take it as given that cars are used to fulfill certain human purposes and that, with respect to these purposes, some cars are better than others, a good one being, roughly speaking, one that fulfills our purposes. Our question, then, is whether we can make sense of the idea that a car can have "a good of its own." Against this possibility it might be pointed out that there would not be any cars, and, so, no good ones, if human beings had not taken an interest in having them, which shows, it might be alleged, that they cannot have a good of their own. But this same sort of argument could be applied to human beings. Suppose it is a fact that my son would not now exist if my wife and I had not had an interest in having children; surely it does not follow from this that, once in existence, he cannot have a good of his own. But if it does not follow in the case of my son, neither can it follow in the case of cars. At most, in short, this sort of thinking can tell us why something has come into being; it cannot tell us whether, once it has done so, it can or cannot have a good of its own, and if the former, in what its goodness consists.

Perhaps it will be said that, though this is true, there are other reasons for denying that cars can have a good of their own. For a time might come when we no longer have any interest in them—for example, because of the development of some alternative mode of transportation. Then, it might be alleged, cars would cease to have any value; were they to cease to be "objects of our interests," they would cease to be, or to have a good. But this line of reasoning surely is defective. Suppose that my Datsun is a better car than Randy's Volvo. And suppose the time comes when neither I nor Randy nor any other human being has an interest in cars. It would still remain true, other things being equal, that my car is a better car than Randy's. All that would have changed is the frequency with which we make use of our good (or not so good) cars and the value we attach to having one. What would not have changed is the relative goodness of the cars, *qua* cars.

Here it will be objected that, if we cease to value cars, they must cease to be good. But this seems to confuse two logically distinct ideas—namely, (*i*) the goodness of things like cars and (*ii*) whether we value them or not. Something can be good and not be valued, just as something can be valued and not be good. This is why talking about "the value of things" is a risky business, especially if it is coupled with talk of goodness as "a value." For then we are apt to suppose that, since valuing is something we do, things are good only if (and only so long as) we value them.[6] In fact, this seems to be precisely what Feinberg has done. Things like cars can have no good of their own, he thinks; rather, "their value consists entirely of their being objects of (our) interests." But the fact, if it is a fact, that the value *we* attach to cars—their value *for us*—stems from their being "objects of our interests" goes no way toward showing that *they* cannot have a good of their own.

Still, we do speak of cars as being good because they fulfill our purposes, and this shows, it might be alleged, that their goodness consists in their fulfilling our purposes, which implies that they cannot have a good of their own. But this line of reasoning gets things backward and confounds, again, the ideas of (*i*) the goodness of things and (*ii*) whether we value them or not. That a car fulfills our purposes is not what makes it a good car; it is not even one of the good-making characteristics of a good car. Rather, a car fulfills our purposes because it is a good car, and it fulfills our purposes because it possesses, to a requisite degree, those characteristics that are good making. Thus, to say that a car is a good one because it fulfills our purposes does not tell us anything about the car, which, *qua* car, makes it good; speaking in this way performs the different function of indicating that we value those cars that are good ones because these are the ones that fulfill our purposes.

Nor will it do to argue that cars cannot have a good of their own because what characteristics are good making in cars depends on what our interests are. For a car has those characteristics it has, including those that are good making, quite independently of our taking an interest in them. Cars do not *become*, say, comfortable or economical by becoming the objects of our interests. They are (or are not) comfortable or economical whether or not we have an interest in them, and whether or not we have an interest in their being comfortable or economical. Of course, manufacturers may try to make cars that are comfortable. But this is only to say that they may try to make good ones, and there is nothing inconsistent in supposing that a thing is made, on the one hand, and, on the other, that it can have a good of its own.

Perhaps, finally, it will be objected that cars are *designed* by human beings with the intention of fulfilling human purposes; only overactive metaphysical glands, it might be supposed, could lead us to the belief that they might have a good of their own. But suppose a good car was produced, not by human design, but by the random operations of a machine. Suppose it just so happened that, on one of its random runs, the machine came up with a good car. Are we supposed to say that it cannot be a good one because it was not designed by humans? Because it was not made with a particular intention? These suggestions lack credibility. If a good car was produced by purely natural means, if, say, one were to "fall into place" as a result of earthquakes, vast temperature changes and the like, that would not make it any less a good one. It would make it an unusual one.

In a word, then, although a good car is one that fulfills our purposes, there seems to be no logically compelling reason to suppose that its goodness depends *entirely* on someone's taking an interest in it. Indeed, there would appear to be no logically compelling reason to suppose that its goodness (as distinct from its value) is in *any* way dependent on this. Sense can be given to the idea that the goodness of a good car is an inherent good, one that it can have independently of our happening to value it because of the interests we take in it. If we were to transport a good car from our world to a world inhabited by beings who did not have the interests we have, it would not cease to be a good car, though it would cease to be valued as one. A good car does not lose its goodness if we lose our interest in it.

Now, whatever may be unclear about the inherent goodness of a good car—for example, whether it should be understood as a property or relation, or as natural or nonnatural—this much at least is clear: it is a kind of goodness that is distinct from well-being, when this is understood to mean "happiness." For we have no reason to believe that a good car is (in any literal sense) a happy one. But a second thing also is clear—namely, that we can make sense out of speaking of cars as having interests, not in the sense that they desire or aim at things, but in the different sense that things can be in their interests, can contribute to their good, *and* that we can make sense out of this without having to bring in the interests of *other* (e.g., human) beings. It is in my Datsun's interests (it contributes to its having the sort of good *it* can have) that I put antifreeze in its radiator in the winter, even though it is not the sort of being that can be interested in what happens to it. True, it also happens to be the case that, by doing this, I do something that is in my interests; and it is also true that my reasons for doing this are tied up with my beliefs about what is in my interests rather than with some "altruistic" concern I have for my car's "well-being"; but none of this shows that, by doing this, I am not also contributing to the goodness that my car, *qua* car, can have. Moreover, since the concept of benefiting something can be explicated in terms of doing what is in its interests, we can meaningfully speak of benefiting (or harming) things like cars. My car is the beneficiary when I put antifreeze in its radiator in the winter.

For these reasons, then, the idea that a car (and by implication, many other "mere things," for example, the interior walls of a house) can have a good of their own appears to be at least an intelligible one. And since cars are admittedly not the sorts of beings who can be interested in things, we have our first reason for denying something that Feinberg would have us affirm—namely, (step 2 of the GP argument) "The only sorts of beings who can have a good of their own are those who are (or can be) interested in things."

The case of plants is at once the same and different. It is different because plants are not (or at least are not normally) the products of human art and contrivance; in their case, therefore, we are less likely to look upon them as mere "instruments" whose possible goodness consists entirely in their serving our purposes well. For this reason it is unnecessary to rehearse most of the arguments just given in the case of cars. The cases are the same, however, in that plants, like cars, can be conceived to have a good of their own. Some plants can be better than others, *qua* the kind of plant that they are. A luxuriant gardenia, one with abundant blossoms and rich, deep green foliage is a *better gardenia* than one that is so deformed and stunted that it puts forth no blossoms at all, and this quite independently of the interests other beings happen to take in them. Now, to one who does not accept this, who thinks that the value gardenias can have "consists entirely of their being objects of other beings' interests," my reply is that, though this may be true as an explanation of why some gardenias have value for us (or are valued by us), it goes no way toward showing that gardenias cannot have a good of their own. For there is, as I have said before, a difference between valuing something and that thing's being good. People who have an interest in gardenias (etc.) would understand very well the idea that they desire to have good ones; and if we were to tell them that there are no good ones, only ones that people desire, and so on, they would think that we did not understand either flowers or the concept of goodness very well. Good gardenias are desired because they are good, they do not become good by being desired. As to what a good one is, that is an important and interesting philosophical question; or, rather, what is an important and interesting philosophical question is whether there are any general truths about the sort of inherent good gardenias and other plants can have. It is to Aristotle and Aquinas that we should look for guidance here. But that "answers to human desires, and aims," is not one of the good-making characteristics of a good gardenia (or any other plant that can have an inherent good) is clear enough. Good gardenias do answer human needs, aims, and so on, if these needs require having good gardenias. But answering human needs is not what makes a good gardenia a good one; it is not even one of the good-making characteristics of a good one; rather, that a good gardenia answers human needs sheds light on why we value those gardenias that are good ones, a very different matter.

Just as in the case of "mere things" such as cars, so also in the case of plants, therefore, sense can be given to our thinking of beings of this sort as possibly having a good of their own. To establish that they do and what, in general, the nature of this good is, that, of course, would require much more by way of argument than I have given here. But that we can at least make sense of the idea that things and plants *can* have an inherent good, that, I think, is clear enough. In the case of plants, too, therefore, we can make sense of the idea that they can have interests, not in the sense that they are interested in things, but in the different sense that things can be in their interests. Even if it is true that I have an interest in my gardenia's flourishing; and even if it is true that it is because of my interest that I water it, give it the proper nutrients, and the like; it does not follow that doing these things cannot be in the gardenia's interests (cannot contribute to *its* good), and this although gardenias are not the sorts of beings that can be interested in what happens to them. Feinberg, therefore, has not shown that in the case of so-called "protective legislation," "the law . . . cannot have as its intention the protection of their (that is, plants') interests" (p. 53), when "*A* has an interest in *x*" is understood to mean "*x* will contribute to *A*'s good." For plants *can* have interests in this (the interest$_1$) sense, even if they cannot have interests in the interest$_2$ sense of being interested in things; and it may be that the intention (or, at any rate, the result) of protective legislation is to protect the interests of plants in just the sense in which they can have them. Plants, like cars, can be the intended beneficiaries of what we do to or for them, if our intention is to do what is in their interests.

A defender of Feinberg might point out that there is one thing I have left out of my argument to this point. This is the idea of "representation." "A rightholder," Feinberg says (p. 51), "must be capable of being represented and it is impossible to represent a being that has no interests." Now, the sense of "has no interests" Feinberg has in mind is the familiar interest$_2$ sense and, as such, his claim about what sorts of beings can be represented is subject to a familiar line of criticism. Granted, trees cannot desire or long for things, from which it follows that we cannot represent their interests in the sense of representing their desires and longings. Still, sense can be given to the idea of representing the interests of trees or the Taj Mahal (Feinberg's example) in the sense of speaking in behalf of what is in their interests—what will contribute to their having the sort of good they can have. And if it be replied that this is a hopelessly muddled way of thinking, it is worth pointing out that even in the case of representing the interests of human beings it is not always their desires that are represented. When a court-appointed attorney represents the interests of a child or a mentally defective person, for example, he does not (or need not) represent what they actually desire. What he may represent is what is in their interests, what will contribute to their good, whether they happen to desire these things or not. So it will not do to argue that plants and things cannot have rights because they have no interests that can be represented. They do. And if it be alleged that, though they may have interests in one sense, they cannot have them in another, and that it is this other sense—the interest$_2$ sense—in which a being must have interests to qualify as a possible possessor of rights, then our reply should be this: That just as no reason has been given for supposing that happiness is the only (or the only relevant) sort of inherent good, so no reason has been given for supposing that desires, wishes, and the like are the only (or the only relevant) sorts of interests that can be represented.

Both in the case of plants and in the case of mere things, therefore, we have sufficient reason to believe that Feinberg is mistaken when he supposes (step 2 of the GP argument) that "The only beings who can have a good of their own are those who are or can be interested in things." And what this shows, if the preceding is sound, is that even if we were to grant Feinberg his goodness principle—the principle, once again, that "The only beings who can have rights are those who can have a good of their own"—it would not follow that neither plants nor mere things can have rights. Quite the contrary, what would follow is that they *can*, if, as I have argued, we can make sense of the idea that they can have a good of their own. If, then, we accept Feinberg's goodness principle and do not suppose, as he evidently does, that the only (or the only relevant) sort of inherent good is happiness, then we can see how the implications of the goodness principle run counter to the implications of the interest principle. Since mere things and plants are not the sorts of beings that can be interested in things, it follows, given the interest principle, that they cannot have rights. But since they can have a good of their own, it follows, given the goodness principle, that they can. And this is to say that, if my earlier arguments are sound, we cannot make use of both these principles as a basis for determining which beings can and which cannot have rights. Yielding, as they do, results that are inconsistent, we must choose to accept one or the other, but not both. Which one, if either, should be accepted is too large a question for consideration here. Here I can only register my own suspicion that it is the goodness principle, not the interest principle, that merits our acceptance, a judgment that, if it should happen to be correct, and if, further, it is true, as I have argued in the above, that plants and mere things can have a good of their own, would yield the interesting (not to say ironic) consequence that Feinberg has provided us with a principle by reference to which we can argue that mere things and plants *can* have rights. And though this much, by itself, certainly would not establish that the principles that constitute an environmental ethic *should* include one that constrains us to respect the rights of trees, or flowers, or flora generally, it would take us some way toward agreeing that they *could* include such a principle.

NOTES

1. I am especially indebted to my colleague, W. R. Carter, whose searching criticisms of two earlier drafts of this essay persuaded me to start anew. I have also profited from the suggestions of my colleagues, Robert Metzger and Alan Sparer. The first two paragraphs and the last sentence of the final paragraph have been added since the original publication of this essay.
2. This essay originally appeared in William Blackstone ed., *Philosophy and Environmental Crisis* (Athens: University of Georgia Press, 1974). Excerpts from an expanded version of this paper appear in "The Rights of Animals" in Tom Regan and Peter Singer, eds., *Animal Rights and Human Obligations* (Englewood Cliffs, N. J.: Prentice-Hall, 1976). I have expressed my debt to Feinberg elsewhere. See my "The Moral Basis of Vegetarianism" (essay 1, above). Henceforth page references are to Feinberg's original paper and occur in the body of my essay.

3. Feinberg cites H. J. McCloskey as a proponent of the interest principle. See McCloskey, "Rights," *Philosophical Quarterly* 15 (1965). For a critical examination of McCloskey's position, especially as it relates to the possibility that animals have rights, see my "McCloskey on Why Animals Cannot Have Rights," *Philosophical Quarterly* 26:104 (1976): 251–257.

4. The argument I develop against Feinberg is premised on this contrast. As it stands, my argument will not cause any difficulties for someone who espouses or implies a contrast different from the one Feinberg implies in the essay under examination. This point has been made clear to me by considering some of the things Professor Feinberg has kindly written to me. It is unclear to me, however, whether, equipped with a richer conception of goodness than the one Feinberg implies here, it is possible to avoid the dilemma I propose at the end of my essay. I am inclined to think it is not.

5. Feinberg is not the only one guilty of failing clearly to distinguish between these two senses of "interest." Consider the following passage from Peter Singer's *Animal Liberation: A New Ethics for Our Treatment of Animals* (New York: A New York Review Book, distributed by Random House, 1975; New York, Avon Books, 1977), p. 9: "The capacity for suffering and enjoyment is *a prerequisite for having interests at all*, a condition that must be satisfied before we can speak of interests in a meaningful way. It would be nonsense to say that it was not in the interests of a stone to be kicked along the road by a schoolboy. A stone does not have interests because it does not suffer. Nothing that we can do to it could possibly make any difference to its welfare. A mouse, on the other hand, does have an interest in not being kicked along the road, because it will suffer if it is." Singer, it is clear, would have us believe that it is meaningless to speak of things as being in the interests of nonsentient beings. This is false. As I explain below, it makes perfectly good sense to speak of what is in the interests of, say, a car or a gardenia. In general, nonsentient beings can have interests, in the sense that things can be in their interests, though, like stones, they cannot be interested in things. The reason we cannot make sense of the idea that something might be in a stone's interests is not that it cannot suffer; it is that we cannot form an intelligible conception of what its good could be.

6. It is commonplace in philosophy to find the pairs of expressions (*a*) "instrumental good" and "instrumental value" and (*b*) "intrinsic good" and "intrinsic value" used interchangeably, as if they were synonymous. This is false; it is both a symptom and a sustaining cause of the failure to see that there is a conceptual distinction between something's being good and its being valued. Things can be good (instrumentally or intrinsically) and not be valued.

9

The Nature and Possibility of an Environmental Ethic

"The Nature and Possibility of an Environmental Ethic" was finished before publication of "An Examination and Defense of One Argument Concerning Animal Rights" but was published some two years after the latter essay. Its place in the development of my thought may be explained in the following way. Both arguments for animal rights and the utilitarian account of the moral status of animals challenge Western culture's dominant environmental paradigm. That paradigm views the natural world *as ours*, having no value in itself, no moral significance apart from human interests. By insisting that sentience (the capacity to experience pleasure and pain), not species membership, gives an individual direct moral standing or legitimate membership in "the moral community," the utilitarians—Bentham, Mill, Singer—challenge this paradigm. But just as the utilitarian account of the moral status of animals increasingly seemed inadequate to me, for reasons given in several of the earlier essays in this volume, so was I increasingly dissatisfied with how the rest of nature must be viewed given the privileged place utilitarians accord to sentience. Why *must* we limit membership in the moral community to all and only those who are sentient? What are the arguments for accepting this qualification for membership as decisive, and how good are they? If we were not to be guilty of divorcing ourselves from one prejudice ("speciesism") only to wed ourselves to another (what we might call "sentientism"), it seemed to me, we could not avoid the task of identifying the arguments in question and subjecting them to an informed, impartial critical review. "The Nature and Possibility of an Environmental Ethic" attempts to take some modest first steps in this direction.

In contesting the privileged position of sentience, this essay continues the development of a line of reasoning briefly sketched in "An Examination and Defense of One Argument Concerning Animal Rights" and more fully articulated in "What Sorts of Beings Can Have Rights?" A genuine ethic *of* the environment, it is argued, is distinct both from a "management ethic," which views the natural order as a system of "resources" calling for "wise management," and from a "kinship ethic," which widens the scope of those meriting direct moral concern to include sentient nonhumans. The concept of inherent value, which comes to play an increasingly important role in arguments for animal rights in some of the earlier essays in this collection, is tentatively applied to inanimate nature. Arguments that challenge (1) the intelligibility and (2) the necessity of viewing nonconscious, nonsentient objects (e.g., trees, flowers, even rivers) as having a good or value of their own are considered and found wanting, and some speculative remarks are offered both about the inherent value of such objects and about the moral principles that an ethic of the environment, rooted in such value, would have us follow. Though the details of an ethic that would recognize the independent value of the flora of the natural order, not just the fauna, are far from complete certainly, the essay, if successful in its limited objectives, helps prepare the way for the development of a "deep ecology" in preference to a "shallow environmentalism," ideas that are explained and explored more fully in the final essay in this collection—"Environmental Ethics and the Ambiguity of the Native Americans' Relationship with Nature."

The arguments against a management environmental ethic may be read as a challenge to, for example, John Passmore, *Man's Responsibility for Nature* (London: Duckworth, 1974). Among those who advocate a kinship ethic, or whose views imply acceptance of an ethic of this type, are Peter Singer, *Animal Liberation* (New York: A New York Review Book, distributed by Random House, 1975; New York, Avon Books, 1977) and Joel Feinberg, "The Rights of Animals and Unborn Generations," in W. Blackstone, ed., *Philosophy and Environmental Crisis* (Athens: University of Georgia Press, 1974), pp. 43–68, and "Human Duties and Animal Rights" in R. K. Morris and M. W. Fox, eds.,

On the Fifth Day (Washington, D.C.: Acropolis Books, 1978), pp. 45−69. A nonutilitarian who has championed sentience as *the* morally decisive capacity is Andrew Linzey, *Animal Rights: A Christian Assessment of Man's Treatment of Animals* (London: SCM Press, 1976). Critics of sentience as morally decisive include John Rodman, "The Liberation of Nature?" *Inquiry* 20 (Spring 1977): 83−131, and "Paradigm Change in Political Science: An Ecological Perspective," *American Behavioral Science* 24, 1 (1980): 44−78; Kenneth Goodpaster, "On Being Morally Considerable," *Journal of Philosophy* 75 (June 1978): 308−325, and "From Egoism to Environmentalism" in K. E. Goodpaster and K. M. Sayre, eds., *Ethics and Problems of the 21st Century* (Notre Dame: University of Notre Dame Press, 1979), pp. 21−35; Richard and Val Routley, "Against the Inevitability of Human Chauvinism," ibid., pp. 36−49; R. G. Frey, "What Has Sentiency to Do With the Possession of Rights?" in D. Paterson and R. D. Ryder, eds., *Animals' Rights—A Symposium* (London: Centaur Press, 1979), pp. 106−111, and Frey, *Interests and Rights: The Case Against Animals* (Oxford: Clarendon Press, 1980), pp. 139−167. Also relevant are W. Murray Hunt, "Are *Mere Things* Morally Considerable?" *Environmental Ethics* 2, 1 (Spring 1980): 59−65, and Jay E. Kantor, "The 'Interests' of Natural Objects," *Environmental Ethics* 2, 2 (Summer 1980): 163−170. An alternative to grounding an environmental ethic in inherent value is to base it on ecological science. For an imaginative attempt in this regard see Don E. Marietta, Jr., "The Interrelationship of Ecological Science and Environmental Ethics," *Environmental Ethics* 1, 2 (1979): 105−207. I dispute Marietta's position in my "On the Connection Between Environmental Science and Environmental Ethics," *Environmental Ethics* 2, 2 (1980): 363−367, and Marietta replies in his "World Views and Moral Decisions: A Replay to Tom Regan," ibid., pp. 369−371.

Of related interest are Robin Attfield, "The Good of Trees," *Journal of Value Inquiry* 15, 1 (1981): 35−54; J. Baird Callicott, "Elements of an Environmental Ethic: Moral Considerability and the Biotic Community," *Environmental Ethics* 1, 1 (1979): 71−81; Alan R. Drengson, "Shifting Paradigms: From Technocratic to Person-Planetary," *Environmental Ethics* 2, 3 (1980): 221−240; Holmes Rolston, III, "Is There an Ecological Ethic?" *Ethics* 85, 2 (1975): 93−109; and R. Routley, "Is There a Need for a New, an Environmental Ethic?" *Proceedings of the 15th World Congress of Philosophy* (Sophia 1973) 1: 205−210. The references cited in the introductions and in the footnotes to essays 8 and 10 also are relevant.

"The Nature and Possibility of an Environmental Ethic" was originally published in *Environmental Ethics* 3, 1 (Spring 1981): 19–34.

I. Introduction

Is an environmental ethic possible? Answers to this question presuppose that we have an agreed upon understanding of the nature of an environmental ethic. Evidently we do not, and one fundamental problem for this burgeoning area of ethics is to say what such an ethic must be like. In this essay, I characterize and defend, although incompletely, a particular conception of an environmental ethic. My modest objective is to show that there is something worth thinking about completing.

II. Two Conditions of an Environmental Ethic

The conception I favor accepts the following two conditions:

1. An environmental ethic must hold that there are nonhuman beings that have moral standing.[1]

2. An environmental ethic must hold that the class of those beings that have moral standing includes but is larger than the class of conscious beings—that is, all conscious beings and some nonconscious beings must be held to have moral standing.

If both conditions are accepted, then a theory that satisfies neither of them is not a false environmental ethic; it is not an environmental ethic at all. Any theory that satisfies (1), but does not satisfy (2) might be regarded as a theory "on the way to becoming" such an ethic, in that it satisfies a necessary condition, but, since it fails to satisfy condition (2), it fails to qualify as a genuine environmental ethic. Only theories that satisfy (2), on the conception advanced here, can properly be regarded as environmental ethics, whether true, reasonable, or otherwise.

Though only a necessary condition, (1) assists us in distinguishing between (*a*) an ethic *of* the environment, and (*b*) an ethic *for the use* of the environment. Suppose we think that only the interests of human beings matter morally. Then it certainly would be possible to develop a homocentric ethic for the use of the environment. Roughly speaking, such an ethic would declare that the environment ought to be used so that the quality of human life, including possibly that of future generations, ought to be enhanced. I do not say developing such an ethic (what I shall call "a management ethic") would be simple or unimportant, but a management ethic falls short of an ethic of the environment, given the conditions stated earlier. It restricts the loci of value to the lives and interests of *human* beings, whereas an environmental ethic requires that we recognize the moral standing of nonhumans.

L. W. Sumner advances considerations that, if accepted, would lead us to an ethical theory that satisfies condition (1) and thereby takes us beyond a management ethic.[2] Sumner argues that the lives and interests of nonhuman animals, not just those of human beings, ought to be taken into account in their own right. Recognition of this fact, he states, marks "the beginning of a genuine environmental consciousness."[3] Other thinkers have advanced similar arguments.[4] Despite many differences, these thinkers share the belief that only *conscious* beings can have moral standing. I refer to theories that embody this belief as *kinship theories* because they grow out of the idea that beings resembling humans in the quite fundamental way of being conscious, and thus to this extent kin to us, have moral standing. I have more to say about kinship theories below (Section IV).

Management and kinship theories are clearly distinct. Management theories direct us, for example, to preserve wildlife if this is in the interest of human beings, including (possibly) the interest of generations yet unborn. Animals in the wild are not themselves recognized as having interests or value that ought to be taken into account. Given a kinship ethic, however, wild animals, in their own right, figure in the moral arithmetic, though precisely how we are to carry out the required computations is unclear. When, for example, there is a clash between the preservation of wild animals and the economic development of the wilderness, it is unclear how conflicting interests are to be weighed. The value of survival of how many caribou, for example, equals the disvalue of how much financial loss to oil investors in Northern Canada?

Whatever difficulties may exist for management or kinship theories in weighing conflicting claims, however, these difficulties seem to be compounded if we move beyond these theories to ones that meet condition (2), for then we are required, it appears, to deal with the possibility that human and animal interests might come into conflict with the survival or flourishing of nonconscious beings, and it is extremely doubtful whether such conflicts can *in principle* admit of rational adjudication.

I do not wish to minimize the difficulties that attend the development of an environmental ethic that is consequentialist in nature (e.g., some form of utilitarianism). There are difficulties of comparison, perhaps themselves great enough to foreclose the possibility of developing a consequentialist environmental ethic. I have more to say on this matter as we proceed. First, though, a more fundamental problem requires our attention. Is it even logically possible for a theory to meet both the conditions I have recommended for an environmental ethic? The answer clearly is no if compelling reasons can be given for limiting moral standing *only* to conscious beings. In the following section I reject three arguments that attempt to establish this restriction.

III. Arguments against the Possibility of an Environmental Ethic

The first argument to be considered I call the "interest argument":

The Interest Argument

1. The only beings that can have moral standing are those beings that can have interests.
2. The only beings that can have interests are those that have the capacity for consciousness.
3. Therefore, the only beings that can have moral standing are beings having the capacity for consciousness.

Now, this argument, as I have argued elsewhere against a similar argument,[5] has apparent plausibility because it exploits an ambiguity in the concept of something having interests. To speak of A's interests in x might mean either (a) that A is interested in (wants, desires, hopes for, cares about, etc.) x, or (b) that x is in A's interest (that x will contribute to A's good, or well-being, or welfare). Clearly *if* the only beings that can have moral standing are those that can be interested in things (have desires, wants, etc.), then only conscious beings can have moral standing. The idea of nonconscious beings having desires, or wants, at least in any literal sense, seems plainly unintelligible. If, however, we mean beings that can be benefited or harmed by what is given or denied them, then it is an open question whether the class of beings which can have moral standing is coextensive with the class of beings having the capacity for consciousness. Perhaps other beings can have a good or value that can be advanced or retarded depending on what is done to them. The interest argument provides us with no resolution of this question, and so fails to demonstrate the impossibility of an environmental ethic.

A second argument, which I shall call the "sentience argument," closely resembles the interest argument and is vulnerable to the same type of objection:[6]

The Sentience Argument

1. The only beings that can have moral standing are those that are sentient.

2. The only beings that are sentient are those that have the capacity for consciousness.

3. Therefore, the only beings that can have moral standing are those that have the capacity for consciousness.

I limit my critical remarks to step (1). How might it be supported? First, one might argue that only sentient beings have interests; that is, one might seek to support the sentience argument by invoking the interest argument, but since we have shown this latter argument is incomplete, at best, this defense of the sentience argument must bear the same diagnosis. A second defense consists in claiming that it is "meaningless"[7] to think that nonconscious beings possibly have moral standing. This is unconvincing. *If* it is meaningless, there ought to be some way of illuminating why this is so, and this illumination is not provided by the mere charge of meaninglessness itself. Such a defense has more the aura of rhetoric than of philosophy.

A third defense consists in arguing that the only beings having moral standing are those having value in their own right, *and* that only sentient beings have value of this kind. This defense, as I argue in a moment, is a token of the argument type I call the "goodness argument." Its major liability is that by itself it provides no justification for its two central claims—namely, (*a*) that only beings that can have value in their own right can have moral standing, and (*b*) that only sentient beings have value in their own right. For reasons to which I come below, I believe (*b*) is false while (*a*) is true. Meanwhile, neither is self-evident and so each stands in need of rational defense, something not provided by the sentience argument itself.

The final argument to be considered is the goodness argument:

The Goodness Argument

1. The only beings that can have moral standing are those that can have a good of their own.
2. The only beings that can have a good of their own are those capable of consciousness.
3. Therefore, the only beings that can have moral standing are those capable of consciousness.

Premise (1) of the goodness argument seems to identify a fundamental presupposition of an environmental ethic. The importance of this premise is brought out when we ask for the grounds on which we might rest the obligation to preserve any existing *x*. Fundamentally, two types of answer are possible. First, preserving *x* is necessary to bring about future good or prevent future evil for beings other than *x*; on this account *x*'s existence has instrumental value. Second, the obligation we have might be to *x* itself, independently of *x*'s instrumental value, because *x* has a good or value in its own right. Given our conditions for an environmental ethic, not all of the values recognized in nonconscious nature can be instrumental. Only if we agree with premise (1) of the goodness argument, therefore, can we have a necessary presupposition of an environmental ethic. How inherent goodness or value can be intelligibly ascribed to nonconscious beings is a difficult question, one we shall return to later (Section V). At present, we must consider the remainder of the goodness argument, since if sound, it rules out the logical possibility of nonconscious beings having a good or value of their own.

"The only beings that have a good of their own," premise (2) states, "are those capable of consciousness." What arguments can be given to support this view? I have examined suggested answers elsewhere at length.[8] What these arguments come to in the end, if I am right, is the thesis that consciousness is a logically necessary condition of having only *a certain kind* of good of one's own, happiness. Thus, though we may speak metaphorically of a "happy azalea" or a "contented broccoli," the only sorts of beings that literally can have happiness are conscious beings. There is no disputing this. What is disputable is the tacit assumption that this is the *only* kind of good or value a given *x* can have in its own right. Unless or until a compelling supporting argument is supplied, for limiting inherent goodness to happiness, the goodness argument falls short of limiting moral standing to just those beings capable of consciousness.

Four truths result if the argument of this section is sound. First, an environmental ethic must recognize that the class of beings having moral standing is larger than the class of conscious beings. Second, the basis on which an environmental ethic must pin this enlargement is the idea that nonconscious beings can have a good or value in their own right. Third, though it remains to be ascertained what this goodness or value is, it is not happiness; and fourth, efforts to show that nonconscious beings cannot have moral standing fail to show this. The conclusion we guardedly reach, then, is that the impossibility of an environmental ethic has not been shown.

IV. Arguments against the Necessity of an Environmental Ethic

We turn now to a second series of objections against an environmental ethic, all of which concede that it is *possible* that nonconscious beings may have value in themselves, and thus that it is *possible* to develop an environmental ethic, but which all deny, nonetheless, that there are good enough reasons for holding that nonconscious beings *do* have a good or value in their own right. There are, these objections hold in common, alternative ways of accounting for the moral dimensions of our relationship to the environment which are rationally preferable to postulating inherent value in it. Thus, while granting the possibility of an environmental ethic, the four views about to be considered deny its necessity.

The Corruption of Character Argument

Advocates of this argument insist that it is wrong to treat nonconscious nature in certain ways—for example, unchecked strip mining—but account for this by urging that people who engage in such activities tend to become similarly ruthless in their dealings with people. Just as Kant speculated that those who act cruelly to animals develop the habit of cruelty, and so are likely to be cruel to their fellow man,[9] so similarly those who indiscriminately destroy the natural environment will develop destructive habits that will in time wreak havoc on their neighbor. Our duties to act toward the environment in certain ways are thus explained without our having to postulate value *in* the environment.

This argument cannot be any stronger than its central empirical thesis that those who treat the environment in certain ways will be inclined to treat their fellow humans in analogous ways. I do not believe there is any hard empirical evidence at hand which supports this hypothesis. Comparing the crime rates of strip miners and accountants would probably provide much hard empirical data against it. Indeed, one cannot help wondering if the very reverse habits might not be fostered by instructing persons to do anything they want to the environment, if no person is harmed, while insisting on strict prohibitions in our dealings with persons. There would appear to be just as much (or just as little) empirical data to support this hypothesis as there is to support the hypothesis central to the corruption of character argument. On empirical grounds, the argument lacks credibility.

The Offense Against an Ideal Argument

This argument differs from the corruption of character argument in that it does not rest its case on an unsupported empirical claim. The argument alleges, quite apart from how those who treat nature end up treating other humans, that those persons who plunder the environment violate an ideal of human conduct, that ideal being not to destroy anything unthinkingly or gratuitously. This argument is open to a fatal objection. It would be an eccentric ideal that, on the one hand, enjoined those who would fulfill it to act in a certain way or to become a certain kind of person, and, on the other hand, held that there was no value in acting in those ways or in being that kind of person. For example, acting with integrity or becoming a compassionate person are intelligible human ideals, but part at least of what makes them intelligible is the implicit judgment that integrity and compassion are fitting ways to behave. But the fitting way to act in regard to *x* clearly involves a commitment to regarding *x* as having value. Honesty is an ideal, not simply because I am a good person if honest, but also because honesty is a fitting way *to act toward* beings possessed of a certain kind of value—for example, autonomy. An ideal that enjoins us not to act toward *x* in a certain way but which denies that *x* has any value is either unintelligible or pointless. Ideals, in short, involve the recognition of the value of *that toward which* one acts. If we are told that treating the environment in certain ways offends against an ideal of human conduct we are not being given a position that is an alternative to, or inconsistent with, the view that nonconscious objects have a value of their own. The fatal objection that the offense against an ideal argument encounters is that, rather than offering an alternative to the view that some nonconscious objects have inherent value, it presupposes that they do.

The Utilitarian Argument

To speak of *the* utilitarian argument is misleading. A wide variety of utilitarian arguments is possible, even including positions that hold that some nonconscious beings do have value in their own right.[10] I restrict my attention to forms of utilitarianism that deny this, focusing mainly on hedonistic utilitarianism.[11]

Abstractly and roughly, hedonistic utilitarianism holds that an action is right if no alternative action produces a better balance of pleasure over pain for all those affected. A theory of this type is "on the way to becoming" an environmental ethic if, as utilitarians since Bentham have argued, animals are sentient, and thus, given the utilitarian criteria, have moral standing. But hedonistic utilitarianism fails to satisfy the second condition of an environmental ethic and thus fails to qualify as an ethic of the environment. Its shortcomings are highlighted by asking, "Why not plastic trees? Why not lawns of astro-turf, or mountains of papier-mâché suitably coated with vinyl to withstand harsh weather?" Stories find their way almost daily into the popular press which illustrate that a plastic environment is increasingly within the reach of modern technology. If, as Martin Krieger argues, "the demand for rare environments is a learned one," then "conscious public choice can manipulate this learning so that the environments which people learn to use and want reflect environments which are likely to be available at low cost."[12] Thus, as Mark Sagoff sees it, "This is the reason that the redwoods are (given Krieger's position) replaceable by plastic trees."[13] "The advertising that created rare environments," Krieger writes, "can create plentiful (e.g., plastic) substitutes."[14]

A hedonistic utilitarianism cannot quarrel over the *source* of environmentally based pleasures, whether they arise from real stands of redwoods or plastic replicas. Provided only that the pleasures are equal in the relevant respects (e.g., of equal duration and intensity), both are of equal value. To the suggestion that pleasures rooted in real redwoods are "higher" or "nobler" than those rooted in plastic ones, the reply must be that there is a long, untold story surrounding the idea of "higher" and "lower" pleasures, that no hedonistic utilitarian has yet succeeded in telling this story, and, indeed, that it may be inconsistent for a hedonistic utilitarian to believe this. Other things being equal, if a plastic environment can give rise to pleasures equal in value to those arising out of a natural environment, we will have just as much or as little reason to preserve the latter as to manufacture the former. Moreover, if the pleasures flowing from the manufactured environment should happen to outweigh those accompanying the natural environment, we would then have greater reason to enlarge the world of plastic trees and reduce that of living ones.

It is open to utilitarians to argue in response that theirs is a theory designed for living in the world as it is, not in the world as it might be, a theory to be used in actual, not wildly hypothetical situations. While it might conceivably be the case that more pleasure would result from plastic than from real environments, this simply is not the way things are.[15] Unfortunately for this type of reply, things seem to be otherwise. As Krieger notes, "Federal environmental policy is such that the rich get richer and the poor get poorer."[16] Commenting on this, Sagoff writes that

> rich people, for example, have the background and leisure to cultivate a taste in beautiful environments and only they have the money to live in or near them. Rising property values in protected areas drive the poor out. If the pleasures of the poor were measured equally with those of the rich, then quicker than you can say "cost-benefit analysis," there would be parking lots, condominiums, and plastic trees.[17]

The empirical point is that, in the world as it actually is, there are grounds for thinking that environmental protection efforts favor the interests of a powerful elite rather than maximizing the pleasures of all, as hedonistic utilitarianism requires. Thus, if protectionist policies do not serve the cause of utility as much as would a plastic takeover, then hedonistic utilitarianism obliges us to move in the direction of a world of plastic trees, even in the world as it actually is. If a *reductio* is possible in assessing theories relating to our duties regarding the environment, hedonistic utilitarianism falls victim to this form of refutation.

The Embodiment of Cultural Values Argument

According to this argument, the natural environment, or certain parts of it, symbolize or express certain of our culture's values. In Sagoff's words, "Our rivers, forests, and wildlife . . . serve our society as paradigms of concepts we cherish," for example, freedom, integrity, power.[18] "A wild area may be powerful, majestic, free; an animal may express courage, innocence, purpose, and strength. As a nation we value these qualities: the obligation toward nature is an obligation toward them."[19] Thus, we are to preserve the environment because in doing so we preserve these natural expressions of the values of our culture.

This argument is not intended to be utilitarian. The claim is not made that the consequences of natural preservation will be better, all considered, if we preserve wilderness areas, for example, than if we allow their development for commercial purposes. Whether we ought to preserve wilderness is not to be settled by cost-benefit analysis. Rather, since our obligation is to the cultural values themselves embodied in nature, our obligation to preserve the natural environment cannot be overridden by or, for that matter, based upon calculations about the comparative value of the consequences of respecting them. The propriety of respect for cultural values is not a consequence of its being useful to respect them.

Because this argument is avowedly nonconsequentialist and not just nonutilitarian, it is reasonably clear that it must stand independently of the corruption of character argument. Moreover, though in some ways similar to the offense against an ideal argument, the two are distinct, for the offense argument involves the principle that certain ways of acting run counter to an ideal of human nature, whereas the embodiment of cultural values argument involves the principle that certain ways of acting violate an ideal of how a member of a particular culture ought to behave. Since it is conceivable that persons might act in accordance with their culture's ideals and yet violate a proposed ideal of human nature (e.g., if one's culture values militancy, while pacifism is an ideal of human nature), and vice versa, there is good reason not to conflate the embodiment and the offense arguments.

What the embodiment argument has in common with the other arguments considered here is the view that environmental objects have no value in their own right. This view is perhaps not so clear in this case because the embodiment argument carries with it "objectivist" presuppositions. Advocates of this argument do hold that the environment itself has certain objective qualities—for example, majesty, power, freedom. These *qualities* are *in* nature no less than are, say, chromosomes. But the *value* these qualities have is not something else that is *in them* independently of the dominant interest of a given culture ("our cultural heritage"). On the contrary, what qualities in nature are valuable is a consequence of what qualities are essential in one's cultural heritage. For example, if freedom is a dominant cultural value, then, since animals or rivers in the wild embody this quality, they have value and ought to be preserved. What *qualities* a natural object expresses is an objective question, but the *value* a natural object has is not something it has objectively in its own right, but only as it happens to embody those qualities valued by one's culture.

The embodiment argument provides an enormously important and potentially powerful basis for a political-legal argument on behalf of the preservation of American wilderness. It is easy to see how one may use it to argue for "what is best" in American society: freedom, integrity, independence, loyalty, and so on. It is the speculative developer rather than the conservationist who seems to be running roughshod over our nation's values. On this view, Disneyland, not Yosemite, seems un-American. Moreover, by insisting that such values as freedom and integrity cannot be trumped even if the consequences of doing so are utilitarian, advocates of the embodiment argument strike a blow that helps to counter the developer's argument that the commercial development of the wilderness will bring about better consequences, more pleasure to more people, than leaving it undeveloped. The embodiment argument replies that, though this may be true, it just so happens to be irrelevant. Given the nature of values such as freedom, integrity, and the like, it is inappropriate to destroy their expression in nature in the name of utilitarian consequences. The rhetorical force of such arguments can be great, and can be a powerful practical weapon in the war for the preservation of nature.

But the embodiment argument does not have comparable philosophical strength. Two problems in particular haunt it. First, how are we to establish what our culture's values are? Sagoff states that we are to do this by consulting our artistic (cultural) history. If we do this, however, we do not hear a chorus singing the same tune; on the contrary, there is much dissonance, some of which Sagoff himself mentions (e.g., the view of wilderness as an adversary to be tamed versus the view that it is to be cherished). Moreover, even if we were to arrive at a cultural consensus, the basis that Sagoff recommends is suspiciously elitist, reminding one of Ross's reference to "the judgment of the best people" in the determination of what is valuable.[20] Implicit in Sagoff's way of establishing what our cultural values are is an evaluative estimate of whose judgment to trust. The cards are stacked against the developer from the outset, since developers normally do not have the time or inclination to dabble in arts, history, and letters. It is not surprising, therefore, that developers take a back seat to the values of freedom and integrity. The argument is indeed potentially a powerful political weapon, but fundamental questions go begging.

A second problem is no less severe. Cultural values can be relative, both between different cultures and within the same culture at different times. Thus, even were we to concede that *our* cultural values up to now call for the preservation of nature, that would entail nothing whatever about what environmental policies ought to be pushed in *other* countries (e.g., in Kenya or India, where many species of wild animals are endangered). Nor would it guarantee even in our own country that future environmental policy should continue to be protectionist. If plastic trees are possible, our culture might evolve to prefer them over real ones, in which case the embodiment of cultural values argument would sanction replacing natural with plastic flora and fauna.

Sagoff recognizes the possibility of significant changes in a culture's dominant values. He observes that we might "change the nature of our cultural heritage"[21] and then goes on to imagine what a changed cultural heritage might be like—for example, imagining a four-lane highway painted through *Christina's World*. But I do not believe he realizes the full significance of the issues at hand. If, as he supposes, hedonistic utilitarianism falls victim to a *reductio* by allowing that a plastic environment might be just as good or better than a living one, consistency requires that we reach the same judgment *re* the embodiment of cultural values argument. That argument, too, allows that a plastic environment might be just as good or better than a natural one, *if* the dominant values of our culture were to become plasticized.

I conclude this section, therefore, not by claiming to have shown that nonconscious natural objects do have a good or value of their own, independent of human interests. I only conclude that the principal arguments that might be advanced for thinking that we can reasonably account for our duties regarding the environment short of postulating such value in nature fail to do so. Thus, neither the possibility of, nor the need for, postulating that nonconscious natural objects have a value that is independent of human interests, has been rationally undermined.

V. Inherent Goodness?

In this final section, I offer some tentative remarks about the nature of inherent goodness, emphasizing their tentativeness and incompleteness. I comment first on five different but related ideas.

1. *The presence of inherent value in a natural object is independent of any awareness, interest, or appreciation of it by any conscious being.* This does not tell us what objects are inherently good or why, only that *if* an object is inherently good its value must *inhere in (be in)* the object itself. Inherent value is not conferred upon objects in the manner of an honorary degree. Like other properties in nature, it must be discovered. Contrary to the *Tractatus*, there is value *in* the world, if natural objects are inherently valuable.

2. *The presence of inherent value in a natural object is a consequence of its possessing those other properties that it happens to possess.* This follows from (1), given the further assumption that inherent goodness is a consequential or supervenient property. By insisting that inherent goodness depends on an object's *own* properties, the point made in (1), that inherent goodness is a value possessed by the object independently of any awareness, is reemphasized. *Its* goodness depends on *its* properties.

3. *The inherent value of a natural object is an objective property of that object.* This differs from but is related to Sagoff's objectivity of the freedom and majesty of natural objects. Certain stretches of the Colorado River, for example, are free, not subjectively, but objectively. The freedom expressed by (or in) the river is an objective fact. But this goes

beyond Sagoff's position by insisting that *the value of the river's being free* also is an objective property of the river. If the river is inherently good, in the sense explained in (1), then it is a *fact about the river* that it is good inherently.

4. *The inherent value of a natural object is such that toward it the fitting attitude is one of admiring respect.* This brings out the appropriateness of regarding what is inherently valuable in a certain way and thus provides a way of connecting what is inherently valuable in the environment with an ideal of human nature. In part, the ideal in question bids us be appreciative of the values nature holds, not merely as a resource to be used in the name of human interests, but inherently. The ideal bids us, further, to regard what is inherently valuable with both admiration and respect. Admiration is fitting because not everything in nature is inherently valuable (what *is* is to be admired both because of its value *and* because of its comparative uniqueness). Respect is appropriate because this is a fitting attitude to have toward whatever has value in its own right. One must realize that its being valuable is not contingent on one's happening to value it, so that to treat it *merely* as a means to human ends is to mistreat it. Such treatment shows a lack of respect for its being something that has value independently of these ends. Thus, I fall short of the ideal if I gratuitously destroy what has inherent value, or even if I regard it merely as having value only relative to human desires. But half the story about ideals of human nature remains untold if we leave out the part about the value inherent in those things toward which we can act in the ideal way. So it is vital to insist that our having ideals is neither to deny nor diminish the further point that this ideal requires postulating inherent value in nature, independently of these ideals.

5. *The admiring respect of what is inherently valuable in nature gives rise to the preservation principle.* By the "preservation principle" I mean a principle of nondestruction, noninterference, and, generally, nonmeddling. By characterizing this in terms of a principle, moreover, I am emphasizing that preservation (letting be) be regarded as a moral imperative. Thus, if I regard wild stretches of the Colorado River as inherently valuable and regard these sections with admiring respect, I also think it wrong to destroy these sections of the river; I think one ought not to meddle in the river's affairs, as it were.

A difficult question to answer is whether the preservation principle gives us a principle of absolute or of prima facie duty. It is unclear how it can be absolute, for it appears conceivable that in some cases letting be what is at present inherently good in nature may lead to value diminution or loss in the future. For example, because of various sedimentary changes, a river that is now wild and free might in time be transformed into a small, muddy creek; thus, it might be necessary to override the preservation principle to preserve or increase what is inherently valuable in nature. Even if the preservation principle is regarded as being only prima facie, however, it is still possible to agree on at least one point with those who regard it as absolute, that is, the common rejection of the "human interests principle," which says:

> Whenever human beings can benefit more from overriding the preservation principle than if they observe it, the preservation principle ought to be overridden.

This principle *must* be rejected by anyone who accepts the preservation principle because it distorts the very conception of goodness underlying that principle. If the sort of value natural objects possess is inherent, then one fails to show a proper respect for these objects if one is willing to destroy them merely on the grounds that this would benefit human beings. Since such destruction is precisely what the human interests principle commits one to, one cannot *both* accept the preservation principle, absolute or prima facie, *and* also accept the human interests principle. The common enemies of all preservationists are those who accept the human interests principle.

This brief discussion of the preservation principle may also cast some light on the problem of making intelligible cross-species value comparisons, for example, in the case of the survival of caribou versus the economic development of wilderness. The point preservationists must keep in mind is that to ask how many caribou lives equal in value the disvalue of how much economic loss is unanswerable because it is an improper question. It confounds two incommensurable kinds of good, the inherent good of the caribou with the noninherent good of economic benefits. Indeed, because these kinds of good are incommensurable, a utilitarian or consequentialist environmental ethic, which endeavors to accommodate both kinds of goodness, is doomed to fail. The inherent value of the caribou cannot be cashed in terms of human economic benefit, and such a theory ends up providing us with no clear moral direction. For the preservationist, the proper philosophical response to those who would uproot the environment in the name of human benefit is to say that they fail to understand the very notion of something being inherently good.

Two questions that I have not endeavored to answer are: (*a*) what, if anything in general, makes something inherently good, and (*b*) how can we know, if we can, what things are inherently good? The two questions are not unrelated. If we could establish that there is something (*x*) such that, whenever any object (*y*) has *x* it is inherently good, we could then go on to try to establish how we can know that any object has *x*. Unfortunately, I now have very little to say about these questions, and what little I do have to say concerns only how not to answer them.

Two possible answers to question (*a*) merit mention. The first is that an object (*x*) is inherently good if it is good of its kind. This is a view I have assumed and argued for elsewhere,²² but it now appears to me to be completely muddled. The concept of inherent goodness cannot be reduced to the notion of something being good of its kind, for though I believe that we can conceive of the goodness any *x* has, if *x* is good of its kind, as a value it has in its own right, there is no reason to believe that we ought to have the attitude of admiring respect toward what is (merely) good of its kind. A good murderer is good-of-his-kind, but is not thereby a proper object of admiring respect, and similarly in the case of natural objects. The type of inherent goodness required by an environmental ethic is conceptually distinct from being good of its kind.²³

The second possible answer to (*a*) is that life makes something inherently good. To what extent this view is connected with Schweitzer's famous ethic of reverence for life, or with Kenneth Goodpaster's recent argument²⁴ for considering life as a necessary and sufficient condition of something being "morally considerable," I do not know, and I cannot here explore these matters in detail. But limiting the class of beings that have inherent value to the class of living beings seems to be an arbitrary decision and one that does not serve well as a basis for an environmental ethic. That it appears arbitrary is perhaps best seen by considering the case of beauty, since in nature, as in art, it is not essential to the beauty of an object to insist that something living be involved.

As for question (*b*), I have even less to say and that is negative also. My one point is that we cannot find out what is inherently good merely by finding out what those things are toward which we have admiring respect. All that this tells us is facts about the people who have this attitude. It does not tell us whether it is the fitting attitude to have. To put the point differently, we can be as mistaken in our judgment that something is inherently good as we can be in our judgment about how old or how heavy it is. Our feeling one way or another does not settle matters one way or the other.

How, then, are we to settle these matters? I wish I knew. I am not even certain that they can be settled in a rationally coherent way, and hence the tentativeness of my closing remarks. But more fundamentally, there is the earlier question about the very possibility of an environmental ethic. If I am right, the development of what can properly be called an environmental ethic requires that we postulate inherent value in nature. I have tried to say something about this variety of goodness as well as something about its role in an ethic of the environment. If my remarks have been intelligible and my arguments persuasive, then, though the project is far from complete, we at least know the direction in which we must move to make headway in environmental ethics. And that is no small advantage.

NOTES

1. By the expression *moral standing* I mean the following: x has moral standing if and only if x is a being such that we morally ought to determine how x will be affected in the course of determining whether we ought to perform a given act or adopt a given policy. In this essay the question of whether beings having moral standing have rights can be regarded as an open question, though in my view they do. See my "An Examination and Defense of One Argument Concerning Animal Rights," *Inquiry* 22 (1979): 189–219, (chap. 6, above). See also in this regard Kenneth Goodpaster, "On Being Morally Considerable," *Journal of Philosophy* 75 (1978): 308–325. Though the class of nonconscious beings includes artifacts and works of art, I normally have natural objects or collections of such objects in mind. For stylistic reasons I sometimes use the more general expression, *nonconscious objects*, and sometimes the more specific, *natural objects* or "collections of natural objects." Also for stylistic reasons I speak interchangeably of "our duties with regard to nature," "with regard to the environment," or "with regard to natural objects or collections of natural objects." I trust that no grievous conceptual errors or partisan causes will be found lodged in my taking this liberty with language.
2. L. W. Sumner, "A Matter of Life and Death," *Nous* 10 (1976): 145–171.
3. Ibid., p. 164.
4. See in particular Peter Singer, *Animal Liberation* (New York: A New York Review Book, distributed by Random House, 1975; New York: Avon

Books, 1977), and Andrew Linzey, *Animal Rights* (London: SCM Press, 1976). For a critical assessment of this position as it is related to the topic of animal rights, see my essay "Examination and Defense," chap. 6 above.

5. See my article "Feinberg on What Sorts of Beings Can Have Rights," *Southern Journal of Philosophy* 14 (1976): 485–498, (chap. 8, above), and "McCloskey on Why Animals Cannot Have Rights," *Philosophical Quarterly* 26 (1976): 251–257. For a defense of McCloskey's position, see R. G. Frey, "Interests and Animal Rights," *Philosophical Quarterly* 27 (1977): 254–259. But see also my reply to Frey, "Frey on Interests and Animal Rights," *Philosophical Quarterly* 27 (1977): 335–337. The occasion for this exchange is McCloskey's important essay, "Rights," *Philosophical Quarterly* 15 (1965): 115–127.

6. Singer in *Animal Liberation* would seem to be committed to this position. See especially pp. 8–9.

7. Singer, p. 8.

8. See my essay critical on Feinberg, n. 5. But see also my discussion of inherent goodness in Section V below.

9. Kant, "Duties to Animals and Spirits," in *Lectures on Ethics*, Louis Infield, trans.(New York: Harper and Row, 1963). Relevant portions are reprinted in Tom Regan and Peter Singer, eds., *Animal Rights and Human Obligations* (Englewood Cliffs, N. J.: Prentice-Hall, 1976), pp. 122–123.

10. See G. E. Moore, *Principia Ethica* (Cambridge: Cambridge University Press, 1903), p. 28.

11. My discussion of the utilitarian argument owes a good deal to Mark Sagoff's important essay, "On Preserving the Natural Environment," *Yale Law Journal* 84 (197): 205–267. I discuss Sagoff's own views below.

12. Martin Krieger, "What's Wrong with Plastic Trees?," *Science* 179 (1973): 446–455, quotations on pp. 451 and 453; quoted by Sagoff, "Natural Environment," p. 206.

13. Ibid., pp. 206–207.

14. Krieger, "Plastic Trees," p. 451; quoted by Sagoff, "Natural Environment," p. 207.

15. R. M. Hare, for example, defends utilitarianism in this manner. See his "Ethical Theory and Utilitarianism" in H. D. Lewis, ed., *Contemporary British Philosophy* 4 (London, 1976), pp. 113–131.

16. Martin Krieger, "Six Propositions on the Poor and Pollution," *Policy Sciences* 1 (1970): 311–324; quotation on p. 318; quoted by Sagoff, "Natural Environment," p. 210.

17. Sagoff, "Natural Environment," p. 210.

18. Ibid., p. 229.

19. Ibid., p. 245.

20. W. D. Ross, *The Right and the Good* (Oxford: Clarendon Press, 1963), p. 41.

21. Sagoff, "Natural Environment," p. 259.

22. See my essay on Feinberg, n. 5 (essay 8, above).

23. Thus, I do not retract my arguments against Feinberg as they relate to the idea of something's being good of its kind. What I do retract is the misidentification, on my part, of inherent goodness with this type of goodness. Recognizing that something is good of its kind does not call forth my admiring respect; recognizing its being inherently good does.

24. Goodpaster, "On Being Morally Considerable," pp. 308–325.

10
Environmental Ethics and the Ambiguity of the Native Americans' Relationship with Nature

Black liberation. Women's liberation. Animal liberation. By now familiar rallying cries, and rightly so. But Indian liberation? One looks in vain to find a champion of the rights of North America's Native Peoples in the learned journals of philosophy. How much this is symptomatic of the prejudices Amerinds have had to fight from the beginning of white contact, when Columbus brought "civilization" to "the New World," it is impossible to say. But *philosophy's* neglect of the Indian liberation movement, especially in a time when philosophers have helped lay the foundations of similar movements, should give our profession pause. The Indian, a frequent victim of a malignant justice, has suffered from a neglect on the part of moral philosophers which cannot be viewed as benign.

The gifted American writer Barry Holstun Lopez was the first person to acquaint me with my own prejudices about Amerinds. The occasion was a conference titled "A Celebration of Animals" held at the University of California at Santa Cruz in November 1979. I was "the philosopher" on the program; others brought their own special expertise to bear on human-animal relations. Lopez brought his "disciplined passion." Rarely have I heard truer words better spoken. Lopez's is a mind we would all do well to know.

It was Lopez who brought Calvin Martin's *The Keepers of the Game: Indian-Animal Relationships and the Fur Trade* (Berkeley: University of California Press, 1978) to my attention, and it was Martin's book in turn which first made me aware of the wildly conflicting claims made on behalf of Native Americans in debates in environmental ethics. On the one hand there are those who are only too willing to call upon these peoples as witnesses for the propriety of a "shallow environmentalism" (the view, roughly speaking, that the things of nature have no value apart from the interests humans happen to have in them); on the other hand, we find advocates of a "deep ecology" (the view, roughly speaking, that nature holds values of its own, in its own right) happy to subpoena their interpretation of the Native American life way as evidence to support the claims of a deep ecology. Which view of the Amerind's relationship with the natural order ought we to accept? And how shall we decide this? These are the central questions explored in this, the final essay in this collection.

Native Americans engaged in practices that were conservationist in result. Both positions—both (1) "the Amerinds as shallow environmentalists" and (2) "the Amerinds as deep ecologists"—can cite these practices as evidence for their respective view. Both, however, must also attempt to explain why Amerinds engaged in practices that were decidedly not conservationist, a tendency that finds its fullest expression in Indian involvement in the fur trade, where Native Peoples overkilled furbearing animals, not only in isolated cases, but systematically, even to the point where local populations of furbearing animals were rendered extinct. This final essay explores whether and, if so, how we can know which position, (1) or (2) above, is the most reasonable, given the Indian involvement in the fur trade. The advocates of neither position, it is argued, can mount a persuasive case for their own interpretation of that involvement or against the interpretation offered by their opponents, and we are left with having to recognize an intractable ambiguity regarding why Amerinds lived as they lived. This recognition has a small but not unimportant role to play in appreciating Indian liberation. We are still captives of that prejudice that allows the legal exploitation of Amerinds if we permit ourselves to exploit them for intellectual reasons. Both the advocates of a deep ecology and of a shallow environmentalism give evidence of this prejudice whenever they appeal to the life way of these peoples as evidence for their respective positions. Respect for the liberation movement of North America's original inhabitants obliges us to cease using Amerinds as evidence for our own favored view of the natural order and our place in it. Those who, as myself, are attracted to a deep ecology will have to work that position out on our own. In addition to the works cited in the introductions and footnotes for essays 8 and 9 and in this essay's footnotes, the following are of particular relevance. Eugene C. Hargrove, "Anglo-American Land Use Attitudes," *Environmental Ethics* 2, 2 (1980): 121—148; Barry Holstun Lopez, ed., "The American Indian Mind," *Quest* (September—October 1978): 1—16; Thomas W. Overholt, "American Indians as 'Natural Ecologists'," *American Indian Journal* 5, 3 (1979): 9—16; George Sessions, "Shallow and Deep Ecology: A Review of the Philosophical Literature," in J. Donald Hughes and Robert Schultz, eds., *Ecological Consciousness* (Washington D.C.: University Press of America, 1981) and "Spinoza and Jeffers on Man in Nature," *Inquiry* 20, 4 (1977): 481—528; and Christopher Vecsey, "American Indian Environmental Religions" in Christopher Vecsey and Robert Venables, eds., *American Indian Environments* (Syracuse: Syracuse University Press, 1981). Two works of fiction by Barry Lopez are certain to be of interest to those concerned about environmental questions. See his *Desert Notes: Reflections in the Eye of a Raven* (Kansas City: Sheed, Andrews, and McMeel, 1976) and *River Notes: The Dance of Herons* (Kansas City: Sheed, Andrews and McMeel, 1979).

"Environmental Ethics and the Ambiguity of the Native Americans' Relationship with Nature" was presented at Moorhead State University in March 1981 as part of a series of lectures I delivered as a Visiting Scholar. It has not been previously published.

Introduction

The title of this essay is misleading. There was no single "Native American relationship with nature," any more than there was a single group of Native Americans. The plurality and diversity of Native American cultures evidently are hard lessons to learn, but their truth is incontrovertible. Michael Dorris says it well, when he writes[1] that

> the original inhabitants of the Americas were a diverse, heterogeneous group of people. They arrived not as a single wing of migration, but in small groups chronologically separated from each other by as much as twelve thousand years. They spoke not a single language but rather their languages derived from well over ten language families, each in magnitude, distinctiveness, and complexity on a par with Indo-European. As a group their cultures shared no common denominator; the society developed by the Native People in California had no more, and probably less, in common with the groups in Michigan than it did with a Polynesia or Spain. There were, in the Americas, as many ethnic groups as there were languages, and the Americas were linguistically among the most diverse areas in the world. In the territory north of the Rio Grande alone at least four hundred separate, distinct, and mutually unintelligible languages were spoken, and at least as many separate societies flourished.

So, no, we have no reason to suppose, and more than ample reason to deny, that Native Americans had a univocal understanding of anything, including nature.

And yet there are discernible tendencies, hints of widely shared vision, common practices amid the sheen of diversity. How tribal wars were fought, why, and to what end, here we find recurrent themes: characteristically, they were fought for "personal reasons," such as to avenge one's honor, and were halted when the limited objective was achieved, this side of "total victory." Or, again, the place and role of the shaman or medicine man in pre-Columbian Indian cultures were palpably similar, and the notion that, though land might be used, it could be no more "owned" than could the air we breathe or the sky over our heads, here, again, we find general agreement. Without wishing either to deny or to diminish the importance of the rich variety of Indian cultures, therefore, it appears permissible in some cases to take note of their similarities. The central objective of this essay is to inquire whether we are in a position to say that the Native Peoples of the Americas shared a particular relationship with nature.

This enterprise—to understand how Amerinds understood nature and related to it—has received increasing attention from philosophers, especially those working in the area of environmental ethics. This essay, therefore, is not simply a project in the history of ideas or comparative anthropology, though elements of both are involved; more than this, understanding the Native American relationship with nature bears on our reaching an informed assessment about how this relationship ought to figure in arguments in environmental ethics. Some writers in this field have identified two main currents of thought, a "shallow environmentalism" and a "deep ecology," labels initially introduced by those who favor the latter view, which accounts for the pejorative element in the name given to the former—a shallow environmentalism must be a shallow way of thinking about the environment! Despite the pejorative aspect of that label, and the laudatory tone of "deep ecology," I use the two labels, my intention being to use them in a neutral way.

How might these two currents of thought be characterized? Bill Devall states[2] that shallow environmentalism "is simply enlightened self-interest based on utilitarian principles of 'the greatest amount of material goods for the greatest number of privileged *Homo sapiens*' "—privileged because, in Devall's words, shallow environmentalism "rationalizes and legitimizes the continued takeover and domination of Planet Earth by one species, *Homo sapiens.*" Nature is viewed as providing humans with "resources," and the moral burden we must shoulder is to "manage" these resources wisely, for the collective welfare of present and future generations of human beings. At its core, Devall writes, "shallow environmentalism is anthropocentric. 'Technique' for management, whether 'wilderness management' or 'wildlife management' or 'management of our natural resources' is all in the name of efficiency. . . . The problem, for shallow environmentalism, is not a metaphysical problem, not a problem of articulating a new spiritual-ethical relationship with nature, not a problem of inter-relatedness, but a problem of inter-dependence of men with men and men with nature."

There is much that is unclear here, but one claim seems just false. Shallow environmentalism, as Devall himself ends up recognizing,[3] is not limited to championing only one kind of value, what Devall, in the passage just quoted, refers to as "material goods." It is perfectly consistent for one who advances the view under discussion to recognize other values in nature—the aesthetic pleasures or the spiritual uplift nature can provide, for example. But while taking note of Devall's exaggeration in this regard, and allowing that some parts of his characterization are somewhat vague, the central ideas are reasonably clear. These involve (1) a central belief; (2) a norm regarding permissible action; and (3) a specification of appropriate attitudes and motivations. These ideas can be roughly summarized as follows.

Shallow Environmentalism

Central Belief: Nature exists for *Homo sapiens* and has no value in its own right (that is, apart from serving human interests).

Norm Regarding Permissible Action: Nature may be used or treated in any way so long as it is used to enhance the quality of human life.

Appropriate Motives and Attitudes. We owe no special respect or reverence to nature, nor are we called upon to "love" it; rather, we are to relate to nature as a system of resources and are to be motivated to manage these resources wisely for the collective human good, for both present and future generations.

Deep ecologists dispute and, indeed, deny the various elements that comprise shallow environmentalism. Nature is not simply a system of "resources" calling for "wise management" by means of enlightened "technique." Nature does not exist *for us*. We are ourselves a part of the natural order, not its sovereign. Aldo Leopold states the basic thrust of deep ecology when he writes[4] that "man is only a member of the biotic team . . . only [a] fellow voyageur with other creatures in the odyssey of evolution," an insight that, once grasped, Leopold thinks, "changes the role of *Homo sapiens* from conqueror of the land community to plain member and citizen of it. It implies respect for his fellow-members, and also respect for the community as such." "We abuse land," Leopold writes in *A Sand County Almanac*,[5] "because we regard it as a commodity belonging to us. When we see land as a community to which we belong, we may begin to use it with love and respect." Nonanthropocentric in its orientation, deep ecology calls for a deepening appreciation and respect for the natural order, "a new spiritual-ethical relationship with nature," one that, in Ervin Laszlo's words, involves

> a reverence for our own kind when our vision is wide enough to see ourselves not only in our children, family, and compatriots, and not only

in all human beings and all living things, but in all self-maintaining and self-evolving organizations brought forth on this good earth and, if not perturbed by man, existing here in complex but supremely balanced hierarchical interdependencies.[6]

By way of general contrast with shallow environmentalism, then, the principal tenets of deep ecology might be summarized as follows:

Deep Ecology

Central Belief: Nature, including its varied and complex ecological systems, has value in its own right, apart from human interests.

Norm Regarding Permissible Action: We are not to treat nature as though it had value only as a means to human ends, but are always to treat it in ways that display recognition of, and respect for, its inherent value.

Appropriate Motives and Attitudes: We are to interact with nature in a spirit of reverence and love, regarding the natural order with that respect appropriate to its independent value.

Now, not all the concepts that figure in the foregoing characterizations of shallow environmentalism and deep ecology are as clear as one might wish; but both characterizations seem to capture, if not all, at least three of the major themes of these respective views, and though one might wish for greater precision in their statement on some future occasion, it is to be hoped that these less precise formulations will serve our purposes well on the present one.[7]

Even in their present form, it is clear that these views might call for the same action in a given case. Thus, for example, both shallow and deep arguments can be, and have been, advanced for wilderness preservation. But the *kind* of argument given in each case will be markedly different, the shallow environmentalist argument resting ultimately on the claim that such preservation will enhance the quality of human life (e.g., by affording people an opportunity for "the wilderness experience"), while the deep ecological argument, while possibly conceding what the shallow argument contends, will go further and claim that such preservation is required if we are to preserve the value wilderness has in its own right. Thus, where the shallow environmentalist will argue for preservation on the grounds that we have a duty to our fellow human beings to preserve wilderness *for them*, the deep ecologist will argue that this is a duty we have *to wilderness itself.* That advocates of the two views can sometimes call for the same act, including, for example, the same legislation, clearly does not mean that they must also agree about the appropriate grounds.

It should also be clear that advocates of the two views need not always agree on particular objectives. For a shallow environmentalist, all that is required to justify human intervention in nature is that such intervention will enhance the quality of human life, and though establishing this in any given case may be far from easy, and while recognizing that this difficulty is compounded because what will enhance the quality of the lives of some may not enhance the quality of the lives of others, it remains true that these difficulties are in principle resolvable if *only* human interests are taken into account. Not so for deep ecology: The propriety of human intervention in nature must not be assessed merely in terms of human interests. There are also the values of nature itself that must be taken into account and weighed, though how, exactly, this "weighing" is to be carried out, or whether one ought to think of natural values as "weighable" to begin with, are murky issues indeed.[8] Internal difficulties to one side, there is the clear possibility that a given intervention in nature (e.g., the construction of a dam) might arguably serve human interests, and so be justified on shallow environmentalist principles, and yet might be destructive of the affected natural surroundings and their inherent value, and so not be justified, given deep ecological principles. Clearly therefore, the debate between advocates of the shallow and the deep can spill over from theory into practice, so that there are practical, not merely intellectual, reasons for assessing their respective merits. Of course, one might argue that anything that truly offends deep ecological principles must be contrary to human interests, and vice versa, there being a "preestablished harmony" between what serves to enhance human life and what enhances the values nature has on its own. If this were true, then the apparent conflicts between the shallow and the deep views, with regard to what ought to be done vis-à-vis human intervention in nature, would be apparent only, not real. But though the possibility of a preestablished harmony cannot be dismissed a priori, this view has failed to attract the numbers of adherents, let alone the number of influential adherents, that both shallow environmentalism and deep ecology can count among their members. It is not for no reason, therefore, that we may assume that the two views, as presently understood by their leading advocates, may lead to opposite conclusions in any given case.

It is against the backdrop of these debates, both theoretical and practical, being waged by advocates of shallow environmentalism and deep ecology that understanding the relationship Native Americans had with nature takes on a correspondingly important theoretical and practical significance. For what we find is this. In the deep ecological camp there are those who argue that the life way of this continent's original inhabitants shows that they accepted a deep ecology. Indeed, some of these thinkers maintain that recognizing this fact not only establishes that it is possible to engage in a way of life rooted in deep ecology—a deep ecology is not, that is, merely a *theoretical* possibility—but, what is more, that we may, or, indeed, we must look to and imitate the Native American relationship with nature if we are to find our way out of our present environmental crisis. Just this last view is set forth by the contemporary Indian activist, Vine Deloria, Jr., a Standing Rock Sioux, when he writes[9] that

> the Indian lived with the land . . . [H]e realized that it was more than a useful tool for exploitation. . . . The only answer [to the white man's environmental problems] will be to adopt Indian ways . . . a total Indian way of life. That is really what [the white man] had to do when he came to this land. It is what he will have to do before he leaves it once again.

Less extreme, but still in the same vein, is this call from the pen of Stewart L. Udall.[10]

> It is ironical that today the conservation movement is turning back to ancient Indian land ideas, to the Indian understanding that we are not outside of nature, but of it. From this wisdom we can learn how to conserve some of the best parts of our continent.
> In recent decades we have slowly come back to some of the truths that the Indians knew from the beginning: that men need to learn from nature, to keep an ear to the earth, and to replenish their spirits in frequent contacts with animals and wild land. And most important of all, we are recovering a sense of reverence for the land.

Others, however, both within and outside the shallow environmentalism camp, stiffly deny the attribution of a deep ecology to Amerinds. These dissenters argue that only a robust romanticism would allow one to picture these peoples as ecological noble savages, that the facts, once objectively set forth and properly understood, show that, deep down, Native Americans were shallow environmentalists after all, that it is partisan wish-fulfillment, not dispassionate scholarship, that would lead one to suppose that these peoples had so intimate a relationship with nature, in W. H. Hutchinson's words,[11] "as to make the Sierra Club seem an association of strip miners by comparison." On the contrary, these thinkers contend, the Amerinds' relationship with nature was thoroughly pragmatic or utilitarian, in the narrow sense that it is human interest, not love of, or respect or reverence for, "the land" that explains the why and wherefore of their intervention in the natural order.

It is this debate—the controversy between those who would credit Native Americans with a life way rooted in a deep ecology and those who judge their life way to be rooted in a shallow environmentalism—it is this debate that serves as the occasion for this essay. My very limited objectives include sketching the competing arguments and critically assessing their respective merits. I begin by sketching certain features of the Native American relationship with nature which are common ground between those who wish to attribute either view, a deep ecology or a shallow environmentalism, to them. Paramount among these features are those that relate to conservation practices among these peoples. It is to a summary of some of these practices that we must now direct our attention.

Conservation Practices Among Native Americans

There is now little question that Native Americans, at least prior to white contact, were generally inclined to engage in practices that were conservationist in result. Father Latour in Willa Cather's *Death Comes for the Archbishop* takes note of this inclination and, in the following passage, contrasts it with his perception of the white man's relationship with nature.

> When they left the rock or tree or sand dune that had sheltered them for the night, the Navajo was careful to obliterate every trace of their temporary occupation. He buried the embers of the fire and the remnants of the food, unpiled any stones he had piled together, filled up the holes he had scooped in the sand. . . . Father Latour judged that, just as it was the white man's way to assert himself in any landscape, to change it, make it over a little (at least to leave some mark of memorial of his sojourn), it was the Indian's

way to pass through a country without disturbing anything; to pass and leave no trace, like fish through the water, or birds through the air.

It was the Indian manner to vanish into the landscape, not to stand out against it. The Hopi villages that were set upon mesas were made to look like the rock on which they sat. . . . The Navajo hogans, among the sand and willows, were made of sand and willows. . . .

In the working of silver or drilling of turquoise the Indians had exhaustless patience; upon their blankets and belts and ceremonial robes they lavished their skill and pains. But their conception of decoration did not extend to the landscape. They seemed to have none of the European's desire to "master" nature, to arrange and re-create. They spent their ingenuity in the other direction; in accommodating themselves to the scene in which they found themselves. . . . When they hunted, it was with the same discretion; an Indian hunt was never a slaughter. They ravaged neither the rivers nor the forest, and if they irrigated, they took as little water as would serve their needs. The land and all that it bore they treated with consideration; not attempting to improve it, they never desecrated it.[12]

A similar contrast is drawn in the Wintu eschatology, as expressed by Kate Luckie and quoted by Cora Du Bois.

People talk a lot about the world ending, but this world will stay as long as Indians live. When the Indians all die, then God will let the water come down from the north. Everyone will drown. That is because the white people never cared for the land or deer or bear. When we Indians kill meat, we eat it all up. When we dig roots, we make little holes. When we build houses, we make little holes. When we burn grass for grasshopper, we don't ruin things. We shake down acorn and pine nuts. We don't chop down the trees. We only use dead wood. But the white people plow up the land, pull up the trees, kill everything. . . . The Indians never hurt anything but the white people destroy all. They blast rock and scatter them on the earth. . . . When the Indians use rocks, they take little round ones for their cooking. The white people dig deep tunnels. They make roads. They dig as much as they wish. They don't care how much the ground cries out. . . . That is why God will upset the world—because it is sore all over. Everywhere the white man has touched it, it is sore. It looks sick. . . . But eventually the water will come.[13]

Most noteworthy, perhaps, among the diverse conservationist practices of pre-Columbian Indians is the case of hunting, a practice that will prove to be of special significance in the argument that follows. To understand this aspect of the Amerinds' original life way we must begin by recognizing that, for the hunting-gathering tribes, hunting was not an avocation, sport, or diversion entered into by members of a leisured class, as was the case throughout Europe before and after white contact. Success in the hunt was absolutely essential to the tribe's survival. It should not be surprising, therefore, that pre-Columbian hunter-gatherers engaged in hunting practices that resulted in the conservation of wild game. For example, in the case of the Mahickan, "It was a law among them not to kill more game than was necessary for their use, none even to barter, which might have produced a temptation to waste their animals. By these regulations their game was preserved undiminished, the consumption being no greater than the natural increase."[14]

The lawlike perpetuation of conservation practices involving wild-life frequently was transgenerational, forming a central element in various aboriginal tribes' system of primogeniture. As W. C. MacLeod relates:[15]

> The beaver is the Indian's pork; the moose, his beef; the partridge, his chicken; the caribou or red deer, his mutton. All these formed the stock of his hunting ground, which would be parcelled out among his sons when the [father] died. He would say to each of his sons: "You take this part; take care of this tract; see that it always produces enough."

Thus was the future reliability of tribal or family hunting grounds not left to chance. Indeed, within these same tracts a kind of crop rotation was practiced. Caribou, for example, were allowed to be killed in one area during one season but not during the next.

To plan wisely for the future clearly requires generous knowledge of the past and present. Native Americans acquired their knowledge of animals in a variety of ways. One was a kind of sympathetic knowledge, an understanding one evidently can secure only by living among animals, an understanding that "knows the ways of animals." Barry Lopez documents well the view that contemporary Eskimos know the ways of the animals they hunt in a way that eludes the untutored perceptions of a non-Eskimo. Indeed, Lopez suggests that some *animals* acquire such knowledge of the ways of other animals, an idea that Eskimos find both intelligible and congenial. An aged Eskimo hunter, when asked who knew more about how to hunt the caribou, an Eskimo hunter or an elder wolf, is quoted by Lopez as saying, "The same. They know the same."[16]

But sympathetic knowledge to one side, there are other, more familiar ways of knowing that we find in Native American approaches to conservation. A kind of census taking, for example, is a useful way to keep track of animal populations and to gauge the impact of past and present hunting practices on the preservation of a reliable stock. Native Americans are known to have kept such censuses. In the case of the beaver, for example, as MacLeod notes,[17] "the number of occupants, old and young, to each 'cabin' of the animals was kept account of; breeders were not killed; each year only young or very old animals were slain." In this way an accurate record was kept of the number, age, and reproductive propensities of the beaver population, all with an eye to insuring that the supply was not overhunted.

Though far from complete certainly, the preceding can be taken as illustrative of conservation practices among Native Americans, a tendency that manifested itself throughout the human interaction with nature, from wild animals to the use of wood from trees. But just because, in pre-Columbian times in any event, conservation was a key element in the Amerind relationship with nature, it does not follow that this relationship was grounded in this or that particular understanding of nature—a deep ecological understanding, say. Rather, these conservation practices provide a point from which to begin the examination of the merits of attributing alternative views about their relationship with nature to these peoples. The grounds for attributing a shallow environmentalism to them concern us first.

Native Americans Viewed as Shallow Environmentalists

Some interpreters of the relationship between Native Americans and nature believe this relationship can be explained without supposing that these peoples viewed nature as having value in its own right, independent of human interests. This is true even of their conservation practices, which can be explained, it is claimed, in terms of the Indians' own interest in (*a*) wanting to survive and (*b*) wanting to minimize the labor and danger involved in the struggle for survival. It does not take much argument to secure agreement that, before white contact, conservation practices were necessary for the survival of hunting-and-gathering Amerinds. To overkill a given species, on which the tribe depended, in a given year, was to insure fewer of that species for the next year, and to continue a campaign of overkill over a period of many seasons was virtually to insure the elimination of a needed resource. There appear to be compelling grounds for maintaining that Native Americans, who "knew the ways of the animals," also knew well the effects of their hunting on the future stock of animals on which they depended, saw the connection between insuring the future availability of these animals and the tribe's survival and welfare, and, for these reasons, if for no other, took the necessary conservation steps to do what they could to husband a sustainable yield of their wild game. So, in any event, argue those who would attribute a shallow environmentalism to Native Americans.

As for (b)—minimizing the effort and danger involved in the struggle to survive—Clifford D. Presnall claims[18] that

> it is apparent that a majority of Indians usually made conservative use of animal products in order to reduce the amount of hard and often dangerous work involved in securing them. The same motivation frequently led to tribal regulation of hunting practices, such as the system of "beloved bear grounds" . . . wherein the Creeks set aside bear preserves from which all hunting was periodically excluded so that the bears would increase enough to permit easy slaughter at certain periods.

In this, and in other similar cases (e.g., the system of primogeniture mentioned earlier), the Indians, according to Presnall,[19] "were evidently seeking a reduction in the labor of trapping, and an increase in the success of their labors." If the Amerinds did not exactly want something for nothing, they at least wanted something for as little as it would cost them, both in terms of labor and risk. We do not demean the Indian—we do not write the Indian off as "lazy"—if we acknowledge the presence in them of the dual desires for ease and safety common to us all.

Now, the desires to hunt easily and safely clearly could conflict with the restraint required to conserve game for the future. That Native Americans were able to conserve as they did shows that they frequently were able to overcome the force of these desires. And yet they were not uniformly successful in tempering their natural interest in ease and safety. Presnall, for example, cites[20] cases where Indians engaged in "wasteful killing of buffalo, and to a lesser extent of antelope, deer, moose, and caribou, by driving them over precipices or into ponds." This, as well as the practice, allegedly common among prairie Indians, of rounding up wild game by the use of fire, was, according to Presnall, a clear instance of a "practice that wasted game but saved the hunters much work." The conservation record of Native Americans, in short, even in pre-Columbian times, arguably is not untarnished by instances of wasteful slaughter, a record that, though it does not show that the general tendency of Native Americans was not to engage in conservation practices, nonetheless does show, if true, that only those, to use Presnall's word, "romantics" about these people's ways would fail to see that the concern for the future did not always outweigh the strong human inclination for easy gratification of an immediate need.

Native Americans Viewed as Deep Ecologists

Those who, like Presnall, attribute a shallow environmentalism to Native Americans think that their relationship with nature can be explained independently of supposing that they viewed nature as having value of its own, and thus independently of claims about how the Indians loved, revered, and respected their natural environment. But it is just this family of concepts (love, reverence, respect) that those who attribute a deep ecology to these peoples believe they find in the Amerinds' life way. How might the case for this view be made?

MacLeod provides a helpful introduction to this view in the following passage. Writing first of the Yukaghin of Northeastern Siberia, he states[21] that

> wasteful killing of animals was taboo. They appear to have rationalized their rude conservation in spiritual terms, however. To explain why the elk disappeared from a certain region they tell a tale which explains that the spirit of the elk disapproved of a case of wasteful killing of elk. An almost identical tale is told by the Micmac Indians of an island off Nova Scotia to explain the disappearance of the moose from their particular area. After an improvident killing of moose the remaining moose, offended, left the island, never to return.

The idea that gratuitous slaughter of animals would "offend" the animals themselves and for that reason lead to a reduction of their supply was not limited to the Micmac or to the case of wild animals. Similar beliefs accompanied the use of the bark and wood of trees. Indeed, as MacLeod notes,[22] in the case of the Kwakitul Indians of Vancouver, "the taking of any bark at all from a tree must be propitiated. The bark peeler stands before the tree, uttering humble apologies and explaining the necessity of taking some bark." One does not apologize to what one regards as of no importance or for an act that one thinks cannot but be viewed as benign. Arguably there is more to the Amerinds' relationship with nature than at first meets the eye. Reflecting further on the hunt in hunting-gathering tribes of the eastern Canadian forests will be suggestive of an alternative vision.[23]

A hunt for these people has the appearance of a consecrated activity, one that required proper spiritual preparation and execution, as well as respectful use of the slaughtered quarry. Regarding preparation, considerable importance was placed on both hunt dreams and physical divination. It was widely believed that it was during dreams of an impending hunt that one's soul spirit, or Great Man, spoke. Knower of the ways of animals, the Great Man imparted all the information necessary for a successful hunt—for example, where certain animals were to be found and how many there were. To insure success, the individual hunter was obliged to listen most attentively to his Great Man and to understand his clues and promptings. Because of the superiority of the Great Man's knowledge, and because it was through the medium of dreams that he spoke, steps were taken to increase the likelihood of dreams some days prior to the hunt. For example, hunters were given sweat baths, or there was intense repetitive singing or chanting.

Rites of consultation or divination served as a check against dream interpretations. These consultations involved not the individual hunter alone, but various senior members of the tribe. Some part, usually a bone, of a deceased animal was placed in fire and, depending on the colors and markings the fire imparted to the bone, relevant information was again imparted. Members of the Montagnais-Naskapi of Quebec and Labrador, according to Frank G. Speck,[24] "generally use the caribou shoulder blade for caribou hunting divination, fish-jaw augury for fishing, and so on." Speck offers the following account of a rite of consultation.[25]

> In the rite of consultation this tablet-like bone is subjected to heat, and burnings, in the form of blackened spots, cracks and breaks, are then interpreted by the cunning and ingeniousness of the practitioner. Imagination suggests the likeness of the marks produced by the heat, to rivers, lakes, mountains, trails, camps, and various animals—the latter either single or in groups. The direction of the burnt marks and their respective locations also are significant. Persons are also believed to be represented by the spots or outlines. Abstract ideas may be represented: life, death, success, failure, plenty, famine, sickness, chicanery, time periods, warnings, encouragement; and general good or bad luck are likewise indicated by the cabalistic markings.

Thus are the bones made to "speak" by what Speck calls "the force of fire."

As important as was proper preparation for the hunt, the ceremonial aspects of the actual encounter between the hunter and his prey are even more striking. Rites of propitiation were common. For example, among the Micmacs, the hunting of bear was surrounded by elaborate ritual, the main features of which are described by Calvin Martin as follows.[26]

> The beast is typically hunted in the early spring, while still in hibernation, and preferably killed with aboriginal weapons; it is addressed, when dead or alive, with honorific titles which serve as euphemisms for its common name; a conciliatory speech is made to the animal, either before or after killing it and sometimes both, by which the hunter sincerely apologizes for the necessity of his act; and the carcass is respectfully treated, those parts not used (especially the skull) being ceremonially disposed.

Finally, significant restrictions were placed on the use that could be made of the slain animal's parts as well as who could eat what, and the like. When, for example, moose, the most preferred food of the Micmacs, was taken, it was the wife of the successful hunter who was delegated with the responsibility of determining what was to be done with each of the animal's parts. Nothing that could be used was wasted, as Martin documents in the following inventory.[27]

> Grease was boiled out of the bones and either drunk pure . . . or stored in loaves of moose-butter; leg and thigh bones were crushed and the marrow consumed; hides were converted into robes, leggings, moccasins, and tent coverings; tools, ornaments, and game pieces were fashioned from antlers, teeth, and toe bones, respectively.

Moreover, even the parts judged to be of no use to the tribe—for example, a certain bone—were not to be treated indifferently or, say, thrown to the dogs, but instead were to be disposed of ceremonially. As for the actual eating, this too was governed by strict laws. Among the Micmac, again, menstruating women were not permitted to partake of beaver, and young warriors could not eat of a bear's heart.

Thus do we find, among the Micmac and countless other Native American tribes, elaborate rituals and prohibitions associated with their interaction with nature, especially with regard to their interaction with wild game. Activities so enmeshed in ritual and ceremony, palpably so valued by those who took part in them and important to those who depended on them, would, it seems, naturally give rise to conservation practices. One does not regard an animal with the respect evident in the Micmac dealings with bear, for example, and then proceed to kill the beast indifferent to the number slain. On the contrary, one kills only what is necessary, and then selectively (e.g., not a young female) and with abject apologies.

Here, then, we have the makings of an alternative account of the Native American relationship with nature, one that differs significantly from the shallow environmentalism sketched earlier. The explanation of the Amerinds' conservation practices lies not wholly or primarily in their own desires for ease and safety, though these may be admitted to to have played some role; rather, these practices were rooted in the Native American's belief that nature (e.g., the animals in the wild) had value in its own right, apart from human interests, and that, because it did, the bounty it provided was to be treated with utmost respect, with reverence and love, both before and after human seizure. To act otherwise was to treat what had value in and of itself as if it had value only as a means to human ends.

The Problem of Overkill

Despite the impressive conservation record of Native Americans, and notwithstanding Father Latour's hopeful observation that "an Indian hunt was never a slaughter," there are known cases of needless overkill, some of which (e.g., buffalo jumps) were alluded to in the above. Considered as isolated episodes, these cases would not pose a serious problem either for those who wish to credit these peoples with a shallow environmentalism or for those who would attribute a deep ecology to them. Neither view implies that all Native Americans always complied with the norm regarding permissible action each view advances. On the shallow environmentalism view, it is perfectly possible that on some occasions some Amerinds killed beyond necessity and thus failed to observe the norm regarding wise management of resources for the collective good, just as, on the deep ecology view, some failed to show respect, or came up short in their love or reverence, and killed beyond necessity. While it would be unconscionable at this late date to denigrate all Indians by regarding them as, say, lazy or sneaky, it would be naive at best to suppose that they all always acted wisely or reverentially. Neither the ascription to them of a shallow environmentalism nor a deep ecology commits one to such naivete.

The problem of overkill, however, is far more serious than this because there are well-documented cases of extensive, systematic overkill, cases where the slaughter of animal species was unchecked and indiscriminate. On the face of it, to engage in practices that threaten the extinction of local wildlife populations, and to engage in them not in isolated episodes but as an ongoing part of a tribe's emerging life way, seem to run directly counter to the wise management of natural resources prescribed by a shallow environmentalism and to the love and reverence for wild game laid down by a deep ecology. And yet Native Americans did just this, and not in small numbers. As Martin notes,[28] "to put it bluntly, the Indian was everywhere, except in the Rocky Mountain trade, the principal agent in the overkilling of furbearers," an involvement that sometimes led to the total eradication of local populations. "By 1635, for example," Martin points out, "the Huron in the Lake Simcoe area had reduced their stock of beaver to the point where Father Paul Le Jeune, the Jesuit, could flatly declare that they had none."[29] Nor were these peoples reluctant participants in the fur trade. "The record seems emphatic on this issue," Martin observes: "the post-contact Indian wasted game with gusto."[30] How, then, in the face of their unbridled, even enthusiastic involvement in the decimation of wildlife can we rationally view the original inhabitants of this continent as either shallow environmentalists or as deep ecologists?

The Amerinds-as-Shallow-Environmentalists Reply

Advocates of the Amerinds-as-shallow-environmentalists view would seem to have a ready reply. Since, on this view, animals are seen as having value only relative to their perceived utility with respect to human purposes, one need only show that the perceived utility of animals in Native American life changed in a way that made their abundant slaughter more useful than the more selective, conservative policy that characterized earlier, precontact practices. And history seems to provide a basis for arguing that just such a change took place. A test case, as it were, is provided by the involvement of the Native Americans of eastern Canada in the fur trade. Arguably what happened is this. Beginning in the sixteenth century, with the early contact of white explorers and trappers, Native Americans were introduced to the material goods of European Iron Age civilization. Eyewitness accounts suggest that these peoples were anything but indifferent to the astonishing goods introduced to their Stone Age culture. As Martin points out,[31]

> presented with the opportunity to exchange their pelts and skins for European trade goods, Indians, whether horticulturists or hunter-gatherers, quickly seized the opportunity to effect the transaction. . . . [One can] illustrate this with the story of Jacques Cartier's reception at Chaleur Bay [Quebec] in 1534. Cartier was literally mobbed by the local, Algonkian-speaking Indians, seemingly Micmac, who insisted that he trade with them for furs. The beleaguered captain found it necessary to fire a volley over their heads to dampen their ardor. "Clearly the strangers who controlled the thunder were heavily endowed with manito," writes Alfred Goldsworthy Bailey, "but even the displeasure of the gods could not keep the Micmac from the source of iron, for iron saved them days of drudgery and enabled them to vanquish their enemies who were as yet armed only with stone, bone, and wood implements."

Nor was the Amerind interest in trade goods confined to iron products. "The white man offered (the Native American)," W. H. Hutchinson writes,[32]

> material goods—iron and woolens and geegaws and alcohol—which he could not resist. These riches, which is what they were, gave his life an expanded dimension it had never known before. No power on earth could keep him from getting these things by raid or trade, once he had been exposed to them. To ask him to have refrained from making his material life fuller and richer is to ask him for far more than we ever have asked of ourselves.

Advocates of the Amerind-as-shallow-environmentalist-view, by alluding to considerations like those advanced in the preceding quotes, can thus seek to explain the dramatic change in Native American hunting practices, from an essentially precontact conservative-minded approach to a postcontact one of virtual plunder, without modifying that view's main tenets. Where, before, the utility of animals had been perceived to be limited to their direct use, as a food source, for clothing, and the like, the coming of the fur trade brought with it a heretofore unimagined utility in terms of what an animal's skin could buy—"iron and woolens and geegaws and alcohol." Given the Amerinds' understandable interest in enriching their own material welfare; given, further, the extraordinary European demand for furs, a demand heightened by the quirks of changing taste in fashion (the beaver hat was all the rage in Europe at the time); and given the diminished supply of fur throughout Europe itself and the inaccessibility of stock in Russia (a war was being fought); given the convergence of all these forces, Native Americans changed their hunting practices, according to the view presently under discussion, without changing their basic perception of, and relationship with, nature. In their role in the fur trade, animals were, like the rest of nature, perceived as having value only in terms of their perceived utility in promoting human purposes.

The Amerind-as-Deep Ecologist Reply

The task of explaining the Native American's involvement in the overkilling of wild animals would seem to be considerably more difficult for those who would view them as deep ecologists. Calvin Martin puts the challenge in the starkest terms when he asks,[33] "Where is the Indian's so-called reverence for Nature in the confused mass of a bison heap or the stillness of a beaver pond?" On the face of it the Amerinds' massive overkill of wildlife seems to provide a compelling argument against regarding them as pioneer deep ecologists. Nor can the depth of this argument be diminished by replying that Native Americans were deep ecologists up to the time of white contact and only turned to the plunder of nature under European influence. For it could not be a very deep ecology that would crumble so easily, upon the first introduction of the baubles of European civilization; and it would be, or at least it would seem to be, to ask far more of modern humanity to turn our back on the treasures of contemporary technology and, with love and reverence, go "back to nature," thereby imitating precontact Native Americans, if they were not themselves able to sustain their alleged deep ecological relationship with nature in the face of "iron and woolens and geegaws and alcohol."

As difficult as this challenge is, the seeds of a possible reply are at hand, thanks largely to Martin's own ingenious interpretation of the Indian's involvement in the fur trade. The main themes of that interpretation, which places special importance on the involvement by the

Native Peoples of eastern Canada and generalizes on the alleged reasons for their involvement, are as follows.

An essential part of the cosmology of the Native Peoples of eastern Canada involved the belief that behind the natural order were personal forces that regulated both that order itself and the outcome of the Amerind interaction with that order. In the case of wildlife in particular, there were, in addition to the animals themselves, keepers of the game—hence the aptness of the title of Martin's book. These keepers of the game regulated the location and supply of the animals, and it was only if the Indians remained on proper terms with the keepers that they were successful in the hunt. Seen in this light the ritualistic aspects of the hunt, summarized earlier, from the divination of hunt dreams to the taboos governing the proper consumption of a slain beast, take on a new significance. For these rituals can be understood as the visible signs that the Native Americans were fulfilling their part of the bargain, as manifestations that these peoples were honoring, in Martin's words, their side of "the contract" they had struck with the keepers. Very roughly, this agreement called for the Indians not to needlessly kill wild animals and not to use the animals' remains frivolously with the understanding that, in return, the keepers would make game available in the required amounts. Not to honor their side of the contract—in particular, to treat the game disrespectfully by overkilling—was to invite the keepers not to uphold their end of the bargain and thus to run the risk of not having access to an essential food source. This "contractual arrangement," moreover, was not, Martin contends, a distant, practically inefficacious force. On the contrary, "the single most important deterrent to excessive overkill in the Eastern Algonkian's mind," he writes,[34] "was the fear of spiritual reprisal for indiscreet slaughter. Prior to European influence, these Indians of the Canadian forest were on amicable terms with the spirits of the game, including the game 'bosses,' or keepers of the game, and it was the vivid, daily awareness of this courteous relationship which more than anything else precluded overkill."

But now there is a problem. For if these peoples stood in this contractual arrangement with the keepers, and assuming that this "courteous arrangement" had the force and vivacity Martin attributes to it, then it seems very unlikely that these peoples would easily abandon their traditional arrangement with the keepers just to acquire the "geegaws" of Europe. And yet they did kill animals to excess. And they did use their skins for trade. How is this apparent contradiction to be explained, or explained away? Herein lies the originality of Martin's interpretation of the Amerinds' involvement in the fur trade.

Martin locates the principal cause of the Amerind involvement in the fur trade in a most surprising place: The epidemics of infectious and parasitic diseases carried by animals and contacted by the Native Americans of eastern Canada and, indeed, throughout the Americas. Native Americans had long realized that humans could contract serious diseases from animals, and we find, beneath the traditions associated with the "courteous arrangement" that bound Indian to animal, notes of distrust and hostility toward the animal sources of human suffering and death. There was even talk of a "conspiracy among the animals," a fear that perhaps someday all the humans would be gone and only the animals would remain. Still, traditional ways, especially the medicine of the shaman, had historically proven effective as a remedy against most of the diseases, and as long as the shaman was equal to his traditional task, the human-animal relationship remained in a state of amicable equilibrium. Rumors of a conspiracy among the animals were just that—rumors.

This equilibrium was dramatically upset, Martin argues, upon the introduction into the New World of contagious Old World diseases, including new strains of diseases (e.g., the Type A strain of tularemia) as well as totally new maladies (e.g., smallpox). The importance of two features of these new diseases cannot be overestimated. First, they *were* transmitted by animals (though not only by animals), *and*, what is more, Amerinds *believed* that they were carried by animals. "It is obvious," Martin contends,[35] "that . . . Eastern Canadian and other North American Indians blamed wildlife for their diseases precisely because they were, indeed, the source of many of their ailments." Second, the shaman, the traditional source of healing power, was exposed as powerless in the face of new diseases that he could not even identify let alone treat successfully. "Native Americans," Michael Dorris observes,[36] " 'out of touch' with other areas of the world for at least ten thousand years, had never experienced the waves of smallpox, typhus, measles, tuberculosis, and syphilis which affected the 'Old World.' Therefore they had no knowledge of these diseases and their medicine had developed no means for their prevention or cure." Nor, of course, had past exposure provided the then extensive Indian population with the opportunity to develop immunities to these diseases. The results were as predictable as they were tragic and immediate. "Some tribes," writes Dorris,[37] "lost five-sixths to nine-tenths of their total population within a period of weeks. . . . Whole Peoples may indeed have died without even knowing the nature or source of their ailment." As for the number of fatalities, Dorris states[38] that "the Native population of North America declined, between 1492 and 1910, from something in excess of ten to fifteen million people to a government estimate of two hundred and ten thousand," principally, Dorris contends, because of the deleterious impact of European diseases, an impact comparable in numbers of fatalities caused to reducing the present total population of the United States to that of, say, greater Cleveland.

> The Native population was dramatically and almost instantly reduced; societies were torn apart; and the New World daily became at once both emptier and thereby more available to exploitation and colonization. Such is the meaning of the oft-used and little-understood term "The Vanishing American."[39]

Clearly, a pestilence was abroad, brought about by the long-rumored "conspiracy among the animals," a scourge in the face of which the traditional ways, personified by the shaman, were powerless. All evidence pointed to the disintegration or the illusoriness of the traditional belief in "the contract" between the game keepers and the Indians. When recourse to traditional chants, propitiations, diviniations, and the other ceremonial trappings associated with human-animal relations failed to bring an end to the spread of untreatable disease, the Amerinds could no longer believe that they were responsible for the apparent dissolution of the once "courteous arrangement" that had obtained. Either the keepers had decided, without good reason, to renege on their part of the bargain, or no "contract" had ever been negotiated to begin with. In either case the traditional hunting regulations and sanctions based on the Amerind relationship with the keepers of the game disintegrated and, given this collapse together with the belief that it was the animals who were responsible for the spread of fatal diseases, these peoples made war on their "animal brethren," killing without restraint to avenge the suffering and death these animals bore, killing even to the point of the extinction of local species. It is into this climate of the decay of traditional ways that the fur trade was introduced into eastern Canada, Martin argues, and it is against this backdrop that the Native American involvement in that trade should be understood. "The fur-for-trade-goods exchange, although it exacerbated this spiritual decay, was thus more a symptom than a cause."⁴⁰ It was not, or at least not primarily, for the "geegaws" of the West that the Amerinds slew animals with such "gusto." The Amerind "holy war" on animals, Martin contends, had mainly spiritual, not economic, causes.

Now, armed with Martin's explanation of the Native American's involvement in the fur trade, those who would attribute a deep ecology to these peoples might follow Martin's lead and argue as follows. The Amerind's role in that trade is not to be explained in the way a shallow environmentalism would lead one to believe: It was not the external allure of the market in European material goods that paved the way for Amerind involvement. Rather, the principal cause is to be found in something internal to the Amerind life way itself—namely, to the collapse of their native cosmology, a spiritual dissolution, involving mythological beliefs about the causes of untreatable diseases. Prior to these epidemics the deep ecology of these peoples had stood, powerful and undisturbed. It was only after the spread of these diseases, and mainly because of beliefs about their causes, that the ecology collapsed from within. Thus are we able, on this view, reasonably to attribute a deep ecology to Native Americans *before* white contact, a relationship with nature that was manifested by those pre-Columbian conservation practices illustrated in the above; and thus are we able also to appeal to their life way as a model worthy of emulation, one that was not so fragile as to collapse under the weight of the first temptation provided by the geegaws of a new technology. Collapse it did, as the Amerind involvement in the fur trade more than amply demonstrates; but the principal cause of their deep ecology's disintegration, as manifested in their rampant overkill of furbearers, was spiritual, not economic.

Problems with the Alternative Replies to the Problem of Overkill

How adequate are the preceding replies to the problem of overkill? Let us begin our assessment with the deep ecological reply, indicate where some of its major difficulties seem to lie, and work our way toward the central issue that separates this from the shallow environmentalism reply.

First, then, there is a problem of generalization. Even if we are on solid ground in understanding the involvement of the hunting tribes of eastern Canada in the fur trade in terms of their "holy war" on furbearing animals, because of their beliefs about keepers of the game and the causal role of these animals in the spread of fatal diseases, it does not follow that *other* Native American hunting tribes or *other* horticultural tribes became involved in the trade for similar reasons. Thus, to the extent that those who would attribute a deep ecology to Native Americans in general would rely on the holy war thesis developed by Martin as a basis for explaining Native American involvement in the trade, to that extent it will be incumbent upon them to show that a similar explanation can be given for the role played in this trade by tribes other than the hunting tribes of the eastern Canadian forests. Providing a kindred explanation is not impossible in principle. That is not the point being urged here. The point that is being urged is that there is a need to provide such an explanation *and* that this need is not met merely by having recourse to Martin's ingenious theory regarding the involvement of those tribes on which he focuses his attention.

Second, the empirical part of the deep ecology reply is decidedly speculative. We simply are not in a position to claim to know that Native Americans took to the fur trade with such gusto because they blamed furbearing animals for the spread of fatal diseases. In saying this we do not say anything that Martin himself has not already said. "All this (i.e., Martin's explanation of Native involvement in the fur trade) is," he has written,[41] "plausible, but frankly conjectural. Nobody knows whether it actually happened" in the way Martin conjectures. Whatever confidence we may have in attributing a deep ecology to pre-Columbian Native Peoples, therefore, if the case for this attribution involves having recourse to Martin's explanation of their role in the overkill of furbearers, must at least be tempered by our uncertainty about the truth of this explanation itself.

But, third, even if something like what Martin conjectures did in fact occur, not only in the tribes of eastern Canada but throughout the Native American population, it would not follow that the principal cause of the Amerind overkill of furbearers bespeaks a deep ecology. Martin's thesis of a "holy war" on the part of Native Peoples against animals, if true, could at most show that the principal cause[42] of this war was not economic but spiritual, in the sense that a previously accepted spiritual-ized understanding of the human-animal relationship, involving the belief in keepers of the game, had disintegrated because of beliefs about the role of animals in the spread of fatal diseases. But the principal cause's being spiritual rather than economic would not establish that that cause had the features necessary for a deep ecological understanding of the Amerind's relationship with nature. The fact, assuming it is a fact, that Amerinds believed that there were invisible spirits *behind* the visible natural order, in a word, does not by itself establish that they also regarded nature itself as having value in its own right.

Indeed—and here we come to the fourth and most fundamental problem—because the "holy war" thesis involves crediting Native Americans with the belief in keepers of the game, this thesis itself stands in the way of arguing for a deep ecological reply to the problem of overkill in preference to a shallow environmentalism reply. The deep ecology view requires us to view Amerinds as acting respectfully toward nature primarily because they believed the things in nature had value in their own right. Once unseen, regulative forces, such as keepers of the game, are introduced behind nature, however, any and all respectful behavior toward nature can be interpreted as behavior directed toward these unseen forces, not toward nature itself. We are, that is, put in the position of having to interpret this behavior either as primarily manifesting disinterested respect for what has inherent value (a deep ecology response) *or* as primarily manifesting interested respect for the regulative forces behind the natural order, *interested* because it is a respect rooted in the felt need to appease the will of these unseen forces in order to secure what is in one's own, or the tribe's, interest (a shallow environmental response). On the former interpretation, the ritualistic preparation for the hunt and the ceremonial use of the parts of a slain animal, illustrated earlier, are examples of the Amerind's love or reverence for wildlife. On the latter, these same practices are exercises in the expedient pursuit of what is in the Indian's own interest: Treat the hunt and the animals slain in certain ways, this latter interpretation implies, and the keepers will provide the necessary animals; fail to treat them in the prescribed ways (treat them "disrespectfully") and the keepers will withhold them. Paradoxically, therefore, the very feature of the Amerind cosmology that makes the holy war thesis, in Martin's word, "plausible"—namely, the evidence for a belief in unseen, regulative forces behind the natural order, the "keepers of the game"—this very feature is a hindrance to the case for attributing a deep ecology to Native Americans. The background presence of such forces as the keepers of the game introduces the possibility, *within the Amerind cosmology itself*, of interpreting respectful behavior toward wildlife and nature generally as grounded in expedience and not, say, "reverence for life."

Of course it is an explanation in terms of expedience, not reverence, that those who wish to attribute a shallow environmentalism to Native Americans are certain to prefer in the present context, an explanation that Martin, for one, openly resists. There was, Martin writes,[43] "a genuine spirituality" that permeated the Amerind's relationship with nature. "Wildlife were revered and propitiated not only out of fear that their favors might be withheld, although there was some sense of that, but also because they were felt to be inherently deserving of such regard."[44] But if we press Martin for evidence for attributing this latter belief to Native Americans, not as an occasional outpouring of their psyches but as embodying their primary views about nature, the evidence he cites turns out either to relate to a different question or to be intractably ambiguous. Thus he writes[45] that "admittedly, mankind need their (i.e., wildlife's) good will to survive—to be physically nourished—yet he also appealed to them for spiritual and aesthetic sustenance. And they furnished it." But this is to confuse the issues rather than to address them. The question at issue is not, Did Native Americans regard wildlife only as a source of physical sustenance? To this question all parties to the dispute may agree with Martin and reply, "No, they also found spiritual and aesthetic sustenance in them." But the central question at issue, and the one Martin's reply fails to address, is, Did these peoples view wildlife and nature primarily as having value apart from human interests, whether these interests were physical *or* aesthetic *or* spiritual? An affirmative answer to this question is not supplied just by insisting that these peoples got much more from their natural environment than simply physical sustenance.

An affirmative answer here is all the more difficult to come by, the more we recognize that the Amerind's relationship with nature was spiritualized in terms of unseen but powerful forces behind and in control of the natural order—for example, keepers of the game. Against this cosmological backdrop, as argued earlier, all outwardly appearing respectful interaction with nature will necessarily have an ambiguous character, since all such behavior may be viewed as growing out of respect for the power held by these forces *or* as growing out of the belief in the independent value of the objects in nature themselves. Martin, for all his acumen, seems to fail to see that, in the nature of the case, one simply cannot point to any known behavior of those Native Americans who, like the Indians of eastern Canada, mythologized their relationship in terms of unseen, controlling forces (keepers of the game, for example), and say, "Here we have an unmistakable case of these people respecting the value they believed nature had in itself." For there is always, in the background, the possibility that it was fear of the keepers, not appreciation of nature's inherent values, that directed these peoples' behavior.

But if we cannot point to their behavior as unmistakably indicative of respect for nature's inherent value, neither can we point to their behavior as disproof of this. The evidence at hand, even including the evidence we have of the Amerind's involvement in the fur trade, is ambiguous, and *intractably* so. Thus, those who, like Presnall, would prefer to view these peoples as shallow environmentalists are, given the intractable ambiguity of their respectful behavior, just as incapable of establishing the correctness of the shallow interpretation as are those who prefer a deep ecological interpretation. Clearly, the case for the shallow environmentalism interpretation cannot be any stronger than the case that can be made against viewing the Amerind's respect as disinterested respect for nature's inherent value. And *that* case cannot be made merely by adducing evidence that, at least sometimes, these peoples did view nature in terms of how it served their own interests, or that, at other times, as in their role in the fur trade, they behaved as if they never thought nature had independent value worthy of respect. Possibly they did. Indeed, possibly their relationship with nature was rooted in their belief that nature had such value and was deserving of such respect. The belief in keepers of the game does not prove that they did; but neither does it prove that they did not. What belief in keepers of the game or other regulative spiritual forces does do is add an ineradicable layer of ambiguity to the respectful behavior of Native Peoples.

This ambiguity of the Native American's relationship with nature is not an ambiguity that could be cleared away if only we had some further facts about how Amerinds behaved toward nature (e.g., whether they prayed in a certain way or made this or that kind of sacrifice). For the ambiguity lies not in what the facts are but in how they should be interpreted. Given any new fact, the same questions will persist: Does it show that they viewed nature primarily as having value in its own right, so that the respect they displayed toward it was rooted in their belief that it was worthy of respect? Or does this fact show that they regarded nature primarily as a system of resources on which they depended for their existence and for whose availability they had to appease the invisible forces behind and regulative of the visible world (e.g., keepers of the game)? No discovery of a new fact about the respectful behavior of Amerinds is capable of removing the ambiguity inherent in the facts we already have. New facts will simply perpetuate the old ambiguity.

At its deepest level the ambiguity of Amerind behavior is the ambiguity of human behavior, the ancient puzzle over whether, as humans, we are capable of acting out of disinterested respect for what we believe has value in its own right or whether, beneath all manner of ceremony, ritual, and verbal glorification of the objects of our attention, there resides, in Kant's memorable words, "the dear self," the true, the universal sovereign of our wills. Perhaps we can understand, though thankfully we can no longer endorse, the view held by some European trappers and settlers, who saw differences in skin color and culture as symptomatic of differences in biological species. But to recognize our common humanity with the original human inhabitants of North America carries with it the recognition of the mysteries of human nature that bind us to them. The behavior of Native Americans can no more prove that sparks of genuine altruism lit their hearts or fired their deeds than can the behavior of any other people. To suppose otherwise—to look upon the Amerinds as "special" in just this respect—is to show them a false respect. Our equals in all that matters most, their behavior, like our own, must remain equally puzzling because equally ambiguous.

Conclusion

Interest in the Native American relationship with nature certainly predates the dawn of our awareness of our environmental crisis, as the extensive body of work from anthropologists and historians shows. But it was not until the recognition of this crisis that philosophers and environmentalists began to turn their attention to the "land ethic" of this continent's original inhabitants. As the practical necessity of developing an enlightened environmental ethic presses itself upon philosophers and policy makers, it is understandable that increasing attention should be given to the Amerind's relationship with nature. The burden of this essay has been to show that further study of this relationship, now or in the future, will not provide a compelling argument for attributing either a shallow environmentalism or a deep ecology to these peoples. While the attention philosophers are beginning to pay to Native Americans is both laudatory and long overdue,[46] and while there is no doubt much to be learned from the study of their diverse cultures, we are not now and never will be in a position to call them as witnesses for the defense of a shallow or a deep way of understanding our own relationship with nature. That relationship is something we must work out on our own.[47]

NOTES

1. Michael Dorris, *Native Americans: 500 Years After* (New York: Thomas Y. Crowell, 1973) p. 4.

2. Bill Devall, "Streams of Environmentalism," first draft, portions of which have appeared in *Natural Resources Journal*, April 1980. In the published version Devall dispenses with the terms "deep ecology" and "shallow environmentalism." I am grateful for Professor Devall's permission to quote from the unpublished version of his essay. K. E. Goodpaster characterizes the difference between what here are called shallow environmentalism and deep ecology in a similar way. "The . . . former path (shallow environmentalism) is merely instrumentalist, utilitarian environmentalism—'human chauvinism'—while the latter path (deep ecology) is the path of the new environmental sensitivity, avoiding arbitrariness in extending its moral concern to a far larger class of beneficiaries: birds, fish, whales, and other animals; plants, trees, and forests; lakes, rivers, air, and land" (from "Egoism to Environmentalism," in K. E. Goodpaster and K. M. Sayre, eds., *Ethics and Problems of the Twenty-First Century* [Notre Dame: University of Notre Dame Press, 1979]), p. 28). The "shallow" and "deep" terminology is traceable to Arne Naess, "The Shallow and the Deep, Long-Range Ecology Movements," *Inquiry* 16, 1 (January 1973): 95–100. Two works that reflect the basic thrust of shallow environmentalism are John Passmore, *Man's Responsibility for Nature* (London: Duckworth, 1974) and Garrett Hardin, "Rational Foundation of Conservation," *North American Review* 14 (1974). A now classic statement in the spirit of the deep ecological position is Aldo Leopold, *A Sand County Almanac* (New York: Oxford University Press, 1949). I argue for the latter and against the former type of position in "On the Nature and Possibility of an Environmental Ethic," *Environmental Ethics* 3, 1 (1981), (essay 9, above). Relevant discussions of these two streams of thought are to be found in William Blackstone, "The Search for an Environmental Ethic," in Tom Regan, ed., *Matters of Life and Death* (New York: Random House, 1980); Holmes Rolston III, "Is There an Ecological Ethic?," *Ethics* 85, 1 (January 1975): 93–109; and Lynn White, jr., "The Historical Roots of our Ecological Crisis," *Science* 155 (1967): 3767.

3. Devall, "Streams of Environmentalism."

4. Leopold, *Sand County Almanac*, pp. 205, 305.

5. Ibid., p. viii.

6. Ervin Laszlo, *Introduction to Systems Philosophy: Toward a New Paradigm of Contemporary Thought* (New York: Gordon and Breach, 1972), p. 288.

7. One way some thinkers have tried to introduce greater precision into the deep ecology position is by using concepts from the science of ecology—e.g., biological diversity and homeostasis. There are deep problems here, however, including the familiar ones over the fact-value distinction and the derivability of "ought" from "is." On this see my "On the Connection Between Environmental Science and Environmental Ethics," *Environmental Ethics* 2, 4 (1980): 363−367, as well as the essay that occasioned that paper—Don E. Marietta, "The Interrelationship of Ecological Science and Environmental Ethics," *Environmental Ethics* 1, 2 (1979): 195−207. I explore the concept of inherent value, albeit very sketchily, in "On the Nature and Possibility of an Environmental Ethic" (essay 9, above).

8. See "On the Nature and Possibility of an Environmental Ethic." A spirited discussion of this and related issues is to be found in Mark Sagoff, "On Preserving the Natural Environment," *The Yale Law Journal* 84 (1974): 205−267.

9. Vine Deloria, Jr., *We Talk, You listen: New Tribes, New Turf* (New York: Macmillan, 1970), pp. 186, 197.

10. Stewart L. Udall, *The Quiet Crisis* (New York: Holt, Rinehart and Winston, 1962), p. 12.

11. W. H. Hutchinson, "The Remaking of the Amerind: A Dissenting Voice Raised Against the Resurrection of the Myth of the Noble Savage," *Westways* (October 1972).

12. Willa Cather, *Death Comes for the Archbishop* (New York: Alfred A. Knopf, 1926).

13. Cora Du Bois, *Wintu Ethnography*, University of California Publications in Archaeology and Ethnology 36, 1 (Berkeley: University of California Press, 1935): 75−76.

14. A. Skinner, "Mahickan Ethnology," *Milwaukee Museum Publications* 2 (1925) (from a manuscript of 1822); quoted in William Christie MacLeod, "Conservation Among Primitive Hunting Peoples," *Scientific Monthly* 43 (December 1936): 563.

15. Ibid., p. 564.

16. Barry Holstun Lopez, *Of Wolves and Men* (New York: Charles Scribners' Sons, 1978), p. 86.

17. MacLeod, "Conservation," p. 564.

18. Clifford D. Presnall, "Wildlife Conservation as Affected by American Indian and Caucasian Concepts," *Journal of Mammalogy* 24, 4 (December 1943): 458.

19. Ibid. On the imputation of "sneakiness" to Indians, Barry Lopez relates the following: "For 100 years or more the Apache have derisively been called 'sneaky.' The term apparently originated in the observation that Apaches moved stealthily about the land. They did so not to be sneaky but because to

leave footprints everywhere was a mark of arrogance." *Quest* (September-October 1978), p. 4.

20. Presnall, "Wildlife Conservation," p. 458.

21. MacLeod, "Conservation," pp. 562–563.

22. Ibid., p. 563.

23. It is appropriate here to acknowledge my great debt to the work of Calvin Martin which, in addition to containing the ingenious theory discussed in the pages below, also directed me to many of the primary sources alluded to in this essay. See his *Keepers of the Game: Indian-Animal Relationships and the Fur Trade* (Berkeley: University of California Press, 1978).

24. Frank G. Speck, *Naskapi: The Savage Hunters of the Labrador Peninsula* (Norman: University of Oklahoma Press, 1935), p. 150.

25. Ibid., pp. 139, 167–168.

26. Martin, *Keepers of the Game*, p. 36.

27. Ibid.

28. Ibid., p. 2.

29. Ibid., p. 1.

30. Ibid., p. 165.

31. Ibid., p. 8.

32. Hutchinson, "Remaking of the Amerind," p. 94.

33. Martin, *Keepers of the Game*, p. 166.

34. Ibid., p. 18.

35. Ibid., p. 144. In discussing this essay Nancy Regan has made the point that Amerinds must have noticed that the Europeans in their midst did not contract the dreaded diseases that were overwhelming the Native Peoples or, if they fell victim to these maladies, tended to survive. And yet these were the same individuals who were busy engineering the intensive exploitation of furbearers! It is not unreasonable to suppose, she argues, that, ignorant as they were of the real causes of the white's immunity, the Indians would view the good fortune of these plunderers as another sign of the nonexistence or dissolution of the "contract" between the Native Peoples and game keepers. She argues that, though Martin fails to draw on this evidence, his theory of Amerind involvement in the fur trade is strengthened not only by the identity of those who died but also by that of those who lived.

36. Dorris, *Native Americans*, p. 6.

37. Ibid., p. 7.

38. Ibid., p. 6.

39. Ibid., p. 7.

40. Martin, *Keepers of the Game*, p. 149.

41. Ibid., p. 143.

42. In discussions of this essay Dale Jamieson has made the point that Martin's position must encounter the problem endemic to social science in general and to anthropology in particular—the problem, namely, of establishing causal connections. Martin's problem is to establish not only that (1) there was a change in the Amerinds' understanding of their relationship with animals at the time that their behavior towards animals changed, but also that (2) this change in their understanding *caused* this change in their behavior. It is unclear how (2) can be established; it is quite clear that it is not established merely by establishing (1). In the absence of compelling arguments to the contrary, one might just as well contend that the change in Amerind behavior vis-à-vis animals brought about the change in their cosmology Martin documents.

43. Martin, *Keepers of the Game*, p. 186. Martin argues that, despite their reverence for the land, Native Americans are miscast as our environmental "gurus" because their understanding of the world was radically different than the Western paradigm bequeathed to us by Judaism and Christianity. My position differs. I argue that they ought not to be cast in this role because we do not, and cannot, know that they were deep ecologists in the first place.

44. Ibid.

45. Ibid.

46. See David Lyons, "The New Indian Claims and Original Rights to Land," *Social Theory and Practice* (Fall 1977): 249–272.

47. I have benefited from discussing the themes addressed in the present essay with Dale Jamieson, Barbara Levenbook, and Nancy Regan. Work on this essay was assisted by a fellowship from the National Endowment for the Humanities for the academic year 1980–1981. It is a pleasure to acknowledge this assistance.

A Select Bibliography On Animal Rights And Human Obligations

The following is a select bibliography, first of books, then of articles, both of mostly recent vintage, which deal mainly with the ethical dimensions of our relations with animals. The bibliography was prepared jointly with Professor Charles Magel, Moorhead State University, and was originally published in *Inquiry* 22, 1—2 (1979): 243—247. It is reprinted here with the permission of Professor Magel and *Inquiry*.

BOOKS

Amory, Cleveland. 1974. *Man Kind? Our Incredible War on Wildlife.* New York: Harper and Row.

Aquis, Ambrose. 1970. *God's Animals.* London: Catholic Study for Animal Welfare.

Batten, Peter. 1977. *Living Trophies: A Shocking Look at the Conditions in America's Zoos.* New York: Thomas Y. Crowell.

Blackstone, William, ed. 1974. *Philosophy and Environmental Crisis.* Athens: University of Georgia Press.

Boas, George. 1966. *The Happy Beast in French Thought of the Seventeenth Century.* New York: Octagon Books.

Carson, Gerald. 1972. *Men, Beasts, and Gods: A History of Cruelty and Kindness to Animals.* New York: Charles Scribner's Sons.

Clark, Stephen R. L. 1977. *The Moral Status of Animals.* New York: Oxford University Press.

Evans, Edward. 1906. *The Criminal Prosecution and Capital Punishment of Animals.* London: Heinemann.

Fisher, James. 1975. *Zoos of the World: The Story of Animals in Captivity.* Garden City, New York: Doubleday.

Frey, R. G. 1980. *Interests and Rights: The Case Against Animals.* Oxford: Oxford University Press, Clarendon Press.

Godlovitch, Stanley and Roslind, and Harris, John, eds. 1972. *Animals, Men and Morals.* London: Gollancz, and New York: Taplinger.

Harrison, Ruth. 1964. *Animal Machines.* London: Stuart.

Hediger, Heini. 1964. *Wild Animals in Captivity*, trans. G. Sircom. New York: Dover.

———. 1968. *The Psychology and Behavior of Animals in Zoos and Circuses.* New York: Dover.

———. 1969. *Man and Animal in the Zoo*, trans. Gwynne Vevers and Winwood Reade. New York: Delacorte Press.

Hume, C. W. 1957. *The Status of Animals in the Christian Religion.* London: Universities Federation for Animal Welfare

———. 1962. *Man and Beast.* London: Universities Federation for Animal Welfare.

Hunt, Mary, and Juergensmeyer, Mark. 1978. *Animal Ethics: An Annotated Bibliography.* Berkeley: Graduate Theological Union.

Linzey, Andrew. 1976. *Animal Rights: A Christian Assessment of Man's Treatment of Animals.* London: SCM Press.

Malcolm, Norman. 1977. *Thought and Knowledge.* Ithaca, N. Y.: Cornell University Press.

Midgley, Mary. 1978. *Beast and Man.* Ithaca, N. Y.: Cornell University Press.

Morris, Richard Knowles, and Fox, Michael W., eds. 1978. *On the Fifth Day: Animal Rights and Human Ethics.* Washington, D. C.: Acropolis Press.

Nozick, Robert. 1974. *Anarchy, State and Utopia.* New York: Basic Books.

Passmore, John. 1974. *Man's Responsibility for Nature.* London: Duckworth.

Paterson, D. A., and Ryder, Richard, eds. 1979. *Animals' Rights: A Symposium.* London: Centaur Press.

Pratt, Dallas. 1976. *Painful Experiments on Animals.* New York: Argus Archives.

Regan, Tom, and Singer, Peter, eds. 1976. *Animal Rights and Human Obligations.* Englewood Cliffs, N. J.: Prentice-Hall.

Regan, Tom, ed. 1980. *Matters of Life and Death.* New York: Random House, 1980; Philadelphia: Temple University Press.

Rosenfield, Leonora. 1968. *From Beast Machine to Man-Machine: The Theme of Animal Soul in French Letters from Descartes to LaMettrie.* New York: Octagon Books.

Ryder, Richard. 1975. *Victims of Science.* London: Davis-Poynter.

Salt, Henry S. 1894. *Animals' Rights.* New York: Macmillan.

Schweitzer, Albert. 1953. *The Philosophy of Civilization.* New York: Macmillan.

Singer, Peter. 1975. *Animal Liberation.* New York: A New York Review Book, distributed by Random House. 1977. New York: Avon Books.

Stevas, Norman St. John. 1963. *The Right to Life.* London: Hodder and Stoughton.

Taylor, Thomas. 1966. *A Vindication of the Rights of Brutes* (1792). Gainesville, Fla.: Scholars Facsimiles and Reprints.

Turner, E. S. 1964. *All Heaven in a Rage*. London: Michael Joseph.

Vyvyan, John. 1969. *In Pity and in Anger*. London: Michael Joseph.

————. 1971. *The Dark Face of Science*. London: Michael Joseph.

Westacott, E. A. 1949. *A Century of Vivisection and Anti-Vivisection*. London: Daniel.

ARTICLES

Auxter, Thomas, 1979. "The Right Not to be Eaten," *Inquiry* 22, 1–2.

Becker, Earnest. 1974. "Toward the Merger of Animal and Human Studies," *Philosophy of the Social Sciences* 4 (June–September).

Benson, John. 1978. "Duty and the Beast," *Philosophy* 53, 206.

Blackstone, William T. 1980. "The Search for an Environmental Ethic," in Tom Regan, ed., *Matters of Life and Death*. New York: Random House.

Broadie, Alexander, and Pybus, Elizabeth. 1974. "Kant's Treatment of Animals," *Philosophy* 49 (October).

Brumbaugh, Robert S. 1978. "Of Man, Animals, and Morals: A Brief History," in Morris and Fox, eds., *On the Fifth Day*. Washington, D.C.: Acropolis Press.

Campbell, Clare, Worden, Alastair, and Ryder, Richard. 1978. "Experiments on Animals. With review discussion of *The Plague Dogs* by Richard Adams," *THEORIA to Theory*, 12, 1.

Carson, Hampton. N.d. "The Trial and Prosecution of Animals and Insects: A Little Known Chapter of Medieval Jurisprudence," *American Philosophical Society Proceedings* 56: 410–415.

Clark, Stephen R. L. 1978. "Animal Wrongs," *Analysis* 38, 3 (June).

————. 1979. "The Rights of Wild Things," *Inquiry* 22, 1–2.

Collins, A. W. 1968. "How Could One Tell Were a Bee to Guide his Behavior by a Rule?," *Mind* 72: 556–560.

Dallery, Carleton. 1978. "Thinking and Being with Beasts," in Morris and Fox, eds., *On the Fifth Day*. Washington, D.C.: Acropolis Press.

David, William. 1976. "Man-Eating Aliens," *Journal of Value Inquiry* 10 (Fall).

Donaghy, Kevin, 1974. "Singer on Speciesism," *Philosophic Exchange* 1 (Summer).

Elliot, Robert. 1978. "Regan on the Sorts of Beings That Can Have Rights," *Southern Journal of Philosophy* 16 (Spring).

Feinberg, Joel. 1974. "The Rights of Animals and Unborn Generations," in W. Blackstone, ed., *Philosophy and Environmental Crisis*. Athens: University of Georgia Press.

————. 1978. "Human Duties and Animal Rights," in Morris and Fox, eds., *On the Fifth Day*. Washington, D.C.: Acropolis Press.

Flew, Anthony. 1974. "Torture: Could the End Justify the Means?" *Crucible* (January).

Fox, Michael, 1978. " 'Animal Liberation:' A Critique," *Ethics* 88, 2 (January).

————. 1978. "Animal Suffering and Rights," *Ethics* 88, 2 (January).

Frey, R. G. 1977. "Animal Rights," *Analysis* 37 (June).

————. 1977 "Interests and Animal Rights," *Philosophical Quarterly* 27 (July).

————. 1979. "Rights, Interests, Desires and Beliefs," *American Philosophical Quarterly* 16 (July).

Fuller, B. A. G. 1949. "The Messes Animals Make in Metaphysics," *Journal of Philosophy* 46 (December 22): 829–838.

Godlovitch, Roslind. 1971. "Animals and Morals," *Philosophy* 46 (January).

————. 1972. "Animals and Morals," in Godlovitch, Godlovitch, and Harris, eds., *Animals, Men and Morals.* London: Gollancz, and New York: Taplinger.

Godlovitch, Stanley. 1972. "Utilities" (using other beings), in Godlovitch, Godlovitch and Harris, eds., *Animals, Men and Morals.* London: Gollancz, and New York: Taplinger.

Goodpaster, Kenneth. 1978. "On Being Morally Considerable," *Journal of Philosophy* 75 (June).

Grene, Marjorie. 1972. "People and Other Animals," *Philosophical Forum* (Boston) 3 (Winter).

Gunderson, Keith. 1964. "Descartes, La Mettrie, Language, and Machines," *Philosophy* 34 (July).

Hanula, Robert W., and Hill, Peter Waverly. 1977. "Using Metaright Theory to Ascribe Kantian Rights to Animals Within Nozick's Minimal State," *Arizona Law Review* 19, 1 (University of Arizona).

Hartshorne, Charles. 1978. "Foundations for a Humane Ethics: What Human Beings Have in Common with Other Higher Animals," in Morris and Fox, eds., *On the Fifth Day.* Washington, D.C.: Acropolis Press.

Haworth, Lawrence. 1978. "Rights, Wrongs, and Animals," *Ethics* 88 (January).

Hyde, Walter Woodburn. "The Prosecution and Punishment of Animals and Lifeless Things in the Middle Ages and Modern Times," *University of Pennsylvania Law Review* 64: 696–730.

Jamieson, Dale, and Regan, Tom. 1978. "Animal Rights: A Reply to Frey," *Analysis* 38 (January).

Levin, Michael. 1977. "Animal Rights Evaluated," *Humanist* 37 (July-August).

————. 1977. "All in a Stew About Animals: A Reply to Singer," *Humanist* 37 (September–October).

Lockwood, Michael. 1979. "Singer on Killing and the Preference for Life," *Inquiry* 22, 1–2.

Lowry, Jon. 1975. "Natural Rights: Men and Animals," *Southwestern Journal of Philosophy* 6 (Summer).

McCloskey, H. J. 1965. "Rights," *Philosophical Quarterly* 15.

————. 1975. "The Right to Life," *Mind* 84 (July).

————. 1978. "Moral Rights and Animals," *Inquiry* 22, 1–2.

McGinn, Colin. 1979. "Evolution, Animals, and the Basis of Morality," *Inquiry* 22, 1–2.

MacIver, A. M. 1948. "Ethics and the Beetle," *Analysis* 8: 65–70.

Malcolm, Norman. 1972–73. "Thoughtless Brutes," *Proceedings of American Philosophical Association* 46: 5–20.

Margolis, Joseph. 1974. "Animals Have No Rights and Are Not the Equal of Humans," *Philosophic Exchange* 1 (Summer).

Martin, Michael. 1976. "A Critique of Moral Vegetarianism," *Reason Papers* (Fall).

Midgley, Mary. 1973. "The Concept of Beastliness: Philosophy, Ethics and Animal Behavior," *Philosophy* 48 (April). Reprinted (1976) in Tom Regan and Peter Singer, eds., *Animal Rights and Human Obligations*. Englewood Cliffs, N.J.: Prentice-Hall.

Naess, Arne. 1979. "Self-realization in Mixed Communities of Humans, Bears, Sheep, and Wolves," *Inquiry* 22, 1–2.

Narveson, Jan. 1977. "Animal Rights," *Canadian Journal of Philosophy* 7 (March).

Nelson, Leonard. 1956. "Duties to Animals," in his *System of Ethics*. New Haven: Yale University Press, pp. 136–44. Also (1972) in Godlovitch, Godlovitch, and Harris, eds., *Animals, Men and Morals*. London: Gollancz, and New York: Taplinger.

Northrup, F. S. C. 1978. "Naturalistic Realism and Animate Compassion," in Morris and Fox, eds., *On the Fifth Day*. Washington, D. C.: Acropolis Press.

Otten, Jim and Russow, Lilly-Marlene. 1977. "Forum: Experimentation on Animals," *Eros*. Department of Philosophy, Purdue University.

Passmore, John. 1975. "The Treatment of Animals," *Journal of History of Ideas* 36 (April–June).

Puka, Bill. 1977. Review of *Animal Liberation* by Peter Singer, in *Philosophical Review* 86 (October).

Pybus, Elizabeth and Broadie, Alexander. 1974. "Kant's Treatment of Animals," *Philosophy* 49.

Rachels, James. 1976. "Do Animals Have a Right to Liberty?" in Tom Regan and Peter Singer, eds., *Animals Rights and Human Obligations*. Englewood Cliffs, N.J.: Prentice-Hall.

———. 1976. "A Reply to VanDeVeer", in Tom Regan and Peter Singer, eds., *Animal Rights and Human Obligations*. Englewood Cliffs, N.J.: Prentice-Hall.

Regan, Tom. 1975. "The Moral Basis of Vegetarianism," *Canadian Journal of Philosophy* 5 (October).

———. 1976. "McCloskey on Why Animals Cannot Have Rights," *Philosophical Quarterly* 26 (July).

———. 1976. "Broadie and Pybus on Kant," *Philosophy* 51 (October).

———. 1976. "Feinberg on What Sorts of Beings Can Have Rights," *Southern Journal of Philosophy* (Winter).

———. 1977. "Narveson on Egoism and the Rights of Animals," *Canadian Journal of Philosophy* 7 (March).

———. 1977. "Frey on Interests and Animal Rights," *Philosophical Quarterly* 27 (October).

———. 1978. "Fox's Critique of Animal Liberation," *Ethics* 88 (January).

———. 1979. "An Examination and Defense of One Argument Concerning Animal Rights," *Inquiry* 22, 1–2.

———. 1980. "Utilitarianism, Vegetarianism and Animal Rights," *Philosophy and Public Affairs* 9 (Summer).

Regan, Tom, and Jamieson, Dale. 1978. "Animal Rights: A Reply to Frey," *Analysis* 38 (January).

Rodman, John. 1974. "The Dolphin Papers," *North American Review* (Spring).

————. 1977. "The Liberation of Nature," *Inquiry* 20 (Spring).

————. 1979. "Animal Justice: The Counter-revolution in Natural Right and Law," *Inquiry* 22, 1–2.

Ryder, Richard (see Campbell, Clare).

Schweitzer, Albert. "The Ethic of Reverence for Life," from *Civilization and Ethics* (Part II of *The Philosophy of Civilization*). Reprinted (1976) in Tom Regan and Peter Singer, eds., *Animal Rights and Human Obligations*. Englewood Cliffs, N.J.: Prentice-Hall.

Seidler, Michael J. 1977. "Hume and the Animals," *Southern Journal of Philosophy* 15 (Fall).

Singer, Peter. 1973. "Animal Liberation" (review of Godlovitch, Godlovitch, and Harris, eds., *Animals, Men and Morals*, London: Gollancz, and Taplinger, 1972), *New York Review of Books* 20, 3 (April 5).

Singer, Peter. 1974. "All Animals Are Equal," *Philosophic Exchange* 1, 5 (Summer).

Singer, Peter. 1977. "A Reply to Professor Levin's 'Animal Rights Evaluated,' " *Humanist* 37 (July–August).

Singer, Peter. 1978. "The Fable of the Fox and the Unliberated Animals," *Ethics* 88 (January).

Singer, Peter. 1980. "Animals and the Value of Life," in Tom Regan, ed., *Matters of Life and Death*. New York: Random House.

Singer, Peter. 1979. "Killing Humans and Killing Animals," *Inquiry* 22, 1–2.

Sprigge, T. L. S. 1979. "Metaphysics, Physicalism, and Animal Rights," *Inquiry* 22, 1–2.

Steinbock, Bonnie, 1978. "Speciesism and the Idea of Equality," *Philosophy* 53 (April).

Sumner, L. W. 1976. "A Matter of Life and Death," *Nous* (May).

VanDe Veer, Donald. 1976. "Defending Animals by Appeal to Rights." in Tom Regan and Peter Singer, eds., *Animal Rights and Human Obligations*. Englewood Cliffs, N.J.: Prentice-Hall.

————. 1980. "Animal Suffering," *Canadian Journal of Philosophy* 10, 3.

————. 1979. "Interspecific Justice," *Inquiry* 22, 1–2.

Weiss, Donald. 1975. "Professor Malcolm on Animal Intelligence," *Philosophical Review* 84 (January).

Worden, Alastair (see Campbell, Clare).

Index

Altman, Nathaniel, 99n
Attfield, Robin, 186
Amory, Cleveland, 98n
Animal experimentation, 61–72, 78–79,
 87, 140
Animal liberation, 27, 43–44, 51
Animal rights, 42–44, 70–72, 90–98,
 113–147. *See also* Rights
Aquinas, St. Thomas, 10, 37n, 82, 180
Aristotle, 31, 180

Bednar, Charles A., 75
Benefits, 154, 158–160, 174–175
Bentham, Jeremy, 8–9, 37n, 42–43, 82,
 92, 99n, 184, 194
Blackstone, William 236n
Broadie, Alexander, 59n, 99n, 146n
Burr, Stephen I., 150

Callicott, J. Baird, 76, 103, 186
Carson, Gerald, 163n
Cather, Willa, 215, 237n
Chessenee, Bartholomew, 151
Clark, Stephen, 103
Consciousness, as criterion of rights, 132
Corruption of character argument, 193,
 196
Council of Europe, 156

Cruelty, 10, 66–68, 72, 82–85, 86, 96,
 111, 174–175
Curtis, Patricia, 74n

Darwin, Charles, 159
Deep ecology, 185, 207, 210–215, 224,
 226–236
Deloria, Jr., Vine, 214, 237n
Descartes, Rene, 4–7, 37n, 153, 158
Devall, Bill, 210, 236n
Diamond, Cora, 2, 41
Domalain, Jean-Yves, 78, 98n
Dorris, Michael, 209, 228, 229, 236n, 238n
Draize test, 79, 84–85, 96
Drengson, Alan R., 186
DuBois, Cora, 216, 237n
Dworkin, Ronald, 91, 100n

Egoism, 54–55, 58
Eibl-Eibesfeldt, Irenaus, 164n
Elliott, Robert, 166
Endangered Species Act, 156
Embodiment of cultural values argument,
 196–199
Environmental ethic, 167, 182, 184–204,
 206–236
Equality of interests, 47–49, 52, 86–87,
 89

Equality of treatment, 49–53
Evans, Edward, 163n

Factory farming, 44–45. *See also* Intensive rearing
Feinberg, Joel, 8, 14, 37n, 38n, 58n, 73n 121, 127, 145n, 146n, 149, 163n, 166, 168–176, 179–182, 183n, 185, 204n, 205n
Fox, Michael A., 2, 41, 58n, 60n
Frey, R. G., 2, 3, 114, 122–124, 144n, 166, 186
Friedrich, Heinz, 164n

Gambell, Ray, 102
Gandhi, Mahatma, 1, 2, 3, 36n
Godlovitch, Stanley and Roslind, 37n
Goodall, Jane, 38n, 164n
Goodness principle, 166, 169, 172, 181–182
"Good of its own," 166, 173, 175–182. *See also* Inherent value
Goodpaster, Kenneth, 186, 202, 203n, 205n, 236n
Gunn, Alastaire, 103

Halverson, Diane, 156
Hannay, Alastair, 113
Hardin, Garrett, 47, 59n, 236n
Hare, R. M., 204n
Hargrove, Eugene C., 208
Harm, 174–175
Harris, John, 37n
Harrison, Ruth, 38n, 40, 44, 59n, 98n
Hedonism, 194
Holzer, Henry Mark, 150
Human interests principle, 201
Hume, David, 26
Hunt, W. Murray, 186
Hutchinson, W. H., 215, 225, 237n, 238n
Hyde, Walter Woodburne, 150, 151, 163n

Inherent Value, 71–72, 93–98, 114–115, 133–144, 166, 173, 175–182, 185, 191, 197, 199–203, 212, 232, 234. *See also* "Good of its own"
Injury, 153–154, 158–159
Intensive rearing, 24–27, 46–47, 49, 51, 87, 140. *See also* Factory farming
Interests, 14, 16, 30–31, 34–35, 86, 108–109, 154–155, 158–159, 168–182, 189–190

Interests principle, 166, 168, 172, 182
Intrinsic evil, 8–10
Intrinsic goods, 22–23, 115, 183n
Intrinsic worth, 28–34
Intuition, 29–30
IWC (International Whaling Commission), 77, 102, 105

Jacobs, Myron, 104, 112n
Jamieson, Dale, 3, 59n, 63, 239n
Jenkins, Peter, 37n

Kant, Immanuel, 10, 28, 37n, 55–56, 58, 59n, 71, 82–83, 86, 93, 96, 99n, 134, 137, 146n, 193, 204n, 235
Kantor, Jay E., 186
Kindness, 68–69, 72, 174–175
Kinship ethic, 185, 188–189
Krieger, Martin, 194–195, 204n

Language, 6–7, 13
Lazlo, Ervin, 211, 237n
Leavitt, Emily Stewart, 156
Leopold, Aldo, ix, 211, 236n
Linzey, Andrew, 120–122, 125, 145n, 186, 204n
Locke, John, 66, 73n, 83–84, 99n
Lopez, Barry Holstun, 206–208, 219, 237n
Lorenz, Konrad, 164n
Luckie, Kate, 216
Lyons, David, 100n, 239

McCloskey, H. J., 38n, 114, 166, 183n
MacIntyre, Joan, 112n
Macleod, W. C., 217, 218, 220, 237n, 238n

Magel, Charles R., ix, x, 63, 73n, 101n, 240
Management ethic, 185, 188–189
Marginal cases, argument from, 116, 147
Marietta, Don E., 186, 237n
Martin, Calvin, 206, 222, 224–233, 238n, 239n
Martin, Michael, 2
Mason, Jim, 42
Mattingly, Steele F., 62
Midgley, Mary, 37n, 159, 164n
Mill, John Stuart, 9–10, 100n, 184
Miller, Harlan, 76
Moore, G. E., 204n
More, Henry, 5
Mowat, Farley, 104, 112n
Muriel the Lady Dowding, 98n

Naess, Arne, 236n
Narveson, Jan, 2, 3, 41, 54, 59n, 116, 144n
Native Americans, 206–239
Nelson, Leonard, 38n
Nickle, James, 73n
Noninjury, principle of, 8–9

Offense against an ideal argument, 193–194, 196
O'Neill, Onora, 59n
Overholt, Thomas W., 208

Pain, 6–26
Passmore, William, 185, 236n
Paterson, David, 59n, 73n, 99n, 114, 146n
Payne, Robert, 105, 112n
Perry, Ralph Barton, 14, 16, 38n
Person, 152–153, 156
Plato, 8, 158
Pleasure, 8–12, 18
Prejudice, 157–160
Preservation principle, 200–201
Presnall, Clifford D., 219–220, 234, 237n, 238n
Pybus, Elizabeth, 59n, 99n, 146n
Pythagoras, 5, 7

Rachels, James, 70, 74n, 100n
Regan, Nancy, 238n
Regenstein, Lewis, 98n, 104, 112n
Rights: moral, 117–119; legal, 117, 121, 149–164; natural, 13–14, 35–36, 43, 117; to be spared undeserved pain, 12–26; to life, 27–34
Ritchie, D. G., 38n, 44, 59n
Rodman, John, 39n, 186
Rolston III, Holmes, 186, 236n
Rosenfield, Leonora, 5, 37n
Ross, W. D., 59n, 198, 204n
Routley, Richard, 186
Routley, Richard and Val, 186
Ruesch, Hans, 98n
Ryder, Richard, 37n, 43, 59n, 63, 73n, 83, 86, 98n, 99n, 114, 146n

Sagoff, Mark, 195–196, 198–200, 204n, 237n
Salt, Henry, 38n
Scarff, James, 103
Schopenhauer, Arthur, 37n
Schweitzer, Albert, 202
Sentience, 125–130, 184–185, 190–191
Sentience argument, 190–191
Sessions, George, 208
Shallow environmentalism, 185, 207, 210–220, 223–226, 232–236
Sidgwick, Henry, 9
Singer, Issac Bashevis, 3, 4, 36
Singer, Peter, 2, 3, 40–58, 58n, 59n, 60n, 69, 73n, 82, 86–90, 98n, 99n, 100n, 103, 105, 112n, 113, 114, 145n, 146n, 163n, 183n, 184–185, 203n, 204n
Skinner, A., 237n
Speciesism, 43–44, 82–83, 86, 88, 90, 184
Speck, Frank G., 221–222, 238n
Stone, Christopher, 164n
Sumner, L. W., 103, 188, 203n

Tinbergen, Niko, 164n

Udall, Stewart L., 214, 237n
Utilitarianism, 9, 41–58, 69–70, 86–90, 95–96, 115, 184, 194–196

VanDeVeer, Donald, 38n, 41, 147n
Vecsey, Christopher, 208
Vegetarianism, conditional, 4, 20, 24, 33
Vivisection, 62–63
Vlastos, Gregory, 38n
Vyvyan, John, 98n

Wade, Nicholas, 73n
Wasserstrom, Richard, 3
Westacott, E. A., 98n
Whaling, 77, 97, 102–112
White, Lynn, jr., 236n
Williams, William, 76
Wray, Phoebe, 103